White Canada Forever is the first comprehensive study of the anti-Oriental attitudes and policies that prevailed in British Columbia between the mid-nineteenth and mid-twentieth centuries. During these years white British Columbians directed recurring outbursts of mass prejudice against the Chinese, Japanese, and East Indians who lived among them. They left behind abundant evidence of their antipathy, much of it hitherto unexamined. In this book W. Peter Ward, drawing upon a rich record of event and opinion in the provincial press, manuscript collections, and successive federal enquiries and royal commissions on Oriental immigration, reveals the full extent and periodic virulence of west coast racialism. He finds its origins in the frustrated vision of a white British Columbia and an unshakeable belief in the unassimilability of the Oriental immigrant. He shows how Canadian attitudes were dominated by a series of interlocking hostile stereotypes, derived from western perceptions of Asia and modified by the encounter between whites and Asians on the north Pacific coast. These images formed a reservoir of racial animus which could readily be tapped by a wide range of circumstances, especially high immigration rates, overseas military activity, and economic conflict—although in the author's opinion economic strains were subordinate to psychological tensions as a source of racial conflict. The resulting public pressure upon local, provincial, and federal governments led to discriminatory policies in the fields of immigration and employment, and culminated in the forced relocation of west coast Japanese residents during World War II.

W. Peter Ward is a member of the history department of the University of British Columbia.

MCGILL-QUEEN'S STUDIES IN ETHNIC HISTORY
DONALD HARMAN AKENSON, EDITOR

MCGILL-QUEEN'S STUDIES IN ETHNIC HISTORY
SERIES TWO: JOHN ZUCCHI, EDITOR

WHITE CANADA FOREVER

Popular Attitudes and Public Policy
Toward Orientals in
British Columbia

W. PETER WARD

McGill-Queen's University Press
Montreal & Kingston · London · Ithaca

Third edition
© McGill-Queen's University Press 2002
ISBN 0-7735-2322-7

Legal deposit first quarter 2002
Bibliothèque nationale du Québec

Printed in Canada on acid-free paper that is 100% ancient forest free
(100% post-consumer recycled), processed chlorine free
Reprinted in paperback 2005

First and second editions © McGill-Queen's University Press,
1978, 1990

This book was first published with the help of a grant from
the Social Science Federation of Canada, using funds provided
by the Canada Council.

McGill-Queen's University Press acknowledges the support of the
Canada Council for the Arts for our publishing program. We also
acknowledge the financial support of the Government of Canada
through the Book Publishing Industry Development Program (BPIDP)
for our publishing activities.

Canada Cataloguing in Publication Data

Ward, W. Peter (William Peter), 1943–
    White Canada forever: popular attitudes and public policy toward
    orientals in British Columbia
    (McGill-Queen's studies in ethnic history; 8)
    Includes bibliographical references.
    ISBN 0-7735-2322-7
    1. Chinese – British Columbia – History.
    2. Japanese – British Columbia – History.
    3. East Indians – British Columbia – History.
    4. Racism – British Columbia. 5. British Columbia – Race relations.
    I. Title. II. Series.
    FC3850.06w37 1990   305'.8'009711
    C90-090418-6
    F1089.7.06w37 1990

To the memory of my father
HENRY GERRIE WARD

CONTENTS

ILLUSTRATIONS

TABLES

PREFACE

This book is a study of anti-Orientalism in Canada—especially in British Columbia—from the mid-nineteenth century to the mid-twentieth century. As an examination of racism within the white community, it is primarily concerned with popular racial attitudes and popular racialist movements. Public policy is of only secondary consideration throughout the work. The differing emphases placed upon these two themes were dictated largely by my conclusions about the ultimate origins of west coast racism. For the most part those who have previously studied the Asian question in British Columbia have assumed, if not concluded, that anti-Orientalism was grounded in economic tensions created by the availability of cheap Asian labour in a maturing industrial capitalist economy. My argument, on the contrary, holds that racism in British Columbia was fundamentally a problem in the social psychology of race relations. To me, economic strains, while in many instances important sources of racial conflict and prejudice, ultimately were subordinate to psychological tensions as the central locus of racial animosity. Consequently my primary task has been to understand the popular mind and its response to Asian immigrants.

Throughout the book I have employed the terms nativism and racism interchangeably. Nativism I use as John Higham defined it: the "intense opposition to an internal minority on the ground of its foreign ... connections."[1] The nativists discussed here were not necessarily natives of British Columbia but rather were members of what came to be the largest, most powerful racial group in the province. In this community nativism was fused with racism to form the tough crust of attitudes which moulded the pattern of race relations that prevailed in British Columbia throughout this century. Racism is here defined as invidious discrimination among differing racial groups; generally such beliefs and actions are based upon assumptions that racial characteristics are fixed, genetically transmitted, and capable of hierarchical ranking on some scale of superiority and inferiority.[2] As employed in this discussion, both concepts—nativism and racism—are intertwined to such an extent that they are virtually synonymous. Together they lie on the dark underside of ethnocentrism, the positive dimension of which is the creation and affirmation of a sense of communal identity by a cultural or national group.

Racism and nativism are among the common consequences of interracial and cultural contact. Since the beginnings of the modern territorial expansion of Europe, which date from the Renaissance, population movement and rates of migration have greatly accelerated, particularly in western societies. Consequently peoples from differing races have increasingly been drawn together into heterogeneous communities. At one time or another most major cultures in the human community have been influenced by this experience to a greater or lesser extent. The intermingling of Europeans and Asians has been particularly common around the Pacific rim. The most extensive contacts between Asian migrants and whites have occurred in Australasia and the western coast of North America, although significant ones have taken place in South Africa as well. In each of these locations the elemental drama of racial encounter has been played out, whites achieving ascendancy and subordinating Asians and indigenous peoples to their rule. In each, the socioeconomic tensions engendered by interracial contact have given rise to racist dogma and conduct. This book examines the Canadian variation on an old and familiar theme.

Curiously, Canadians have been slow to acknowledge their nativistic past. In recent years they have clung tenaciously to the myth of the ethnic mosaic: the belief that the nation has evolved more or less harmoniously as a multicultural society, and the related assumption that this was and is a desirable condition.[3] Perhaps one reason for the persistence of this belief is the collective need for a national mythology which distinguishes Canada from, and represents her as superior to, the American "melting pot" to the south. But whatever the explanation, the history of west coast race relations suggests that the Canadian commitment to multiculturalism has been tenuous at best. It would seem that the limits of tolerable diversity have been much more narrow than today we commonly believe. Before the mid-twentieth century, racial and cultural homogeneity was the touchstone for west coast whites; the character of the community which they envisioned was to be fixed by the dominant charter group—that of Anglo-Canadian British Columbians.

This book is a substantially revised and expanded version of an earlier, unpublished study which owed much to the patient counsel of Roger Graham of Queen's University. The fruits of his advice are apparent in these pages too. I have also benefited from the suggestions of several of my colleagues at the University of British Columbia, in particular, Margaret Prang, Allan Smith, Keith Ralston, Edgar Wickberg, and Alan Tully, who have read some or all of the manuscript and have offered helpful comments. My chief obligation, however, is to George Rawlyk of Queen's University. Throughout the entire life of this project he has been both critic and friend. Time and again his tough questions have forced me to clarify my thoughts while his encouragement has sustained my sometimes failing enthusiasm. I am greatly in his debt.

Grants from the Canada Council and the Committee on Research of the Faculty of Graduate Studies at UBC made possible the research necessary for this book. Publication was assisted by a grant from the Social Science Federation of Canada. An earlier version of Chapter 8 appeared in the September 1976 issue of the *Canadian Historical Review*, and the kind permission of the publishers to reprint it here is acknowledged with thanks.

My wife, Pat, gave me that assistance which is beyond measure and price and for which my simple thanks seem most inadequate recompense. This book is dedicated to the memory of my father, who first taught me to write and then gave me his interest in history.

PREFACE TO THE SECOND EDITION

This book concludes with the most dramatic expression of racism in Canadian history, the Japanese evacuation of 1942. During the spring and summer months of that year, some 20,000 men, women, and children of Japanese ancestry who lived in coastal British Columbia (more than 90 per cent of the Japanese Canadian population) were dispossessed of most of their property and forced to move inland, either to special camps built for their reception, to work sites in western and central Canada, or in a small number of instances to new homes which they found for themselves. The process destroyed the tightly knit Japanese communities which lay scattered along the coast and stripped most Japanese Canadian families of their modest, hard-won wealth. It also laid bare the limits of Canadian liberal democracy.

The federal government ordered the evacuation, which was carried out with the active participation of all three levels of government. The policy rested on a broad groundswell of popular support and, while some liberally minded individuals and institutions offered the evacuees a helping hand, no significant public protest questioned either the decision to expel the Japanese Canadians from their homes or the many ensuing acts which put the expulsion machinery in motion. To the extent that the public voice is a reliable guide, Canadians were of one mind on the wartime Japanese question.

As this book reveals, the evacuation decision and its aftermath were the culmination of a long history of white hostility toward Asians in British Columbia. Racism had been deeply ingrained in the community from the late 1850s, the earliest days of Chinese immigration, and Japanese migrants arriving later fell heir to this harsh legacy. The book describes its most enduring features and offers an explanation for its virulence and persistence.

But the history of Asians in Canada does not end with World War II, nor does the Canadian experience of racism. Until the 1970s Asian immigration remained at low levels. Asian communities across the country became more fully integrated into Canadian society and the most visible signs of anti-Asian prejudice, especially their legal disabilities, gradually faded. Strident hostility toward Chinese, Japanese, and East Indian Canadians seemed a thing of the past. Over the past two decades, however, immigration from Asia has swelled to unprecedented levels and serious race relations problems have surfaced once again. Given the cyclical nature of racial tensions in the past, it seems obvious that we have been passing through yet one more cycle of racism.

While this is no doubt true, we also should realize that the circumstances surrounding relations between Canadians of Asian and European ancestry in the post-war years differ in important ways from those before 1945; this fact has fundamentally altered the character of race relations in the country. The most important change occurred in Canadian law. After World War II the many legal disabilities once imposed on Asians in Canada gradually were removed. During the later 1940s the extension of the franchise to Asian Canadian citizens held great symbolic as well as practical meaning. Not only did it create a place for them in the political community but it acknowledged them as full members of Canadian society. Meanwhile, the lesser legal restrictions on Asian opportunity in Canada were dismantled piece by piece. Discrimination remained deeply embedded in immigration law, however; it perpetuated a white Canada policy until 1962, when new immigration regulations eliminated race as a significant factor in immigrant selection.

Since the 1960s the national government has taken still more energetic steps to establish legal equality in Canadian race relations. The Canadian Bill of Rights and the Charter of Rights and Freedoms offer equal protection in law to all Canadians, regardless of race, while the latter holds out the possibility of positive discrimination to overcome racial disadvantages. In recent years successive federal administrations have signalled their commitment to legal racial equality in a number of ways: their support for multiculturalism, their redress of Japanese Canadian wartime claims, and their creation of a national race relations institute, to name only three. Indeed, the most significant difference between the present and the past in Canadian race relations is the existence of broad legal protection for the rights of racial minorities today where little existed a generation ago.

These alterations in law stemmed in large part from the transformation of Canadian perceptions of Asian minorities and the civilizations of Asia, as well as changing beliefs about the character of Canadian society. Most important, the conviction that Asian immigrants were a threat to Canada's cultural destiny disappeared rapidly after the Second World War. The dispersal of the Japanese Canadians destroyed what had seemed the source of greatest alarm before 1942: a cohesive, disciplined minority newly arrived in British Columbia from an aggressive military power. More generally, Asian immigrants had gradually become acculturated and within two generations were as fully integrated into Canadian society as were many early-twentieth-century immigrants from Europe. Unlike most Europeans, moreover, the Chinese, Japanese, and East Indians in Canada were largely cut off from their countries of origin after the war's end, as, to a greater or lesser extent, they had been since before World War I. Deprived for so long of cultural nourishment from their home countries, the three minorities fell prey to the powerful assimilationist pressures of Canadian society. In the process they ceased to appear to be a threat to the majority.

Similarly, the countries from which they and their ancestors had come took on new meanings in Canadian eyes. Japan quickly ceased to be the menace many Canadians had considered it since at least the early 1930s. First a conquered, war-torn nation, later a new-born democracy and home of an economic miracle, the image of post-war Japan in Canadian eyes was not hostile but benign. The communist regime of China roused some alarm in cold-war Canada, but several factors offset this concern. The Soviet Union always appeared the more serious threat in a world bristling with nuclear weapons. Because of its enormous demand for imported wheat, China was a major Canadian trading partner, with unlikely friends among conservative prairie farmers. National interest and a thinly disguised anti-Americanism also promoted sympathy for China among Canadians who wished some leeway in foreign policy matters under the American umbrella. India was considered to be a case for benevolence and charity; newly independent, democratic, and a Commonwealth member led by a dignified statesman, it seemed a deeply impoverished state with special claims on the Canadian conscience. In various ways Canadians' perceptions of the Asian minorities in their midst were refracted through these new national stereotypes, all of which replaced an older sense of a looming Asian threat with images of common interest and a measure of goodwill.

In the recent past more and more Canadians have had contact not just with images of China, India, and Japan but with the countries themselves. The growth of international travel, both for business and recreation, has given unprecedented numbers of middle-class Canadians an opportunity to see something of Asia for themselves and form their own impressions of these nations. As a result, tourism has helped undermine traditional perceptions of Asia and her diverse peoples among the leading class of contemporary Canadians – leading, that is, insofar as public opinion, politics, and policy formation are concerned.

Meanwhile, the self-perceptions of Canadians have gradually changed as well. The insistent demands of French Canadian nationalists, the waning identification of English Canadians with Great Britain, the growing ethnic diversity of the population, and the increasing assertiveness of second and third generation ethnic Canadians have challenged older, rather comfortable assumptions about the cultural essence of our society. The 1960s saw widespread acceptance of the view that Canada was a bicultural community; the 1970s endorsed the notion that it is a multicultural society. In fact, multiculturalism has become a national government policy, placing the power of the state behind a dramatically new vision of the Canadian community. From an intellectual point of view this emergent sense of national character provides ample room for ethnic and racial diversity. A multicultural Canada is big enough to include all peoples and cultures. Perhaps more important, by embedding this concept in governement policy we have established new social norms, standards to which minorities can appeal in the face of discrimination.

These broad changes in popular thought have been tied to others which, though rather less widely shared, equally helped to introduce the fundamental changes in law that have altered the structure of Canadian race relations in recent years. Members of Canada's postwar political elite subscribed to the liberal internationalist idealism of the later 1940s and 1950s which strongly condemned racism, their convictions strengthened by post-war revelations of German and Japanese wartime atrocities. At least some among them also realized that Canadian commitments to the United Nations and the Commonwealth required an end to legal forms of racial discrimination. A small number even saw uncomfortable parallels between the treatment of the Japanese in Canada and wartime crimes against other minorities.

Slowly the idea of legal racial equality won wider acceptance among the public as well. During the years immediately after the war some liberal Protestant churches, civil rights groups, and left-leaning politicians made common cause with Japanese Canadian organizations in their quest for just treatment from the Mackenzie King government. This was the first time in the long history of the Asian presence in Canada that a significant number of white Canadians mounted a sustained campaign to end discrimination against Canadians of Asian ancestry. While a small minority, they were the vanguard of growing numbers of liberal-minded Canadians who, over the years, became convinced that the west coast Japanese had been victims of a monumental injustice during and after World War II. In itself this conviction became a powerful argument for the protection of minority rights in law. It is no exaggeration to state that the Japanese expulsion of 1942 and its destructive consequences provided the major historic justification for the legal protection of minorities in Canada. More generally, the post-war years have seen the growth of a host of articulate interest groups dedicated to the defence of minority rights. Just as legal reform created a basis in law for defence of the rights of racial minorities, so these organizations established a basis in public opinion for defence of minority interests.

If law and opinion have altered the context for Asian-white relations in post-war Canada, so have changes in the character of the minorities themselves. Here, however, the situation is complex, for the Chinese, Japanese, and East Indian communities in contemporary Canada each consist of two primary segments: one made up of the descendants of migrants who arrived by and large during the late nineteenth and early twentieth centuries, and one composed of those who have come since the early 1960s and their Canadian-born children. The former segments are dominated by those who are three or more generations removed from the land of their ancestry, many of whom have lost all but the sentimental aspects of their original culture. The latter segments straddle the gap between the old world and the new, their weight gradually shifting from one world to the other with passing time and succeeding generations.

The numbers of Chinese and East Indian (though not Japanese) immigrants in the recent past have vastly exceeded those of the first phases of Asian migration, and the Chinese and East Indian communities in Canada have grown rapidly as a result. Most of the newcomers have settled in large cities, dramatically altering their social composition. Today Toronto has the most numerous Asian population of any Canadian city, although that in Vancouver is proportionately the largest – perhaps one resident in six is of Asian ancestry. But, unlike settlement patterns in the past, the new Asian immigrants are no longer concentrated in British Columbia. Now they are widely distributed across the country, particularly in the central and western provinces.

Immigration law has also filtered the incoming population in ways which have eased the task of absorbing newcomers into Canadian society. The strong preference for skilled, well-educated, or well-to-do migrants, or those with close relatives already resident here, has tended to favour the admission of family groups and people whose cultural values are more closely aligned with Canadian norms than once was the case. At the same time the international character of the modern consumer culture, one of the leading features of our age, has meant that Asian immigrants and Canadians now hold more in common than at any time in the past. Although many recent arrivals from Asia have not yet been fully incorporated into Canadian society, integration has proceeded swiftly. As a result, the Chinese, Japanese, and East Indian minorities are now much more fully a part of mainstream Canadian society than they were at any time before World War II.

At the same time, however, each minority possesses a strong sense of its own identity and each asserts its uniqueness in many ways. Among some recent immigrants the tendency has been to perpetuate old world institutions. East Indians, for example, have re-established their familiar religious organizations: the Hindu, Muslim, and Sikh temples of their homeland. Language schools – long a common feature of Asian immigrant communities – attempt to transmit leading elements of traditional cultures in a new world setting. The more westernized among recent migrants, however, show greater selective affinity for their cultural traditions and tend to identify with the individualistic and materialistic elements of modern Canadian culture.

The long-established segments of each Asian minority have drawn on both their Canadian experiences and their ancestral inheritances when asserting their community identities. Because racial discrimination has loomed so large in their new world experiences, it looms large in minority self-consciousness as well. This is particularly true of the Japanese community, for reasons which are obvious. But whatever the limits imposed by racism in each minority's past, each has also had a rich and complex experience in Canada. In recent years the Chinese and Japanese communities, in particular, have proclaimed a powerful sense of their own unique histories through a series of museum displays, photo exhibits, and memorial volumes, all of which proudly reveal their collective pasts to group members and outsiders alike. Meanwhile, the celebration of old world cultural traditions remains an important element in the identity of each group, as the new Sun Yat-Sen Classical Chinese Garden in Vancouver, for example, indicates. As well, in their various cultural and community centres across the nation today, Chinese, Japanese, and East Indians each work to sustain and share a vital sense of collective identity.

The growing willingness to defend community interests is another mark of this vitality. During the past decade in particular the Japanese and Chinese minorities have sought redress for past wrongs more energetically than at any previous time, the Japanese, at least, with some success. They have also taken a more aggressive stand against contemporary racism. At one time these tasks had been left to consular officials and traditional community leaders, largely ethnic businessmen, who acted as brokers between the minority and Canadian elites. But now direction comes from the community's newer leaders, many of them professionals, who insist that Canadians live up to the ideals embedded in their liberal democratic rhetoric. Thus, the presence of three assertive, self-conscious Asian minorities has come to play an important role in altering the race-relations equation in late-twentieth-century Canada.

But despite the altered circumstances of the past 40 years, racism persists. In one form or another it has been with us, through hard times and boom times alike, since the end of the war. As in the early years of Asian immigration, it has raised its public face when immigration rates have been on the rise. For the most part, however, its crude and overt forms have long vanished. Today's racist sloganeers no longer address public meetings; they scrawl on public washroom walls. The hot rhetoric of racism has been replaced by more subtle codes, words whose ambiguities often cloud their central message but whose meaning is clear to most observers. Racism still pervades the workplace and the schoolyard. It still imposes indignities, limits, and even dangers on minority group members. We may have chained the beast of prejudice but we have not destroyed it, and it still roams among us on an unacceptably long leash.

Vancouver
June 1990

PREFACE TO THE THIRD EDITION

Studies of the past are written at a particular moment and in a particular context, reflecting an author's understandings at that time and place; this one is no exception. It took first form in the early 1970s as a doctoral dissertation written at Queen's University. I then reshaped it into the book you see here, pruning the detail and the scholarly apparatus that thesis writers use to display their craft skills, while sketching its broad frameworks in bolder outline. It has remained in print since it first appeared in 1978 and the publishers now wish to extend its life. Needless to say, I'm pleased. But time waits for no one and contexts are ever changing. Canadian historical writing, indeed Canadian society itself, have evolved since the book was first published. Initially I considered revising it and adding a section on the post–World War II years. But in the end I decided to leave the text as it is. A thorough revision would require a very different study, reflecting our own preoccupations and circumstances a well as the twisting path that connects this book's past with its present. If this study can still speak to us from the late 1970s, so be it.

Certainly the subject remains timely. Canada is one of the major migrant receiving nations in the modern world. Roughly 15 million immigrants have come here since the dawn of European settlement, half of them since 1950. In absolute terms these numbers may seem small when compared with those entering the United States, the leading destination in the Americas for migrants during the past two centuries. Yet in relative terms they are not: at the turn of the twenty-first century about 17 per cent of Canada's population is foreign born, twice the proportion of immigrants in American society.

Sheer numbers apart, the social, cultural, and economic impact of immigrants on Canada has been enormous. Since the first days of European colonization, generation after generation, wave upon wave of immigrants has touched Canadian shores. First they displaced, and then overwhelmed, the native peoples of northern North America, who gradually became a minority in their own land. Before the mid eighteenth century most immigrants were from France. From then until the end of the nineteenth century the leading groups came from the British Isles though, toward the end of the century, small groups of other Europeans and Asians also swelled the immigrant tide. From the turn of the twentieth century until the 1960s the largest numbers continued to come from Britain, though an ever-widening stream from continental Europe broadened the cultural range of new arrivals. Since then, the diversity of newcomers' backgrounds has widened still further as migrants from around the globe have expanded the pool of recent arrivals – over the past two decades the largest numbers have come from South and East Asia. Clearly, the history of modern Canada is a history of growing cultural pluralism.

This book was one of several studies published during the later 1970s and early 1980s that re-evaluated the place of immigration in the national experience. Together they supplanted older understandings of immigration to Canada that were concerned mostly with the first immigrant groups, French and British. These studies had evolved at a time when nation building was the leading motif in Canadian historical writing. It emphasized the concept of progress in the national experience and lauded the newcomers' contributions to the growth of the new nation. As well, the historians of the mid-century decades were preoccupied with the creation and maintenance of a national consensus and, with the notable exception of the historic French-British cleavage, they paid little attention to cultural differences and conflicts or to prejudice and discrimination. By and large, immigrants of other origins fell between the cracks of what was in many ways a celebratory history. At best they were subsumed within a broad category of "others," a "third force" in the Canadian experience.

During the 1970s and 1980s the emergence of new leading approaches to the study of the past – social history, labour history, feminist history - deeply influenced historical writing in Canada, as elsewhere. Concern for everyday life, for the powerless, for conflict and dissent, for social inequality, and for cultural differences stood high on historians' agendas at the time. From this vantage point, the absence of a broad, inclusive history of migration was one of several glaring omissions in Canadian historical writing and a number of younger historians tried to fill the gap. Some of their work extended the political preoccupations of the earlier generation of nation-building historians onto the new terrain of immigration history. Adopting the standpoint of the host country, they examined immigration policy formation and assessed the reception that newcomers received once they entered Canada. Freda Hawkins' first study of federal immigration policy, and Abella and Troper's work on Jewish exclusion during the 1930s are obvious examples.[1]

White Canada Forever was another of these studies. Its goal was to examine the place of immigrants in the popular mind, exploring the influence of cultural stereotypes on popular politics and public policy. When, as a new graduate student, I first began to read about the long history of anti-Asian feeling in Canada, I quickly grew dissatisfied with arguments suggesting that prejudice and discrimination were rooted in economic conflicts between racial groups competing in a capitalist wage economy. While the past offered many examples of racial conflict in workplace settings, it seemed to me that racist outbursts also occurred in situations where no obvious economic conflict existed. Not only that but it was quiescent at times when economically rooted racism might be thought to have flourished, the early and middle 1930s for example. Ultimately I concluded that the mass prejudice against Asians, endemic in British Columbia from the mid nineteenth to the mid twentieth century, was a product of social and psychological tensions rooted in a regional community then in the early stages of its social formation. It was attempting to accommodate Asian and European immigrants in a culturally pluralist society, one based on hierarchies of power that favoured Europeans over other racial and cultural groups. Recurring outbursts of racism were a reflection of underlying anxieties roused by this plural condition and by the dominant group's desire for a culturally homogeneous community.

In tandem with this new interest in Canada as an immigrant receiving community emerged a growing concern for minority groups themselves. In broadest terms its most important contribution was to challenge the view that newcomers were subject to historic processes over which they had little control with another that revealed them as independent historical actors. During the past two decades immigration history has been one of the liveliest areas in Canadian historical writing. The new ethnic history and its historians have done much to undermine older notions about the bicultural nature of Canadian society and its presumed openness to newcomers, and also to encourage a more inclusive recognition of its growing diversity. Leading themes in the new history of minorities include the maintenance of ethnic institutions, the presence of ethnic conflict and social inequality, the recurrence of labour and political radicalism, and the persistence of traditional family and social structures. Among the many works in this area several stand out, including Donald Akenson's studies of Irish rural settlement in Ontario, Franca Iacovetta's and John Zucchi's works on community and family life amongst Italian immigrants, Carmella Patrias' examination of political activism within the Hungarian-Canadian community and Gerald Tulchinsky's survey history of the Jews in Canada.[2] In their various ways, all are histories of the immigrant experience seen from the viewpoint of the immigrants themselves.

The interest of historians in diversity, marginality, and the lived experience of ordinary people also resonated with the Canadian state's growing commitment to pluralism in politics and public policy. One consequence of the federal government's embrace of the multi-cultural model has been growing practical support for the study of ethnic history. This development also coincided with a popular reappraisal of the history of Canadian ethnic and race relations. Gradually we have come to acknowledge the gulf that has sometimes existed between the egalitarian liberal democratic values we have long professed and the historic inequalities so evident in the everyday experience of ethnicity and race. The Japanese Canadian community's quest for redress for its wartime losses was merely the first of a number of attempts to seek collective acknowledgement for past wrongs and to win compensation for those affected.

Asian immigrants occupy a distinctive place in Canadian history as well as in historical writing about Canada. More than any other minority groups, historically they have been subject to wide-ranging discrimination, from formal legal restrictions on their admission and civil rights to endless casual acts of petty prejudice based upon presumed racial and cultural characteristics. More recently they have become the largest among the many minorities entering the country, creating vital growing communities in our larger urban centres. These reasons alone are enough to justify the ongoing scholarly interest in Asian Canadians, particularly in the Chinese, East Indian, and Japanese communities, whose presence here now extends for much more than a century.

Over the past decade two books have made particularly important contributions to the study of Asian Canadian history, both concerned with the Chinese community in Vancouver. Kay Anderson's *Vancouver's Chinatown* examines the city's Chinese community as a mental construct, a set of ideas historically fashioned within the larger society of European Canadians that have imposed an identity upon the Chinese minority, legitimating and reproducing the hierarchies of dominance and subordination that characterized the long history of urban race relations.[3] Anderson views these processes as a case study of much broader and far more enduring cultural processes. "It is in the context of that long rise to hegemony of a European historical bloc," she states, "that the category of Chinese needs to be situated, because out of the quest for power the classification acquired its meaning of non-white, non-Christian – in short of "them" as opposed to "us" (247). One of Anderson's points of departure is *White Canada Forever*, whose argument she labels "liberal" and "idealist" and therefore unable to account for the persistence of prejudice. For Anderson the explanation lies in "the ideology of racial difference that informs it" (19). However, she herself fails to explain why this ideology has had such an enduring life in Canada and elsewhere, though her book certainly offers many examples of its deployment in the interests of the dominant community.

Wing Chung Ng's recent book, *The Chinese in Vancouver, 1945–80*, departs sharply from this debate in a carefully wrought study of community struggles over cultural identity during a period of renewed Chinese immigration and settlement.[4] Ng rightly points out that studies of racism can contribute relatively little to an understanding of the immigrant experience. Racist attitudes and policies certainly impinged on the experience of Asians in Canada, and often imposed important restrictions on their lives, but at most they set boundaries within which minority group members continued to live their lives. In contrast with my work and Anderson's, Ng stresses the fundamental importance of adopting the immigrant perspective rather than that of their hosts. He is particularly critical of Anderson's assumption that the racial definitions that European Canadians imposed on Chinese Canadians left them a subject population, lacking the capacity to shape their own destinies. Quite the contrary, he offers ample evidence that they possessed their own voices and used them creatively to fashion their own sense of community, both within minority society and Canadian society at large.

One of the other leading developments in the literature of the Asian Canadian experience since *White Canada Forever* appeared has been the emergence of new voices from within minority communities. Some of the most articulate among them have spoken in fiction, others in autobiography, still others in fictionalized history. Joy Kogawa's powerful novel of Japanese life in pre-war and wartime British Columbia, *Obasan*, comes immediately to mind, as do Paul Yee's stories of Chinatown life. Denise Chong's *The Concubine's Children* walks the line between family biography and history in a finely drawn portrait of family life in British Columbia's early twentieth-century Chinese communities. Tara Singh Bains' *The Four Quarters of the Night* is a powerful account of one man's journey from the Punjab to the west coast of Canada.[5]

While immigration history has flourished in Canada in the years since the late 1970s, in many respects this work is little more than well begun. Looking ahead, there are a number of broad issues that the coming generation of scholars should consider. While the history of minorities is now commonly written from the newcomers' perspective, all too often attention is paid only to their experience in Canada while their home country origins are neglected. The few exceptions make clear how much is overlooked in this process. John Zucchi's study of early Italian migration to Canada, for example, reveals how significant immigrants' old world ties can be to their new world experience.[6] If we are to understand migrants' lives in their new homes we need to know who they were in their old ones, why they chose to leave, what distinguished them from those who stayed behind, how they remained connected to their roots, and what they hoped to achieve by migration. Canada's immigration history begins in the many communities that sent their members abroad, not when they arrived in this country.

We also need to think more carefully about the migrant's voyage itself. Much of our immigration history has been written as though migrants journeyed along a predetermined path from their home countries to this one. But we should realize that, for many immigrants, Canada was only one of several possible destinations. Many countries in the Americas opened their doors at the same time that Canada did and migrants often shopped around for the best opportunities. In other words, the immigrant experience includes not only those who formed part of a permanent community in Canada but also those who sojourned here and then returned home as well as those who arrived here and moved on when seeking their fortunes.

Finally, we need to recognize that minority communities disappear as well as persist, and that this disappearance is another leading feature of the immigrant experience. The recent emphasis some historians have placed on the construction of group identities should not blind us to the powerful assimilationist forces of modern mass culture and the difficulties most minorities face over time in attempting to maintain strong collective identities. Across the generations, the disintegration of ethnic communities has been a fundamental part of the migration experience for most Canadians, whatever their cultural origins. Ironically, in most cases the final stage in the formation and maintenance of group identities is their ultimate loss, as newcomers and their descendants adopt – and often contribute to – the multiple identities accessible to us all in modern mass society.

November 2001

NOTES

1. Freda Hawkins, *Canada and Immigration: Public Policy and Public Concern* (Montreal: McGill-Queen's University Press, 1972); Irving Abella and Harold Troper, *None is Too Many: Canada and the Jews of Europe, 1933–1948* (Toronto: Lester and Orpen Dennys, 1982).

2. Donald Harman Akenson, *The Irish in Ontario: A Study in Rural History* (Montreal: McGill-Queen's University Press, 1984); Franca Iacovetta, *Such Hardworking People: Italian Immigrants in Postwar Toronto* (Montreal: McGill-Queen's University Press, 1992); John E. Zucchi, *Italians in Toronto: Development of a National Identity, 1875–1935* (Montreal: McGill-Queen's University Press, 1988); Carmela Patrias, *Patriots and Proletarians: Politicizing Hungarian Immigrants in Interwar Canada* (Montreal: McGill-Queen's University Press, 1994); Gerald Tulchinsky, *Taking Root: The Origins of the Canadian Jewish Community* (Toronto: Lester, 1992); Tulchinsky, *Branching Out: The Transformation of the Canadian Jewish Community* (North York: Stoddard, 1998).

3. Kay J. Anderson, *Vancouver's Chinatown: Racial Discourse in Canada, 1875–1980* (McGill-Queen's University Press, 1991).

4. Wing Chung Ng, *The Chinese in Vancouver. 1945–1980: The Pursuit of Identity and Power* (Vancouver: UBC Press, 1999).

5. Joy Kogawa, *Obasan* (Toronto: Lester and Orpen Dennys, 1981); Paul Yee, *Tales from Gold Mountain: Stories of the Chinese in the New World* (Toronto: Groundwood Books, 1989; Denise Chong, *The Concubine's Children: Portrait of a Divided Family* (Toronto: Viking, 1994); Tara Singh Bains and Hugh Johnston, *The Four Quarters of the Night: The Life-Journey of an Emigrant Sikh* (Montreal: McGill-Queen's University Press, 1995).

6. Zucchi, *Italians in Toronto*.

This the voice of the west and it speaks to the world:
The rights that our fathers have given
We'll hold by right and maintain by might,
Till the foe is backward driven.
We welcome as brothers all white men still,
But the shifty yellow race,
Whose word is vain, who oppress the weak,
Must find another place.

CHORUS:

Then let us stand united all
And show our father's might,
That won the home we call our own,
For white man's land we fight.
To oriental grasp and greed
We'll surrender, no never.
Our watchword be "God save the King"
White Canada for ever.

cited in Khushwant Singh,
A History of the Sikhs, vol. 2, 1893-1964.

PART ONE

SINOPHOBIA ASCENDANT

1

JOHN CHINAMAN

"John Chinaman" was what they usually called him, though sometimes they also dubbed him "the heathen Chinee" or "the almond-eyed son of the flowery kingdom." These were names nineteenth-century North Americans commonly gave the Chinese immigrant. They were part of the rhetoric of race of white America. Essentially the names were terms of derision, not as disparaging as the twentieth century's Chink, but with heavy overtones of mockery and contempt. Together they revealed something of the animus with which both Canadians and Americans greeted the Oriental immigrants who touched the Pacific margin. But if these terms reveal the flowering of west coast racialism, they scarcely describe the dense and prickly nature of its foliage. From the mid-nineteenth century onward, a luxuriant anti-Orientalism flourished on the western coast. It took many forms and displayed many hues. Whatever its appearance, however, it was always firmly rooted in the rich, hard clay of public opinion. Racist attitudes were broadly shared among those in the farthest west. Thus it is here, at the level of popular thought, that this study must begin.

West coast whites, both north and south of the international border, were always extremely open about their racial prejudices. They uttered them in the legislature, on the street, in the press, at the meeting hall—in fact almost everywhere opinions were exchanged. But despite its many sources, a few central ideas always dominated their comment. Most of these conceptions were highly stereotyped. Taken together, they conveyed a vivid image of the Oriental. It was neither a full nor an accurate picture, but that proved no deterrent to its general acceptance. The chief significance of this image lay in the strong influence it had upon the configuration of race relations in west coast communities, whether in Canada or the United States. Like most ideas, these paid little heed to political boundaries. The racial stereotypes of British Columbians are of primary concern here, however, and as the Chinese preceded other Asians to these shores, this study must first explore the image of John Chinaman in that province, its nature and its origins.

The image was formed from a cluster of stereotypes, virtually all of them unflattering to the Chinese they described. "A stereotype," according to social psychologist Gordon W. Allport, "is an exaggerated belief associated with a category,"[1] be it a racial or religious category, or other generalized social grouping. Many racial stereotypes take their origin from a kernel of truth. Others persist without any basis in fact, sometimes even in spite of evidence to the contrary. These two forms of stereotypes are inherently irrational. Still others are largely true, but in most cases they are formed from highly selective observations which emphasize some racial characteristics while neglecting others entirely. Stereotypes are usually thought to be negative or hostile, but they can also be positive or favourable. Whatever their content, they are a normal feature of human perception and thought, for these processes always advance with the aid of such generalizations.[2] Our concern is with one pattern of negative stereotypes, a set of beliefs which etched a derogatory image of Asian immigrants upon the minds of white British Columbians.

The west coast image of the Chinese immigrant derived from two major sources. First among them were conceptions of China and the Chinese character firmly embedded in Western, or European and North American, thought. Usually these impressions were based upon the accounts of merchants, diplomats, and missionaries who had travelled in China. During the early nineteenth century most of their reports disparaged Chinese society. Yet western views of the Orient had not always been hostile. Indeed, from the time of Marco Polo to the end of the eighteenth century, western intellectuals had celebrated China's glories—her arts, her riches, and her enlightened social order. It was not until after 1800 that a strong note of contempt for the Chinese began to creep into western thought. When viewed charitably, China seemed a curious, exotic, irrational place. But to many western men the barbaric in Chinese life seemed more apparent than the quixotic. Popular accounts of China repeatedly contended that ignorance and perversity, cruelty and poverty, were the common characteristics of her people.[3] In the United States, for example, stereotypes emphasized "Chinese deceit, cunning, idolatry, despotism, xenophobia, cruelty, infanticide, and intellectual and sexual perversity."[4] The prevailing view was that, whatever Chinese society had once been, it had long since grown decadent. Widely shared in western nations, these sentiments ultimately became the warp of the racial attitudes which white British Columbians wove for themselves.

The first whites on the North Pacific coast undoubtedly brought their culture's impressions of Asia with them. Furthermore, although they lived on the fringes of their own civilization, they were not far removed from the core of its popular thought. They read the current literature of Great Britain and North America and, in the process, further exposed themselves to prevailing notions of China. They also circulated these ideas among themselves in school textbooks and newspapers, among other forms of communication. And by all their accounts life in the "flowery kingdom" was a crabbed and narrow thing. Typical was one school geography which used the yardstick of progress (that common gauge of any nineteenth-century society) to measure Chinese civilization. "What they appear to have been 2,000 years ago, they are still," it reported.[5] It was an oft-told tale. In British Columbia popular literature repeatedly emphasized that widespread poverty, loathsome disease, cruel vanities, and low regard for life were all characteristic of Chinese society. The Chinese were a truly backward people, suspicious of foreigners and ignorant of the West's great achievements.[6] Judged by all western standards, they were clearly inferior.

These conceptions of the Chinese character found a receptive audience in British Columbia. The remarks of a prominent public figure, G. M. Sproat, on the debased nature of the Chinese worker, were perhaps representative. Sproat described China as a "vast reservoir of helotry." There the Chinese labourer had for centuries been

forced to regulate his life, in a very direct and exclusive manner, in reference to the primitive human instinct of self-preservation, or at any rate, a low animal existence with a few coarse enjoyments. The long continued, uniform operation of overmastering external conditions, has compelled him, and it also has enabled him, to subsist on the very least which in his case will merely maintain the nerve force that drives his muscular machinery. . . . The repression of the natural development of the man, which ought to be moral and intellectual as well as physical, together with an inherited inaptness, prevents his advancing much beyond the ways and means which the passion of self-preservation inspires and stimulates.

These influences, Sproat concluded, had moulded the character of the Chinese labourer; it had become one "of a fixed, persistent type, alien, beyond any control or chance of change, to everything that concerns western civilization."[7] Sproat and many others held that, because of their low condition, the Chinese could never be absorbed into Canadian society. On the contrary, they would forever remain an inferior, alien presence in the community. Therefore they were most unsuited for emigration to Canada.

Pacific coast residents also clung to the West's fear of the Yellow Peril. Ever since Napoleon had warned of the sleeping giant of the East, the twin themes of race war and Asian inundation had recurred in European thought. During the late nineteenth and early twentieth centuries, in particular, these notions circulated widely in North America.[8] The assumption was that, because of its great population, when China awoke it would be a force with which to reckon. The Chinese "would over-run the land like grasshoppers,"[9] a provincial politician warned in 1879, and his were not uncommon sentiments. In British Columbia the Yellow Peril proved an especially heady brew in times of high racial tension. As one provincial journalist remarked soon after the Vancouver riot in 1907:

A struggle is coming beyond any possibility of doubt, and such a struggle as history cannot parallel. The tide-like sweep of the Teutonic tribes across Europe, before which the Roman Empire went down like grass before the scythe, will appear small by comparison with the advance of the Orient when once it has begun in earnest. If the racial assertion of forty millions of Japanese has challenged the astonished Occident, what may we expect when the four hundred millions of China, the two hundred and fifty millions of India and the other people sufficient to swell the aggregate beyond seven hundred millions assert themselves?[10]

The western image of China, then, was one major source of the Chinese stereotypes which imbued popular thought in British Columbia. But far more important as a source of racial imagery was the contact between whites and Chinese which immigration made possible. Once resident on the eastern Pacific rim, Chinese immigrants offered their hosts occasion for close observation. This greater intimacy led to social and economic conditions which engendered the majority of stereotypes accepted by west coast whites. Thus many of these racial assumptions were home-grown, not borrowed. While broadly similar to attitudes which prevailed in the American west coast states and the Australasian colonies, they were largely generated by local circumstances.

This is not to say that British Columbians ever came to know the newcomer well. On the contrary, they had only a superficial knowledge of the Chinese in their midst, even though the two races lived side by side. Much of their understanding was formed, not by direct observation, but by contact with the image of John Chinaman itself.[11] As is often the case with stereotypes, those linked with this central image had a self-perpetuating tendency. They acted as a filter through which the Chinese were perceived: they screened out many of the immigrants' characteristics and magnified a few others. In effect, they acted as prophecies concerning the Chinese character. Sometimes these prophecies were fulfilled, and once fulfilled, they were reaffirmed. Thus, in this circular process, the stereotypes were perpetuated. West coast racialism continually fed on itself. Contact with popular attitudes, rather than with the Chinese themselves, was quite enough to keep it alive.

What, then, was the content of these stereotypes? What Chinese characteristics were singled out for emphasis? What were the main features of the image of John Chinaman? One persistent belief was that he was unclean. Only occasionally was his personal hygiene called into question, but his seeming neglect of sanitary conventions drew repeated comment. After orderly communities replaced the tent cities of the gold rush years, the state of sanitation in British Columbia's Chinatowns provoked constant complaint. Neighboring residents considered them physically offensive for they seemed to exhale foul smells and parade disagreeable sights. In 1884, for example, before the installation of underground sewers, the back alleys of Victoria's Chinatown displayed "all the combined waste from the laundries, saloons, restaurants, and other places on Johnson and Government streets ... while oozing from the outhouses is the rankest of filth, all combined rendering the atmosphere of the place so poisonous with stench as to be almost unbearable. The boards of the yard were covered with a green slippery slime."[12] The Chinese practice of preserving large barrels of human waste to fertilize and bleach vegetable crops provoked a similar response.[13]

This picture of Chinatown squalor was linked with the common assumption that the Chinese thrived in overcrowded housing. The popular understanding was that the Chinese lived in rooms crammed with four or five times as many occupants as any white would tolerate. According to rumour, they slept three and four a bed, sometimes even in shifts. A few whites saw this as another sign of Chinese frugality; many others, however, considered it further proof that the race was debased. Most believed that such living conditions were a threat to the public health. "Their quarters," it was predicted in 1884, "would be centres from which contagion would spread all around, and thus diseases not otherwise dangerous might readily become epidemic."[14]

That the Chinese threatened pestilence was a matter of general agreement. It was a commonplace in the late nineteenth century that the Orient was ravaged by virulent, disgusting diseases. White British Columbians shared these assumptions and until long after the turn of the century the public mind linked Chinese immigrants with the possibility of epidemics. Smallpox, cholera, and leprosy were particularly feared, especially during the years before immunization became a standard public health procedure. In 1881, when

2,000 Chinese arrived in Yale, some of them afflicted with scurvy, they spread panic among local whites who feared an outbreak of smallpox.[15] Three years later a cholera epidemic in Asia aroused concern for the primitive state of sanitation in Victoria.[16] But leprosy was by far the greatest source of consternation. Many British Columbians considered the Chinese an inherently leprous people and believed that they had introduced the affliction to the province. Infrequently a case of leprosy was discovered among the Chinese and the victim was then sequestered. But despite its small basis in fact, the myth of the Chinese leper grew to substantial proportions, and it proved a source of potent imagery for provincial Sinophobes. "Our dainty Victoria belles," claimed a short-lived labour newspaper, itself infected with animus, "are having their fine linen done up today by leprous hands, lepers in whom leprosy may be in a dormant state, or active, but concealed from view, may possibly be at this very hour employed in numbers in a large portion of our would-be aristocratic residences. How long will it take before the pest breaks out? No one knows; the poison may be in the blood of dozens even now."[17]

A further assumption common in British Columbia during the 1870s and 1880s was that most Chinese women were prostitutes and concubines.[18] As a group they were usually considered even more depraved than their white counterparts. One witness told the Royal Commission on Chinese Immigration in 1884 that the former flaunted their vices, seeming "to glory in their shame, and ... to advertise their depravity in all possible ways," while the latter "shrink from the eyes of the public, and seek to hide themselves from view, ashamed to own their fall."[19] The common belief was that Chinese harlots jeopardized the moral welfare of the entire white community, not just the Chinese quarter, and when "the gross clasps of a lascivious Chinawoman can be procured for fifty cents or less" the young and innocent were believed in special peril.[20] The Victoria *Colonist* had complained a decade earlier, "Chinese women are in the habit of luring boys of tender age into their dens after dark, and several fine, promising lads have been ruined for life in consequence."[21] They were ruined, of course, by a particularly virulent form of syphilis with which, at least one doctor claimed, virtually all Chinese were infected when they entered the province.[22] It was also assumed that the inmates of Chinese brothels were young girls sold into slavery—mere waifs imprisoned in harlotry by evil procuresses who had purchased their girls with the profits of their own lives of infamy. Police raids on these dens of iniquity inevitably revealed at least one young captive "with the blush of innocence still fresh on her cheeks."[23] Clearly, common beliefs about Chinese sexuality emphasized moral depravity, not erotic sensuality.

The Chinese opium fiend was another popular conception. Many west coast residents shared the widespread assumption that, both in China and abroad, the Chinese were addicted to the pleasures of the pipe. This attitude was not especially common during the early years of Chinese immigration, but during the late nineteenth and early twentieth centuries, it enjoyed growing currency. Respectable opinion in British Columbia held the opium habit to be debilitating and in consequence deplored it. But if the vice had been thought confined to the Chinese alone, it would have seemed little more than proof of Oriental degeneracy. The claim was, however, that whites in growing numbers were smoking opium, too; consequently, "hundreds of men and women.... [were] irredeemably lost by the vice."[24] For this the Chinese were at fault. They had introduced opium to Canadian society and corrupted many whites by teaching them to smoke it. Furthermore, they controlled the drug trade and China was their source of supply. There were also suggestions that the Chinese opium peddler especially wished to enslave a white woman with the poppy and then defile her with his own embraces or prostitute her to his countrymen.[25] Occasionally it was even hinted that Chinese drug peddlers were part of a plot to dull "the bright-browed races of the world."[26]

Further hints of corruption completed the picture of Chinese depravity. Among the most enduring were those which involved gambling. From the 1880s onward, the west coast seemed preoccupied with the Chinese gambler and his den. This understanding permeated popular views of the Chinese immigrant. It became a continual goad to the police officer and the mission worker as well as a source of lurid imagery for the writer of popular fiction.[27] The Chinese were considered a grave source of lawlessness in other ways as well. According to popular belief, they had a penchant for petty theft as well as serious crime. In the eyes of their critics, the Chinese could be trusted only when watched. They reputedly escaped punishment for most of their crimes. A frequent explanation for this that the Chinese shared a universal disregard for truth. As one observer noted, they considered the "adherence to truth ... an admission of weakness." Instead they placed a much higher value on "duplicity" and "capacity to deceive," for their morality permitted "whatever contributes to immediate success in the object they desire to obtain."[28] Because of their guile, their offences went unreported and their testimony in court could not be trusted. Furthermore, through secret societies the Chinese systematically conspired to commit and conceal crimes. These societies allegedly controlled Chinatown's opium dens and gambling halls and also extorted money from their countrymen. "Tong" wars among them erupted on occasion. To outside observers the Chinese secret society often seemed an insidious device to evade the law with impunity. It was a further sign of the depths of Chinese debasement.

Whites also believed that the Chinese threatened the economic status of the west coast workingman—his wages, his job, and his stable economic environment. Indeed, in the minds of many this conviction was far more firmly fixed than those stressing Chinese depravity. That the threat was grave there was little doubt. In the first place, it was widely assumed that the Chinese hoarded their wages and sent them back to China, that they spent as little as possible and invested nothing in the community, and that therefore their earnings were forever lost to British Columbia. But much more important was the apparent willingness of the Chinese labourer to accept lower pay than his white counterparts. In doing so he imperilled the livelihood of every white wage earner in the province. The root of the problem was thought to lie in the Chinese character itself. Moulded by a debased civilization, the Chinese were accustomed to low pay, meagre fare, and wretched living conditions. They could survive, and even prosper, on living standards far below those of the western worker. Second, it was commonly agreed that, unlike other immigrants, the Chinese brought no families to support and thus refused to shoulder any community responsibilities. This, in turn, increased their capacity to work for low wages. Third, it was generally accepted that the Chinese worked on a contract labour basis, bound in virtual slavery to labour brokers who habitually sold their services below the market rate for whites. For all these reasons, therefore, the Chinese appeared to undermine the place of whites in the British Columbian labour market. As a branch of the Knights of Labor argued in 1884,

Chinese labor is confessedly of a low, degraded, and servile type, the inevitable result of whose employment in competition with free white labor is to lower and degrade the latter without any appreciable elevation of the former. Their standard of living is reduced to the lowest possible point, and, being without family ties, or any of those institutions which are essential to the existence and progress of our civilization, they are enabled to not only live but to grow rich on wages far below the lowest minimum at which we can possibly exist. They are thus fitted to become all too dangerous competitors in the labor market.[29]

The Chinese threat to the economy was also alleged to deter immigration. White settlers would never bless the province's shores, one journalist declared in 1875, until the Chinese evil was removed. Certainly it would be a "delightful relief to both sight and senses not only of residents of Victoria but of visitors, if that pleasant little city could be freed from the forbidding presence and vile habitations of the majority of the Chinese residents, and the comfortable cottages of white laborers, with happy wives and troops of smiling children substituted in their place."[30] Later, Chinese employment on railway construction was strongly condemned on the same grounds. Many British Columbians hoped that the Canadian Pacific Railway would quickly populate the west. Therefore, one newspaper argued, it was "of the very first importance that the labor should be performed by those who shall become settlers.... If hordes of Mongolian slaves are brought in to do the work ... the country shall have its railway; but nothing more! The grand opportunity of peopling its vast plains and fertile valleys will have been missed."[31] A group of Victorians predicted even more dire consequences in 1882, a year of high Chinese immigration. "Unless some immediate and urgent steps are taken to restrict this heathen invasion," they declared, "the rapid deterioration and ultimate extinction of this Province as a home for the Anglo-Saxon race must ensue."[32] The Sinophobes agreed that, as long as a substantial number of Chinese remained in the province, its growth would be retarded.

If John Chinaman, the workingman, seemed a threat to most British Columbians, there were others who viewed him in a somewhat different light. By and large both parties accepted the same set of stereotypes but each placed a different construction upon them. As one perceptive observer noted in 1884, "industry, economy, sobriety, and law-abidingness are exactly the four prominent qualities of Chinamen as asserted both by their advocates and their adversaries."[33] The former, a small group of whites, found much to praise in Chinese immigrants. The group included many entrepreneurs who regularly hired Chinese workmen. Colliery owner Robert Dunsmuir praised them for their frugal, industrious, peaceable, and temperate ways. Moreover, he asserted, they always fulfilled their business contracts.[34] Their apologists claimed that it was precisely these characteristics that made the Chinese and their labour necessary.[35] In 1885 it was argued that the province's canneries and coal mines, and the railway to the Pacific "would not have succeeded without the aid of Chinese labor."[36] Yet for every employer who unreservedly favoured hiring Chinese there was probably one who considered the practice a regrettable necessity and another who believed it entirely unnecessary. Moreover, as often as not, even the entrepreneur's praise for the Chinese workingman was based upon the premise that he was inferior, and therefore only useful as a source of industrial labour.[37]

Frequently those who employed Chinese servants found them praiseworthy too. For some a houseboy was merely a useful domestic aid. "The conditions of life would be very much easier in the development of our resources," a Vancouver businessman remarked at the turn of the century, "if white men and their families had servants like the Chinese to do the dirty work for them. I think it is the destiny of the white man to be worked for by the inferior races."[38] Others considered Chinese servants more favourably. Perhaps typical was Mrs. W. A. Baillie-Grohman, an upper middle-class Englishwoman who lived in British Columbia for more than a decade at the end of the nineteenth century. On the average, she observed, Chinese domestics were good,

comparing more than favourably with the ordinary Western help, which is generally an untrained white girl who has to be taught all her work, and who expects to be treated as an equal. It is scarcely fair to compare poor John with the trim English maid in her cap and apron, who has been well trained in modern civilities as well as her duties, nor can his culinary productions compare with those of a finished European cook; but with the average plain cook and the inefficient housemaid the contrast would be all in his favour.[39]

But if Mrs. Baillie-Grohman thought her Chinese servants more than adequate, on the whole she regarded them with a mixture of curiosity, amusement, frustration, and respect. Whatever their domestic talents, as men they were simple, credulous, and superstitious. They were not at all likely to rise above their servile status. Mrs. Baillie-Grohman's relations with her Chinese "boys" were highly paternalistic, a condition which reflected the great social distance between them. Like most of those who relied upon Asian help, she bore no overt racial animus. Hers was the prejudice of *noblesse oblige*.[40] Yet like other employers she shared many stereotypes with the most outspoken of Sinophobes.

One Chinese stereotype, however, loomed far larger than all the rest—that of the unassimilable Asian. It was a belief which truly obsessed the west coast imagination, far more so than any other perceived racial characteristic. That the Chinese could never be assimilated was an axiom among whites in the Pacific coast province. "They are not and will not become citizens in any sense of the term as we understand it," remarked the royal commissioners in 1902, at the end of their lengthy enquiry into Asian immigration.[41] This conclusion merely reiterated the community's consensus. What constituted assimilation, and why it was impossible, was never clear in the public mind, for few British Columbians had any real understanding of racial and cultural intermingling as social processes. One means of assimilation, miscegenation, was dismissed out of hand, however. The prospect was so remote to many whites that it scarcely entered their minds.[42] The common belief was that the physical assimilation of Chinese could never take place. Culturally as well, it was usually assumed, the Chinese would always be apart from the host community. Because their character was considered immutable, there seemed no chance for acculturation. The ultimate promise of Chinese immigration thus seemed the creation of a permanent, alien presence in the heart of the west coast province.

These, then, were the convictions which informed British Columbian thought on the Chinese immigrant from the late 1850s to the early 1920s. Some were drawn from popular nineteenth-century views of China embedded in the thought of the West. Miners from the California goldfields—where Sinophobia flourished throughout the 1850s—brought others to British Columbia during the Fraser River gold rush. Direct observation and interracial contact also moulded these perceptions. They were further reinforced by that consciousness of race which pervaded western thought in the nineteenth and early twentieth centuries. For this was an age in which the concept of race had become a basic category of social analysis.[43] Racialism often influenced political, scientific, and literary ideas and marked them with the doctrine of white supremacy. Popular thought bore similar imprints, usually more bold in design and vivid in tone. The "scientific" racialism of European and American intellectuals left no sharp impression on British Columbian anti-Orientalism. Yet that sensitivity to race so characteristic of the period was undeniably influential, for, if nothing else, it stimulated racial awareness amongst west coast whites.

Once these beliefs rooted themselves in the minds of British Columbians, they proved remarkably enduring. Most of them existed in embryo early in the gold rush decade, and during the recession years of the later 1860s they began to take more mature form. By the early 1880s, when Chinese immigration increased sharply, a mosaic of negative stereotypes was clearly stamped upon west coast thought. Over the next two generations its pattern did change slightly. The stereotype of the Chinese prostitute, for example, was replaced by those of the gambler and the opium fiend. But on the whole, popular impressions of the Chinese remained fixed throughout the late nineteenth and early twentieth centuries. This was particularly true of those which stressed their economic threat and their unassimilable nature. In view of the rapid pace of social and economic change in British Columbia during these years—as its population increased at an extraordinary rate and its industrial economy quickly matured—the static nature of these ideas might seem somewhat surprising. Yet the self-perpetuating tendency of stereotypes kept them very much alive, and they were nourished as well by recurring social, psychological, and economic tensions.

It has been argued that, in their attitudes toward the Chinese, British Columbians were divided along class lines, that only workingmen felt genuine animus (and then only because of the Asian labour threat) while wealthier British Columbians regarded the Chinese as romantic and exotic.[44] But this suggestion is simplistic and misleading. Stereotyped views of the Chinese were widely shared across class lines. Trade union rhetoric, while emphasizing the economic menace, employed the full potential of negative Chinese imagery. Similarly, middle-class British Columbians, employers and housewives included, usually reflected the same attitudes. In the words of those who investigated the question in 1902, "the great mass of the white people of British Columbia of all professions, trades and callings, and the Indians, are not favourable to the Chinese and desire further immigration of the labour class excluded."[45] Admittedly there were some who commended the Chinese. But such commendation usually came from men and women who believed that the Chinese had only a limited role in the life of the province. Even Christian church leaders, when offering the Chinese immigrant their fellowship, stigmatized his character and demanded his speedy assimilation.[46] This is not to say that all white British Columbians shared all of these conclusions, nor that all of those who did held them with equal conviction. Nevertheless the hostile image of John Chinaman permeated the thought of white British Columbia. It reflected the consensus.

But what of British Columbia's Chinese themselves? Was there substance to the image of the Chinese immigrant? Did appearance and reality converge? In terms of numbers, the Chinese constituted a significant racial and cultural minority in British Columbia from 1858 onward. During the gold rush years the region's population ebbed and flowed continually, a common characteristic of placer mining frontiers, and the west coast Chinese, like their white counterparts, were constantly in motion. Although it is impossible to be precise, their numbers probably reached a peak of about 4,000 in 1860 and thereafter dwindled to about 1,500 by the end of the decade.[47] During these years the Chinese population varied in size from 15 to 40 per cent of that of the fluctuating white community. The impact of this high percentage was mitigated, however, by the highly fluid nature of frontier mining society and the extreme porosity of the mining frontier's setting. Over the next fifty years the Chinese community in British Columbia grew steadily. Immigration, not natural increase, was the major source of growth; while the rate rose and fell, it seldom dropped below 1,000 a year. Peaks of migration occurred between 1881 and 1884, 1899 and 1904, 1910 and 1914, and in 1919, when, on the average, more than 4,000 Chinese immigrants annually entered Canada. Thus by fits and starts the small Chinese community of 1871 grew to substantial size. By the early 1920s more than 20,000 Chinese lived in British Columbia. (See table 1, p. 170.) Yet these were years of rapid population increase for the province's white population as well; between 1871 and 1921 it grew in geometric proportion, at least doubling in size in every census decade but one. This growth rate was higher than that of the Chinese community. Thus the Chinese, who were more than 20 per cent of the size of the white population in the early 1880s, numbered less than 6 per cent in 1921, on the eve of Chinese exclusion.

The social background of the Chinese immigrant is also worthy of note. Almost all who came to Canada were from the Sze-yap area in the province of Kwangtung southwest of Canton. Having come from a region scarcely thirty miles in radius, they formed a culturally homogeneous group. The great majority were peasants schooled in the intensive, wet-rice agriculture of the district. A small but significant minority, however, were merchants. Political unrest and social disorder were chronic in Kwangtung during the late nineteenth and early twentieth centuries. Land shortages, demanding landlords, and escalating pressures for increased agricultural productivity all helped to create acute rural poverty in the district. Together these conditions stimulated the migration process. Economic motives, above all else, prompted most immigration. But despite his desire for financial gain, the Chinese immigrant seldom intended to remain abroad for life. "He left in order to remit whatever savings he could afford to aid his family in China. In effect, he left to sojourn elsewhere, with the clear intention of returning to his home, of supporting it in the meantime, and of eventually being buried in his village."[48] This was always especially true of recent emigrants. Traditional kinship patterns in southeastern China facilitated this form of migration. There individuals and families were tightly bound together in an intricate network of lineage associations. Often these kinship units performed important social welfare functions and thus permitted temporary male migration by assuming some of the absent migrant's family responsibilities. One consequence of the sojourner condition was that by far the great majority of Chinese in British Columbia, especially during the nineteenth century, were males of working age who preserved strong transpacific ties and lacked a commitment to permanent settlement in Canada. Thus Chinese society in British Columbia was no replica of that of the homeland. Demographic, social, and economic factors had truncated it severely, and it clung to a mentality that was based on transience.

Once they arrived in British Columbia, the Chinese quickly found various sorts of work. During the era of the gold rush most followed the advancing mining frontier. These were the gleaners of the goldfields: they frequently worked abandoned or unprofitable claims, often for small returns. Others became labourers, cooks, laundrymen, teamsters, and merchants and thus provided some of the ancillary services which the mining community required. In towns and villages a few found work as houseboys in the homes of the well-to-do. Throughout the 1870s this employment pattern changed little. But between 1881 and 1885 more than 15,000 Chinese arrived to work on the Pacific railway, and during the next four decades, as the provincial economy matured, they entered many new occupations. To some extent they remained a reservoir of unskilled labour and did the rough work of a pioneer industrial economy. Railway construction and land clearing were two of many such tasks. But other Chinese workers entered the ranks of the skilled and the semi-skilled, especially in the saw mills and canneries of the province. The Chinese cannery worker of the turn of the century was typical. Most provincial salmon canneries employed him to make, pack, and seal tins. He possessed significant industrial skills, a fact acknowledged by his employer, and he stood on a middle rung in the province's labour hierarchy. Other immigrants from China took up agriculture. Chinese market gardeners became fixtures in British Columbia, particularly near Vancouver and Victoria where by 1900 they had monopolized the business. Still other Chinese found petty commerce attractive, increasingly so after the turn of the century. Many Chinese grocers, laundrymen, peddlers, shopkeepers, and restaurateurs provided services to the white community while others dealt exclusively with a Chinese clientele.

In some respects Chinese industrial workers stood apart from the white labour force in British Columbia. For one thing, their work was often organized on a contract labour basis. Apparently there were two forms of the practice although, as evidence is rather scanty, the nature and extent of each is unclear. Of the first very little is known, but most likely it closely resembled the credit-ticket system common in California during the 1850s and 1860s.[49] Chinese lenders, either in China or North America, advanced money to immigrants to pay their travel expenses. Each immigrant was then bound to the lender until the debt was repaid. Some lenders employed the immigrants themselves; others sold their labour contracts to other Chinese employers. None of these contracts, however, had any legal force in Canada. They could only be enforced through the social sanctions of the Chinese community.

The other form of contract labour developed somewhat later. It involved Chinese work gangs employed in a small number of industrial pursuits. At the turn of the century, for example, Chinese cannery workers were almost invariably hired on a contract basis. Chinese bosses recruited workers, some of whom were skilled and therefore in high demand, and then contracted with cannery managers for their services. The contractor assumed the financial risk of abnormally low production for, in a poor year, he might not recoup the wage advances his workers demanded before signing up. In any case, most contractors made their profits on the provisions with which they furnished their employees, not on the labour contract itself. In 1901, a typical year, the canneries employed about 6,000 Chinese for up to four months on this basis.[50] Outside the industry, however, the practice was not common. From the 1880s onward it had been adopted in railway construction, but the Chinese employed in other industries generally formed part of the regular labour market.

Low wage rates, high levels of transience, and strong work discipline also characterized the Chinese industrial labour force. Wages varied from one industry to the next and gradually increased over time as well. But, generally speaking, for equivalent work the Chinese earned one-third to one-half less than their white counterparts. (Chinese common labourers, for example, received $.75 to $1.25 per day at the turn of the century; whites usually earned from $1.50 to $2.50.)[51] Many Chinese workers were transient. They frequently accepted seasonal or short-term employment and in consequence moved from one job to the next, in and out of the industrial labour force, often suffering unemployment in the process. The immigrants quickly accepted the rigorous work discipline of British Columbia's primary industries. They readily submitted to the long, toilsome hours of the mine, mill, and construction gang, as well as their low work status. The occasional strike demonstrated that they were by no means servile, but they were nevertheless a notably tractable element in the west coast labour force. Submissiveness, transience, and low rates of pay were to some extent consequences of the sojourner condition. Its chief imperative was the search for work. Wages and working and living conditions were usually secondary considerations. As long as Chinese immigrants earned and saved more than they could in China, they seemed willing to forgo a settled, comfortable life.

An intricate social structure also grew up within the west coast Chinese community. Some of its roots were transplanted from China; others, however, were North American hybrids. One imported institution was the kinship system of southeastern China, a complex network of relations among families bound together by descent from a common ancestor. Until the mid-twentieth century the Chinese immigrant's primary kinship links lay in China, not in Canada.[52] Consequently few Chinese saw themselves as immigrants making a fresh start in a new homeland. Two other cultural institutions brought from China were the joss house or temple and the Chinese theatre. Yet the Chinese community in British Columbia also evolved its own characteristics. A fragment of Chinese peasant society, it very early generated its own elite, one composed of merchants (a marked departure from practice in China where the mercantile class enjoyed low social status.) Other important innovations were the many voluntary associations, adapted from models in China, which the immigrants formed for personal and community welfare, social contact, political activity, and self-defence, among other purposes. These institutions offered the newcomer shelter when he first arrived, help in seeking a job, loans when he needed them, companionship in lieu of his family, and ultimately even returned his bones to China when he died. The presence of Chinatowns in British Columbia, particularly those in Victoria and Vancouver, greatly strengthened these institutions. They provided a physical focus for the cultural, social, and economic activities of the Chinese, thus enlarging their sense of community.

In some respects, then, the reality of Chinese life in British Columbia was as it appeared to west coast whites. By western standards, Chinatowns were often overcrowded, malodorous, and unclean. Prostitution, gambling, and opium smoking were prominent features of Chinese social life largely because the community was transient and overwhelmingly male. But at best Chinese stereotypes were only partial truths. Often they were a good deal less. Although Chinese secret societies, for example, were popularly considered nothing more than dens of lawlessness and conspiracy, their illegal activities were far less significant than their unpublicized social and political functions. Similarly, the economic threat of the Chinese was far less substantial than was generally believed. Undoubtedly interracial competition for work did exist. But the structure of employment and work in British Columbia minimized direct conflict. The Chinese frequently accepted jobs and wage rates which few others would. They also provided manpower in times of inadequate labour supply. Furthermore, in some industries they alone performed selected tasks, thereby eliminating all competition for such jobs, which were recognized as their preserve. In sum, the assumption that the Chinese would usurp the white labourer's place was more often based on anticipated competition than on open economic conflict.

The most deeply rooted of all Chinese stereotypes—the belief that they were unassimilable—had only a limited basis in fact. It was a highly circumscribed "truth." As we have seen, the concept of the unalterable Chinese character was firmly fixed in nineteenth-century thought. In British Columbia it seemed confirmed by the Chinese immigrant's own conduct. The mere presence of China-town, with its curious mixture of the exotic and the repulsive, was taken as proof that the Chinese were forever confirmed in their foreign habits. In a thousand other ways as well, the Chinese seemed to stand apart, actively resisting assimilation. Yet white nativism barred the way to acculturation as surely as did the so-journer mentality. Neither influence was openly acknowledged in popular thought, but the prospect of cultural intermingling was never seriously entertained by either race and on the part of west coast whites, spurious racialist doctrine precluded its very prospect. The Chinese were condemned to permanent alien status.

Why, then, did the image of John Chinaman enjoy such a long and vigorous life? Why did it often contain nothing more than a germ of truth? Why, even when accurate, was it so intensely deprecatory? To answer these questions is the purpose of this book and therefore only partial explanations can be offered at this point. But the roots of an understanding lie in the recognition that, during the late nineteenth and early twentieth centuries, British Columbia was a plural, or segmented, society.

Social scientists have defined two theories of the plural society. The first equates democracy with pluralism and has been largely employed in describing the modern western democratic polities. In essence it states that the plural society is comprised of a multiplicity of political, social, and economic interests and institutions. Power in such societies is held by many interests and is diffused throughout many institutions. Democratic forms are preserved by the system of checks and balances which flows from this diffusion of power. Social integration is preserved through each individual's affiliation with many institutions and his commitment to common social values. When used in this sense, the term pluralism describes a mechanism which creates and sustains social integration within the state.[53] The second theory suggests that, on the contrary, the plural society is marked by cultural diversity and significant social cleavage. It is a society sharply divided into two or more distinct segments. As M. G. Smith has stated, pluralism can take three forms. Cultural pluralism may create institutional differences in a society without any corporate social differences attaching themselves to these distinctions. Social pluralism is a condition in which institutional differences, based on culture, coincide with the boundaries of clearly defined, closed segments within a plural society, thus creating a community in which all segments share power and are of roughly equal status. Structurally plural societies, Smith declares, are those in which the segments are not only closed but are linked in a hierarchical relationship, one of them dominant and the others subordinate in varying degrees. In such a community, cohesion or integration is usually enforced by political control, military force, economic circumstance, or combinations of the three.[54] This theory has most often been used to describe colonial communities in which a minority has governed a culturally distinct majority. It emphasizes the disintegrative nature of the plural society. Admittedly this model—the structurally plural society—does not fit British Columbian society exactly, in particular because it was characterized by majoritarian dominance. Nevertheless this model does isolate the most prominent features of race relations in the west coast province: segmentation and racial hierarchy. It is in this sense, therefore, that the term plural society is used here.

As a structurally plural society, the west coast community was made up of three components, white, Asian, and Indian. None of the three was homogeneous but each segment possessed a significant degree of internal coherence, social, cultural, or merely racial. By the late nineteenth century the Indians of the province had been pushed to the margins of British Columbian society; they constituted a discrete entity and enjoyed only a low level of integration into community life. They form no part of the present study and therefore need not detain us here. On the other hand, whites and Asians, for the most part, lived in much closer proximity. Orientals formed one highly visible social component in the more populous communities in British Columbia. Yet the level of social integration of the two was not much higher than that of west coast Indians, at least prior to World War I, and this was especially true of the Chinese.

To a considerable extent, the Chinese and white communities shared economic bonds; work and commerce brought them together in the impersonal relationships of the marketplace. Beyond this, however, the two groups diverged in fundamental ways. Culturally, they possessed widely different social norms and values. Kinship patterns and religious beliefs were two of many basic social characteristics which sharply separated the segments. On an institutional level whites and Chinese shared few of the same social organizations, excepting the Protestant missions. Each segment arranged its life about its own set of institutions—the Chinese about their clan, locality, fraternal and community societies, the whites about myriad political, social, economic, and religious associations. Furthermore, the two segments were linked in a hierarchical relationship, the Chinese community subordinated to the white. Access to political influence and major economic resources was clearly the prerogative of the whites. Some avenues to economic gain, and even wealth, were open to the Chinese, but formal and informal sanction greatly narrowed such possibilities. And, lacking the franchise, the Chinese had no political power whatsoever. Fundamentally these conditions conform to Smith's concept of structural pluralism. The two segments in west coast society—the white and the Chinese—enjoyed a form of coexistence based on the supremacy of the former, the subordination of the latter, and their differential access to power.

The fact of segmentation in west coast society profoundly influenced patterns of racial perception within the dominant white community. Pluralism heightened its awareness of race and thus encouraged the circulation of negative Asian stereotypes. The plural condition did not, in any simplistic manner, create the concept of John Chinaman, but it did stimulate the image's growth and broad acceptance. Furthermore, pluralism raised white British Columbia's awareness of its own "somatic norm image," that set of idealized physical characteristics which a community accepts as a self-image. According to the Dutch student of comparative race relations, H. Hoetink, "the somatic norm image [of all groups in a society] is the yardstick of aesthetic evaluation and ideal of the somatic characteristics of the members of the group." The image is not merely an individual preference; it is broadly shared, socially determined, and culturally transmitted. In a segmented society it forms a central part of at least the dominant group's self-perception, and it strongly influences social behaviour and aspiration.[55] In British Columbia, the dominant segment's somatic norm image was founded upon race—more specifically, upon whiteness. Whiteness became the primary symbol of the homogeneous society which west coast residents hoped to create. And it was because of the plural condition that whiteness came to form the core of the host community's identity. This was the image which best enabled whites to distinguish themselves from John Chinaman and his undesirable characteristics.

But why did the plural fact arouse racial awareness at all? Why did the white response to Orientals exhibit such animus and such vigour? Hoetink contends that in segmented societies, because of psychological tensions deriving from fundamental social cleavage, all racial groups yearn for a racially homogeneous community. Most plural societies, he suggests, are therefore inherently unstable and tend toward racial and cultural homogeneity. This end can be reached through intermingling or through the elimination of one or more segments by another. Societies in which either solution would destroy the socio-economic position of the dominant segment often meet this need psychologically, by regarding the other segments as "foreign bodies, outsiders, even aliens, however economically necessary or desirable."[56] Whatever the means by which homogeneity is achieved, however, each segment longs for homogenization on its own terms—in accordance with its own norms, values, and images. It was precisely this longing, this desire for racial homogeneity, which white British Columbia harboured and Asian immigrants challenged. "The main objection to the Chinese," a west coast senator succinctly put it in 1886, "is that they are not of our race and cannot become a part of ourselves. We cannot build up a homogeneous people in Canada with races of that description, a population totally alien to ours."[57] The multiracial nature of the west coast province stirred a profound psychological impulse within the white community to strengthen its collective identity by striving for a homogeneous society. The unremitting hostility evidenced by the Chinese image was one manifestation of this drive.[58] Social pluralism was unacceptable to nativists in British Columbia. John Chinaman seemed unassimilable and therefore he thwarted the drive toward the goal of homogeneity. To many whites he was nothing but an unfortunate wen on the face of their community; his very presence marred its fair appearance. At the bottom of west coast racialism lay the frustrated vision of a "white" British Columbia.

2

THE ROOTS OF ANIMOSITY

In the beginning it was gold that lured the Chinese to British Columbia, just as it had drawn them before to California.[1] The first of them arrived from San Francisco in June 1858, on board the steamer *Oregon*, at the height of the Fraser River gold rush. Initially they were few in number and were soon submerged beneath the incoming tide of more than 25,000 white miners. But over the next two years, while the flood of miners receded, the Chinese community continued to grow. By 1860 estimates placed the Chinese population of the two west coast colonies, Vancouver Island and British Columbia, at about 4,000, most of it on the mainland.[2] Within two short years the Chinese had become a large and visible segment of the colonial population.

The gold rush transformed white society on the northern Pacific coast. The most obvious change was in size, for the small fur trade and agricultural settlements of previous years suddenly swelled to substantial proportions. But changes wrought in the composition of colonial society were equally important. Before 1858 virtually all whites on the mainland had been agents of the Hudson's Bay Company. On the island a handful of colonial officials had governed a few company employees and a small number of farmers. With all the air of an English country village, Victoria was a community profoundly British in origin, manner, and sympathy. The argonauts of 1858 rudely shattered this idyll. For they were international citizens of a remarkably different community—the gold mining frontier of the Pacific rim. Most of them came from nearby American territories, but some arrived from as far away as Australia. Whatever their origins, they were part of a floating population, one continually on the move from one gold-field to the next. Moreover, while most early arrivals came from south of the forty-ninth parallel, only a minority of them were Americans; the majority were of many nationalities. Thus a rootless, polyglot tide of humanity inundated Britain's little outpost on the Pacific. The Brit-

ish colonial residents successfully defended their political dominance by clinging tenaciously to civil authority. The mining community's power, on the other hand, was that which comes from
numbers, and with this strength it imposed its own unique culture
on west coast society.

One facet of this culture was the mining frontier's attitude toward the Chinese, for many miners' racial beliefs were formed long
before they set off up the Fraser. It is likely that they were drawn in
part from the nineteenth-century western image of China. But
these miners had often been schooled on other frontiers where their
attitudes had congealed into racial prejudice. This was especially
true of the mining towns of Washington, Oregon, and California in
which, during the 1850s, anti-Chinese feeling was virulent. In California the question first prompted a popular outcry in 1852, following heavy Chinese immigration to the state. The state governor,
campaigning for re-election, warmed to rising public feeling and
bitterly denounced Chinese immigrants. At the same time mass
meetings of miners forbade Asians to work in the mines, and in
several cases the Chinese were expelled from their camps. Thereafter the California mining community remained unrepentently
anti-Oriental, and as the miners trickled northward into Oregon
and Washington they took their prejudices with them.[3] This same
animosity was common in the goldfields of Australia and New Zealand.[4] By 1858 anti-Chinese sentiment was indelibly stamped on
the culture of the placer mining frontier. Undoubtedly, when the
gold seekers arrived in British Columbia to search out fresh diggings, they carried their prejudices with them, along with their
shovels and gold pans.

Thus, when the Chinese first set foot on the western shores of
British North America, two converging streams of thought inclined
west coast whites against them. One was the Sinophobia ingrained
in western beliefs. The other was the racism born of mining camp
life. Yet for all the animosity that had characterized race relations
on the American Pacific coast, no immediate outburst of sustained
white hostility greeted the Chinese when they first appeared on the
Fraser. Initially there was some harassment, and a little anti-
Chinese agitation, but no discriminatory legislation was enacted at
the outset.

That genuine enmity was present, however, there can be little
doubt. In isolated instances the miners made their prejudices abundantly clear. In the summer of 1858, when a boat filled with Chinese passengers arrived at Fort Hope, an angry crowd of Califor-
nians lined the river bank and stopped them from landing. In the

end they did disembark, but only when a Hudson's Bay Company official intervened, revolver in hand.[5] Later, when the Chinese entered the Cariboo, they met further ill-will. Soon after they arrived local miners threatened to drive them from the district.[6] On one occasion angry whites drove a group of Chinese miners off the Hudson's Bay Company steamer *Otter*,[7] and on another the hostility of white miners was so intense that it forced a number of Chinese to quit the gold-fields and return to China.[8]

There were other early signs of open racial animus. The first colonial newspaper, the *Victoria Gazette* (published by two San Franciscans), was outspokenly critical of the Chinese. In a noteworthy editorial—the first analysis of the Chinese question published in the colonies—it appropriated the rhetoric of the California goldfields. In both California and Australia, the paper suggested, the Chinese had done far more harm than good; in particular they had degraded the status of labour by accepting low wages. Furthermore, female Chinese immigrants had spread gross immorality in both areas. As far as British Columbia and Vancouver Island were concerned, the Chinese were not without their usefulness; there were mining districts in which only the Chinese could earn remunerative wages. But in future they should be confined solely to these inferior diggings. In the long run, the *Gazette* claimed, anticipating arguments that were to be heard for years to come, the presence of Chinese in the colonies was not beneficial.

It must be borne in mind that few Chinese work as miners for *themselves*, being mainly employed in a species of slavery by companies; and they are, with few exceptions, not desirable as permanent settlers in a country peopled by the Caucasian race and governed by civilized enactments. No greater obstacle to the coming of the class of immigrants needed in British Columbia could be devised, than the presence of Chinamen in large numbers throughout the upper mining region of British Columbia.[9]

Other early observers also viewed Chinese immigrants with mixed concern, hostility, and contempt. Colonial Governor James Douglas noted their growing numbers with a sense of unease. "They are certainly not a desirable class of people, as a permanent population," he told colonial officials in London in the spring of 1860, "but are for the present useful as labourers, and, as consumers, of a revenue-paying character."[10] A few weeks earlier, a public meeting in Victoria, called to discuss the financing of road construction, had entertained a motion for a poll tax on Chinese immigrants. During the debate the Chinese were denounced as "a nuisance—a moral scourge—a curse." To the meeting's great amusement the chairman disdainfully declared that "the Chinaman came to this country but produced nothing; he didn't even *reproduce himself*. . . . All he wanted was to get as much gold as he could in a short time and then leave."[11] One of the first surveyors in British Columbia saw even more cause for alarm in the Chinese presence. The "offscourings" of Shanghai, Hong Kong, and Canton arrived in the colonies as virtual slaves, he charged. Their labour in the mines, while it might yield initial profit, could never benefit the region permanently. Ultimately, he warned, their immigration would prove detrimental, just as it had in Australia and California. In large numbers they did "infinite mischief" and would discourage future white immigration.[12]

But if Sinophobia touched British Columbia during the gold rush years, by no means all whites shared its basic tenets. To those who could afford servants, for example, the Chinese were most welcome. High wage rates, a shortage of labour, and the relative absence of women had made domestic help scarce; Chinese men were often willing to accept housework and therefore it was they who invariably met the demand. One leading Victorian, Dr. J. S. Helmcken, recalled that the first Chinese domestics in town came from San Francisco, brought in by Americans who could not find white servants. During the early years of the gold rush, Helmcken asserted, "the Chinese were believed by all to be an advantage and an improvement,"[13] all, at least, who could afford the blessings of hired help in the kitchen. Mrs. Florence Goodfellow, who lived in Hope during the 1860s, similarly recounted that "a shipload of coolies" once arrived from China and "all of the families got some for houseboys."[14] Yet ultimately the householder's approval of Chinese help was class-bound and paternalistic. It was founded on the assumption of Chinese inferiority. As Mrs. Goodfellow remarked, "ours was a good boy and it wasn't long before he was quite a help." Help he was, but *boy* he was too.

Masters aside, there were other whites who in a sense favoured the Chinese. One early observer noted (albeit with alarm) that many British Columbians were "enchanted by the copious Chinese immigration to their shores"; it offered new labour for the goldfields and marked the dawn of a new era in the colonies' commercial relations.[15] Another, a miner, lauded their temperate behaviour. Rev. Edward White, an early Methodist missionary from Canada, also saw much virtue in them. In 1860 he reported:

Although the popular cry of California and with many here is 'Stop them! drive them back;" I say, let them come! While we are trying to get their country open to our commerce and our christianity, it is right that we should treat them kindly who come to our shores, even though they may carry off a large portion of our *precious dirt*. And they seem bound to do it; for while others are grumbling and hesitating, or in too many instances drinking and gambling, the Chinese go at once to the mines, work hard, and spend as little as possible. I have not seen one of them either drinking or gambling since I came to this coast.[16]

In the same year a grand jury at Lillooet declared that the Chinese were "a steady source of profit to the trader and materially increase the revenue of the colony, and in addition greatly benefit the country by the extreme development of its mineral resources; they are also a well-behaved, easily governed class of the population."[17]

Victoria's other early paper, the *Daily British Colonist*, at first applauded the Chinese too. Amor de Cosmos, its youthful editor, argued that their trade was beneficial for the merchants of the city. Looking ahead, de Cosmos saw great promise in their immigration. Chinese labour, he speculated, would help to prove the vast wealth of British Columbia, which consequently would attract the British immigrants so necessary for colonial growth. In addition, the Chinese were "pioneers of the great work that lies before us—the uniting [of] the commerce of the Atlantic and the western shores of the old world with the East by railway enterprise across the continent.... It now assumes a more tangible form by the initiative taken by native Chinese merchants themselves in consigning vessels laden with laborers and Chinese produce to our port."[18]

Time, however, soon tempered de Cosmos's initial enthusiasm. A year later he still held their presence an economic benefit but he also admitted that "Chinamen are not the most desirable population." In March 1862 he further allowed that the California experience had revealed the "social evils connected with a Mongolian population," including "their inferior civilization, their language, their religion, their habits of living—all so hostile to the customs and prejudices of the higher and dominant race." Even more serious was their competition with white labour. Despite these many drawbacks, however, the *Colonist* still maintained that there was ample room for the Chinese in the two colonies. As farmers and fishermen they could find ready employment. Furthermore, "in our gold mines there must, in the nature of things, be extensive auriferous districts in which the cheap labour of China could be profitably employed both to themselves and to the State without at all interfering with the more civilized, more energetic, and more valuable white miner." But there was also much to be learned from the experiences of Australia and California. There, when the numbers of Chinese grew, white interests were adversely affected and antipathy was the result. The lesson for British Columbia and Vancouver

Island seemed clear. "Our policy should be shaped so as to invite a Chinese immigration without being overwhelmed by an excessive number, and check their immigration gradually without oppressing them."[19]

A lengthy volume on the two coastal colonies by an early resident, Matthew Macfie, reflected much the same attitude. Countering the argument against Chinese immigration, he declared that Chinese labour did not reduce the wages which white labour earned; on the contrary, the Orientals engaged only in menial occupations and therefore did not compete with skilled labourers. "Nor," he declared, "can their presence at the mines at all interfere with the enterprises of the superior race; for it is well known that they are unable to resort to those mechanical appliances requisite in the working of rich diggings; that they always keep at a respectful distance from the whites, and are content with such small returns as may be yielded by abandoned 'claims', from which the whites have already taken the cream." Macfie dismissed fears that the Chinese might overrun and devastate the colonies. He agreed that their "social and domestic habits" were unclean, but on the other hand they were extremely industrious and law-abiding, more so than any other group in the colonies. As to the charge that they "diverted" wealth from "*white* industry," he noted that in reality the white community suffered no actual loss, for without the labours of the Chinese this wealth would not have been created in the first place. In any case, their presence alone brought commercial advantage to the colonies. He concluded that,

whether, therefore, we consider the antiquity of these Mongols, their natural ingenuity, or the encouragement afforded by their national institutions to talent, integrity, and industry, the most cogent reasons exist for our extending to them a cordial welcome. Let the colonists show the fruits of a superior civilization and religion, not in ridiculing and despising these Pagan strangers, but in treating them with the gentle forbearance due to a less favoured portion of the family of mankind, and they will continue to be useful and inoffensive members of society.[20]

Clearly some white colonists approved of the Chinese immigrant from the outset. They valued him as a source of cheap labour and as a market for the colonial merchant community. Chinese labour seemed to promise rapid economic development as well as domestic comfort. The Chinese left something to be desired as consumers, for they dealt with their own countrymen whenever possible; nevertheless they remained a significant source of trade and therefore their custom was valued. But ultimately this favour was highly qualified for behind the open reception which it offered lay several derogatory assumptions about the Chinese. De Cosmos and Macfie were only two of many who reflected these attitudes. Like most other whites, they were intensely ethnocentric. They shared the firm conviction that, intellectually, socially, and culturally, the Chinese were their inferiors. Orientals were less civilized and less progressive than whites, and therefore less valued as immigrants. In fact, their chief utility stemmed from this inferiority for they could be used to benefit the colony without requiring an offer of whole-hearted acceptance in return.

Given the history of violent Sinophobia on other gold rush frontiers, it might well be asked why the first response to the Chinese in British Columbia was relatively restrained. One major reason was the general absence of direct economic confrontation between the two races. As long as the gold rush economy prospered, and the Chinese accepted economic roles ancillary to Occidentals, white miners shared no significant economically-based racial grievances. In addition, the vastness of the frontier, and its capacity to absorb (and even submerge) large numbers of miners, rendered the Chinese less visible and reduced the potential for friction even further. Thus, while anti-Chinese feeling was always latent in the mining community, there were few occasions which might activate it during the gold rush years. The fact that a number of colonists welcomed Chinese immigrants, even in a qualified fashion, was another important influence for it limited the breadth of the opposing consensus. Then, too, whether through decisive administrative action or the British reputation for strong and impartial authority, the level of social violence on the mining frontier of British Columbia was much lower than that of the American Far West. Consequently the vigilante racial disturbances so common south of the border were comparatively infrequent in the gold-fields of the colony. Moreover, most of the transient mining population had no commitment to settle in British Columbia, and therefore was untroubled by the long-term implications of multiracial immigration. The mining community certainly did not feel the concern for racial homogeneity evidenced by later generations. Because of these conditions, anti-Chinese feeling remained only an undercurrent throughout the gold rush era. Hostility was always present but violent protest was largely absent.

As the 1860s progressed, however, the gold rush spent its force, mining returns slumped, men left the colony, and depression replaced the prosperity of earlier years. Growing numbers of miners found themselves out of work. In these adverse circumstances the anti-Chinese attitudes of white British Columbia slowly began to harden. The qualified praise of the Chinese immigrant vanished from public view. Henceforth criticism bore a new and sharper edge. One observer in the Cariboo in 1868 was pained that "nearly all the largest and best paying claims are being worked principally by Chinamen, while white miners are unable to get a day's work." "Chinamen," he declared, "are a curse in a mining country."[21] His impressions were later confirmed by the editor of the *Cariboo Sentinel.*

There are few claims at present working on this creek but what few there are, are entirely worked by Chinamen while dozens of white men are loafing around on the point of starvation. It makes my very blood boil to see these d----d heathen enjoying the comforts of life while poor white men have to go many a day with an empty stomach. It is an uncontroverted fact that the Chinamen are a *curse* to any country they inhabit and the blight they have caused by their presence here is every day more apparent.[22]

It was during these depression years that the initial signs were seen of sympathy for discriminatory legislation. The first formal anti-Chinese measure—the cancellation of all votes cast by Chinese in the Cariboo during the election of 1863—was merely the whimsical act of a returning officer.[23] Two years later, however, when prosperity had vanished, the Assembly of Vancouver Island entertained the colony's first anti-Chinese motion. The member for Salt Spring Island, G. E. Dennes, urged the House to tax incoming Chinese ten dollars each. But Dennes received no support from his fellow legislators. Among the most prosperous and prominent of the colonists, they were members of that social class most likely to support Chinese immigration. As Dr. Helmcken declared, he was "glad to see Chinamen come into the country, and thought them a valuable addition to the population." He felt the aim of whites should be "to elevate the Chinamen to our own standard, not to place them in a lower position."[24] Early in 1871, on the eve of Confederation, the colonial legislature debated a similar measure, a $50 poll tax for the Chinese in the colony. On this occasion the motion was withdrawn on the advice of the governor.[25]

By the early 1870s, then, a set of negative assumptions about the Chinese were firmly fixed in west coast thought. The white community's feeling toward the Chinese had hardened into antipathy. Yet the process of hardening had been slow, and despite its prevalence popular racialism had remained largely quiescent throughout the colonial era. Racial incidents had been sporadic and no mass anti-Chinese movement had emerged. Furthermore, the host society had imposed no legislative sanctions upon the Chinese, although the possibility was certainly entertained. Compared with those on other mining frontiers, race relations in British Columbia con-

tinued to be less tense, less violent, and less bound by formal discrimination. The reasons for this condition during the prosperous
gold rush years have already been explored, and they apply as well
to the later 1860s. Even during those difficult years, economic
conflict between the races was not serious. As the colony's white
population dwindled when faced with financial adversity, so did
that of the Chinese community. Furthermore, both whites and Chinese clung to their distinctive economic roles. When the major de-
posits of placer gold were exhausted, white miners adopted more
highly-organized, capital-intensive mining practices; the Chinese,
on the other hand, remained largely independent and continued to
pan for gold in the traditional fashion. Thus even the straitened
years of the decade did not precipitate racial conflict. Economic
strains were not so intense as to prompt a popular outburst.

Soon after British Columbia entered Confederation, however,
the complexion of the Chinese question changed. Once a matter of
private prejudice, henceforth it became a public issue. For the first
time west coast nativists began to act in concert, and during the
next ten years they formed a succession of ephemeral protest organizations. At the same time provincial politicians became the Sinophobes' leading spokesmen. These were signs that, as the depths of
depression passed and British Columbia achieved a measure of social and economic stability, the racial consciousness of the province's 9,000 whites was growing stronger. To some extent this was
due to the growing sense of communal identity which white society
had begun to articulate after 1871. British Columbians soon established the basic criteria for full admission to their new community, a
major one being whiteness. Thus, in defining the nature of their
own society, west coast whites had decided whom to exclude, as
well as include. In this climate of growing public prejudice, the first
concerted attempts were made to promote formal discrimination
against the Chinese.

When the new provincial legislature first met, John Robson, a
prominent journalist and political workingman's friend, lost little
time in assailing the Chinese. He was the member from Nanaimo,
where anti-Chinese feeling had been keen since the Vancouver
Coal Company hired a hundred Chinese workmen in the later
1860s. Robson believed that this act had taken jobs from whites,
thus preventing them from settling in the country with their families. He also feared that Chinese labour might be employed on the
proposed Pacific railway. Spurred by these fears, he asked the legislature to impose a yearly poll tax of $50 on all Chinese residents and
to forbid them employment on all public works.[26] Robson's propos-

als won little favour in the House, but this was no sign that his colleagues disagreed with his assertions. Premier J. F. McCreight, for one, openly accepted Robson's view of the Chinese threat; he refused to support the proposed tax only because he believed it beyond provincial authority. So broad was the anti-Chinese consensus that the House soon approved, without dissent or debate, a bill which excluded all Chinese from the provincial franchise.[27] Henceforth they were to enjoy no political power in British Columbia. The law further implied a fundamental assumption about the Chinese: they could never be admitted to west coast society on terms of equality with whites. The House also passed another discriminatory act, of little practical but great symbolic importance. This measure exempted all Chinese from registering vital statistics with provincial officials.[28] Few if any Chinese were likely to be discomfited by this practice. But the act was an open assertion that Chinese immigrants had no integral role to play in west coast society. The province's first legislators were founding a white community, one in which, at best, there was only a subordinate place for newcomers from Asia. Their initial legislative program made these racial views explicit.

During the next six years popular agitation and legislation directed at the Chinese were fitful. In 1873 a short-lived anti-Chinese society, probably composed of workingmen, called for revision of the Sino-British treaty which permitted Chinese immigration to Canada.[29] New attempts to impose a Chinese poll tax met with no more success than the first; yet because of the ongoing Chinese presence, public anxiety persisted. On four occasions during its 1876 session the legislature earnestly discussed ways to prevent "the country from being flooded with a Mongolian population, ruinous to the best interests of British Columbia, particularly her laboring classes."[30] Unable to find a satisfactory method, however, it adopted no plan of action. At a public meeting in Victoria several speakers denounced the Chinese as the "grasshoppers" of British Columbia, a plague which would eventually devour the province, and called for their expulsion. Meanwhile the Victoria Municipal Council, urged on by Councillor Noah Shakespeare, forbade the employment of Chinese on all local public works.[31] But these early attempts at discrimination were merely sporadic. It was not until 1878 that the Chinese question assumed a new sense of urgency and British Columbians began systematically to seek legislative answers.

In the spring of the year Chinese immigration to British Columbia appreciably increased. Victoria's streets were thronged with recent arrivals, a fact which many whites viewed with mounting concern. The provincial election campaign in May reflected this rising alarm. Several candidates promised new legislation to restrict Chinese immigration while Premier A. C. Elliott declared his government's resolute opposition to the Chinese. Some suggested that future legislation should be patterned on measures enforced in Australia, where heavy annual poll taxes had reduced the number of Asian residents. Others urged restrictions on Chinese employment and heavy license fees for trades dominated by the Chinese.[32]

Once the dust of the campaign had settled, the new premier, George A. Walkem, called the legislature into session. From the outset the House seemed anxious to give prevailing anti-Chinese feeling legal force and it quickly prohibited Chinese employment on public works projects in the province. Then the Walkem government introduced the Chinese Tax Act, which exempted Chinese residents from other provincial taxes but required all those over twelve years of age to pay a fee of $10 quarterly. Those who refused were to be subject to heavy penalties. Several members of the House disagreed that the measure offered the best way to discourage Chinese immigration, but none denied that this end was a desirable objective. As a result, the bill was approved.[33] When enforced, however, the act had a short and troubled life. First it aroused angry complaint from provincial cannery operators. Then the Chinese themselves protested; in Victoria they went on strike for several days in late September. They refused to work for white employers and left more than 250 positions vacant. Finally Mr. Justice J. H. Gray of the Supreme Court of British Columbia declared the act *ultra vires* the provincial jurisdiction.[34]

While the act was still in force, however, a group of Sinophobes formed a new organization to further popular protest. Early in September 1878 a small number of labouring men in Victoria formed the first trade union in the province, the Workingmen's Protective Association. From the outset it was essentially a vehicle for anti-Chinese agitation, despite its professed concern for working-class conditions in general. Those who addressed its inaugural meeting discussed little more than the evils of Chinese immigration. The association's constitution urged "the mutual protection of the working classes of British Columbia against the great influx of Chinese" and the use of "all legitimate means for the suppression of their immigration." It also required members to pledge that they would "neither aid nor abet or patronise Chinamen in any way what ever or patronise those employing them" and would "use all legitimate means for their expulsion from the country." The WPA met and publicized its sentiments throughout the fall of 1878. It also circulated a widely signed anti-Chinese petition and took a census of the Chinese in the city, advertising the names of their employers in order to encourage a boycott. In December a new branch of the WPA, boasting forty members, was formed in New Westminster.[35]

But the WPA shared the fate of many protest movements whose ends elude their grasp. Within a few months it had wilted away, almost as suddenly as it had blossomed. The wheel of public opinion had begun to turn once more, and as the community grew more accustomed to the numerous recent arrivals from China, popular hostility subsided. One sign of flagging concern was the sensationalism to which the association's chairman, Noah Shakespeare, stooped in order to revive it. In January 1879 he titillated one of its final meetings with the sight of a queue recently shorn from a Chinese prisoner at the local jail. At his urging, he boasted to his listeners, the heads of all long-term prisoners, especially those of the Chinese, were in future to be shaved. This particular queue, he declared, would become a family heirloom.[36]

Shakespeare also led the new Anti-Chinese Association which in the fall of 1879 filled the gap left by the demise of the WPA. "No Surrender" was to be the new association's motto. At gatherings in Victoria and New Westminster the ACA denounced the Chinese, condemned their employment on railway construction, criticized past failure to halt their immigration, and urged a Queensland Act for that purpose. It circulated petitions to both provincial and federal governments which requested measures to restrict Chinese immigration. In addition, it sent a delegation to meet Andrew Onderdonk, chief contractor on the western section of the Pacific railway, and demand that he refrain from employing Orientals.[37] But the agitation of the ACA was even more sporadic than that of its predecessor, and it lacked the underpinnings of an aroused public opinion. Thus it soon fell prey to the same fate.

The brief lives of the WPA and its successor exemplify two characteristics of anti-Orientalism which were to prove recurrent in British Columbia. First, popular anti-Orientalism was a cyclical phenomenon. It rose and fell continually, driven by social, economic, and psychological tensions. At no time did it disappear entirely; on the contrary, a base level of animosity persisted in west coast thought. Yet prejudice was always a fluid commodity, whose level varied constantly with changing time and circumstance. Second, the nativistic societies which promoted anti-Orientalism were usually short-lived. For the most part they consisted of an organizational core to which a loose group of individuals was attached.

Whatever the source of the attraction—a popular leader or a set of shared fears and convictions—these organizations were difficult to organize, to discipline, and therefore to perpetuate, except when widespread hostility was independently aroused. Unable to preserve a broad following, and likewise unable to achieve their objectives quickly, they suffered grave deficiencies as effective institutions. In some instances a skeletal organization did persist, but only without a popular following. Thus the ultimate significance of these anti-Oriental societies lies not in their strength or support so much as the fact of their constant rebirth. It underscored the cyclical nature of white British Columbia's obsession with race and allowed repeated articulation of the nativism embedded in west coast culture.

After 1878 the provincial legislature again became the chief public forum for debate on the Chinese question. The Walkem government announced its intention to use "every legitimate means" to obtain the ends of the defunct Chinese Tax Act.[38] What means those were, however, was by no means apparent. The fate of the act had raised serious doubts about the legislature's competence to deal with the problem. Consequently the House felt it could only appeal to Ottawa for redress, a policy which it followed for several years. Most immigration restrictionists, in fact, were forced to turn to Parliament for satisfaction, and Parliament seemed unwilling to fulfil their hopes. In the Commons an attempt to prevent Chinese employment on the Pacific railway was defeated in 1878. During the following year a federal select committee reported that Chinese labour should not be employed on Dominion public works and that Chinese immigration should be discouraged. But no action was taken on either recommendation.[39] During the early 1880s the government of Sir John A. Macdonald seemed content to fend off repeated requests for anti-Chinese legislation. This response, however, was certainly not the result of neglect or indifference. The prime minister was well aware that the railway to the Pacific would require vast numbers of workmen and he feared that such a measure would tie the hands of the railway's contractors. In 1882 Andrew Onderdonk bluntly informed Macdonald that, if the railway was to be completed within a reasonable length of time, Chinese labour would have to be employed.[40] Accordingly the prime minister ignored all entreaties to the contrary. And when railway construction commenced in earnest, a new surge of Chinese immigration soon followed.

3

AGITATION AND RESTRICTION

In the spring of 1882 the pace of work increased on the Fraser canyon section of the railway to the Pacific. Government contractor Andrew Onderdonk required a large reservoir of inexpensive labour to forward his construction program, but none could be found in British Columbia, for the community was not yet sufficiently populous. Nor could enough white navvies be lured northward from the United States, at least at wages he was willing to pay. As a result, Onderdonk adopted the same expedient that other American railroad contractors had found — the extensive use of Chinese labour. In 1882 he already had some 1,500 Chinese under his employ, and over the next four years he imported perhaps 15,000 more. At no one time were there more than 7,500 actually on the job, for the Chinese work force was an extremely mobile one. But in a community of perhaps 35,000 whites the Chinese immigrant once more bulked large in the provincial population.

White British Columbia was quick to notice the sharp rise in Chinese immigration, an increase which seemed even more alarming because the United States had recently passed a law excluding all Chinese immigrants. "Finding the Golden Gate closed against it," one journalist predicted, "the yellow wave will roll in on our shores in increased volume."[1] In the province's two major centres of population, Victoria and New Westminster, rumours spread of massive immigration. According to reports in the spring of 1882, already there were half as many Chinese as whites in the province. More than 10,000 had so far arrived and up to 24,000 more were reputedly on the way. These rumours were an unmistakeable sign of growing racial tension, in the midst of which federal and provincial elections were held. The two campaigns provided outlets for renewed outpourings of anti-Chinese feeling. The federal election also stirred to life the ashes of the Anti-Chinese Association. By then, however, it was no longer just a focus for spontaneous protest. It had become instead a vehicle for the political ambitions of its president, Noah Shakespeare, now the mayor of Victoria and a successful Conservative candidate in the federal contest; after his victory the ACA again disappeared.[2] Nevertheless, as the election atmosphere made clear, political channels for nativistic protest were open in British Columbia. Consequently whites felt little need for pressure group activity, and soon after the elections hostility began to ebb. Coastal residents quickly grew somewhat accustomed to the sight of Chinese transients. Meanwhile the newcomers themselves soon disappeared from view: no sooner had they arrived than they passed inland to their work camps on the railway.

Although coastal residents came to accept the Chinese influx with little outward protest, along the railway line animosity was easily aroused. In May 1883, near Lytton, a minor dispute between a white foreman and a Chinese bookman flared into an open interracial brawl. In the first assault white construction workers armed with pick handles were forced into retreat, outnumbered by their rock-throwing adversaries. But that night, under cover of darkness, a mob of club-wielding whites attacked the sleeping Chinese, catching them unawares. Nine were beaten unconscious before they could flee, two of whom later died. The Chinese camp was then burned to the ground. Despite an outburst of indignation and a reward of $500 offered by the government, the guilty—although known—were never brought to justice.[3] If this incident was any indication, racial tension lay close to the surface in white construction gangs. Probably most navvies would have agreed with British novelist Morley Roberts who, wandering along the line near Kamloops, considered the Orientals he saw to be "the very scum of China."[4]

On Vancouver Island the coal-mining town of Nanaimo became another focus of interracial friction. Since the late 1860s Chinese had worked in the several mines of the district. Mine managers employed many as unskilled labourers for surface and underground work while the miners themselves hired others on the butty system to load and push carts. Yet Chinese employment in the mines was a longstanding source of complaint. Many miners believed that the Chinese ignored accepted mining practices, could not understand English, refused to follow directions from whites, and cared nothing for safety when working underground. These suspicions seemed confirmed in 1879, when a Chinese miner was blamed for a mine explosion which took seven white and four Chinese lives.[5] Furthermore, there were lurking fears that the Chinese mine labourer might rise above his station and challenge the skilled white miner for his job. In 1883, when colliery owner Robert Dunsmuir hired Chinese scabs to break a lengthy strike, animosity was especially intense. Faced with the intransigent strength of Dunsmuir, the miners dropped their demands one by one. In the end their only ultimatum was that all Chinese workers be discharged, but even this was denied them and the miners were forced to accept all of Dunsmuir's terms.[6] This was only the first of several similar confrontations in the Nanaimo district. Chinese strikebreakers were employed in the mines during the major labour struggles of 1903 and 1912-14, refreshing once again the miners' longstanding hostility.

As long as shiploads of workers from China arrived to work on the railroad, provincial politicians were anxious to combat what they saw as a major problem. In 1884 Sinophobes in the legislature mounted a major attack, not just on incoming immigrants, but on those already in the province. The House approved three measures, one forbidding further Chinese immigration and two which imposed discriminatory restrictions upon all Chinese residents; these included a $10 annual poll tax and a ban preventing them from acquiring crown lands.[7] But with the railway still far from completion, the federal government could not yet countenance any restriction on immigration. It disallowed the Chinese Immigration Act six weeks after its passage. Then the act which levied the Chinese poll tax was struck down by the courts. In the end only the prohibition on land acquisition was allowed to stand. Nevertheless continued west coast pressure had begun to take effect, for at the same time as the Immigration Act was nullified the prime minister promised an early investigation into Chinese immigration as well as a measure to regulate it.[8] Persistent pressure from British Columbia had forced him to accept the principle of immigration restriction, although he would not enforce it until the railway's end was in sight.

The Royal Commission on Chinese Immigration, Macdonald's promised investigation, sat during the summer of 1884. Its two commissioners were J. A. Chapleau, federal secretary of state, and Mr. Justice J. H. Gray of the Supreme Court of British Columbia. Gray came to the investigations with well-fixed preconceptions. "The object of the Commission," he told its first sitting in Victoria, "is to obtain proof that the principle of restricting Chinese immigration is proper and in the best interests of the Province and the Dominion." He admitted that "evidence on both sides is required to arrive at a just decision," but the essential task was to inform parliamentarians "in a shape and way that would justify them in passing a prohibitive or restrictive Act. They will have also to be put in possession of proof that would justify them before their constituents, in the event of their supporting a restrictive measure against the Chinese."[9] The commission gathered testimony on the American Pacific coast and then at public hearings held in several British Columbian centres. In all, they received fifty-one submissions, most of them from prominent business and professional men, civil servants, and local politicians in British Columbia.

Although Gray and Chapleau prepared separate reports, a procedure made necessary by limitations of time, the two reached similar conclusions. Both commissioners implicitly accepted the prevailing view that the Chinese were inferior. Yet, once they had examined the evidence, both agreed with the entrepreneurs' claim that, whatever their liabilities, the Chinese were an asset to the province. Chapleau, in particular, emphasized the advantages of Chinese labour. It "is a most efficient aid in the development of a country, and a great means to wealth," he declared. If its use were continued, he speculated, the rich Pacific province "would literally shoot ahead as one of the great seats of commerce and industrial activity."[10] There were evils attending Chinese immigration to be sure, Chapleau admitted, but proper legislation and supervision could deal with them effectively. Nor was Gray an alarmist, even though he had approached the investigation with negative preconceptions. There was no evidence, he pointed out, to indicate that Chinese immigration now endangered the country, and therefore none to suggest any need for immediate or stringent legislation. It was equally clear, however, that public sentiment was aroused and that British Columbians (with some notable exceptions) vigorously opposed any further immigration from China, even though they did not wish Chinese residents expelled. Gray discerned three strains of opinion on the question. One, expressed by a "strongly prejudiced minority," called for total exclusion. A second, that of an "intelligent minority," held that the problem could be solved without legislation if the marketplace were left to regulate itself. A majority, however, favoured "moderate restriction, based upon police, financial and sanitary principles, sustained and enforced by stringent local regulations for cleanliness and the preservation of health."[11]

On the basis of these conclusions the commissioners made their recommendations. The principle which should govern future legislation on Chinese immigration, Gray stated, was "*a policy of judicious selection*. Take what is good, reject what is bad, study the interests of the country, consider its circumstances." But at the same time, Chapleau cautioned, great care should be taken to insure that existing "great interests and enterprises" not be harmed. These ends, they believed, could best be achieved by imposing a head tax of $10 on all Chinese immigrants, preventing the objectionable—the diseased, deformed, and impoverished—from landing, and creating a special tribunal to register the Chinese and then enforce laws, administer justice, and collect taxes among them.[12]

But while the commissioners had spoken, they had not uttered the words white British Columbia wished to hear. When published late in February 1885, their report was greeted by an outburst of irate abuse. In Victoria an angry public meeting dismissed their proposals as "so much folly" while the city council petitioned the House of Commons in protest.[13] By this time the provincial government had grown impatient, too. Its own restrictive policies had been rendered ineffective and Ottawa, which had the authority, seemed most reluctant to act. Meanwhile large numbers of Chinese immigrants had arrived in 1884 and more were expected in the coming months. In protest, therefore, the provincial House re-enacted the disallowed Chinese Immigration Act, hoping either to halt the influx itself or to force federal officials to do likewise.[14] The measure was quickly enforced, and on at least one occasion Chinese arriving by ship were prevented from landing. But this immediately jeopardized the coming season's work on the railway. Onderdonk told George Stephen, president of the CPR, "a large number of Chinamen will necessarily have to come from Oregon and California in the Spring to work on your road above Kamloops. It would be well for you to see that this local act is dissallowed [*sic*] immediately or it will embarrass us very much in getting the men into the country."[15] Again the pliant Macdonald government disallowed the act.

But Macdonald had already committed himself to immigration restriction and he was under growing pressure to implement his commitment. Not only was the British Columbia legislature an irritant but in February and March eastern Canadian unions deluged the Commons with anti-Chinese petitions.[16] Perhaps these smacked as much of the unions' growing desire to exercise political influence as they did of pressing concern for the Chinese threat, but no doubt this concerted campaign urged Parliament onward. At the peak of the petitioning movement, Macdonald introduced an amendment to the Franchise Act, then under protracted and acrimonious debate in the Commons, to prevent any "person of Mongolian or Chinese race" from voting in federal elections.[17] Some objections were raised during the debate which ensued. As one member commented, "I do not think they are a desirable class of persons, but I think that, as British subjects, in British colonies, we ought to show them fair play."[18] But most of the debaters opposed granting the franchise to naturalized Chinese residents, Macdonald as much as anyone. As he told the House:

The Chinese are foreigners. If they come to this country, after three years' residence, they may, if they choose, be naturalized. But still we know that when the Chinaman comes here he intends to return to his own country; he does not bring his family with him; he is a stranger, a sojourner in a strange land, for his own purposes for a while; he has no common interest with us, and while he gives us his labor and is paid for it, and is valuable, the same as a threshing machine or any other agricultural implement which we may borrow from the United States on hire and return it to the owner on the south side of the line; a Chinaman gives us his labor and gets his money, but that money does not fructify in Canada; he does not invest it here, but takes it with him and returns to China; and if he cannot, his executors or his friends send his body back to the flowery land. But he has no British instincts or British feelings or aspirations, and therefore ought not to have a vote.[19]

Yet franchise restrictions were scarcely enough to satisfy west coast nativists, who day by day were growing more irate at procrastination in Ottawa. In Victoria, during the spring and summer months of 1885, popular Sinophobia reached unprecedented heights. On the evening of May 21, in the wake of earlier public protest, nearly a thousand citizens gathered at Campbell's Corner. By the flickering light of torches they paraded down to the new electric light on Blanshard Street. They marched to patriotic airs played by the Blue Ribbon band and carried banners proclaiming anti-Chinese slogans:

NO YELLOW SLAVE SHALL EAT OUR CHILDREN'S BREAD
DOWN WITH THE DRAGON FLAG
LET NO CHINESE LEPER CROSS OUR THRESHOLD
CUT OUT THE CHINESE CANCER

Standing on top of a wagon, labour leader J. M. Duval addressed the crowd, now swollen to more than 2,000. As one they endorsed his impassioned appeal for federal anti-Chinese legislation. Then they resolved to form a new league to forward their cause.[20] One week later the Anti-Chinese Union was founded in Harmony Hall, Victoria's labour temple. City Councillor W. A. Robertson, a self-proclaimed workingman's friend, became its first president.

The ACU held well-attended meetings into the new year. Persistently they reiterated their nativistic demands, including stricter law enforcement within the Chinese community and further restrictions upon Oriental employment. They also tried, with little success, to encourage the immigration of white replacements for

Chinese domestics. At this point, moreover, the working-class roots of this anti-Chinese impulse became more evident, for the ACU became a recruiting ground for the local labour movement. In October the union heard an organizer from Seattle who urged workingmen in the audience to join the Knights of Labor. His appeal was successful, for when the meeting ended seventy-five took out membership. The Knights then embarked on their own anti-Chinese program. They planned to interview local industrialists and determine whether or not they were willing to discharge Chinese employees in favour of whites.[21] The ACU, however, continued to lead the agitation, their cause furthered by the weekly *Industrial News*, a violently Sinophobic labour journal which was published by Duval.

Early in July, after several months of agitation in Victoria, Parliament approved the long-awaited Chinese Immigration Act. The Commons gave the measure little more than a cursory glance. In the Upper House the bill raised the ire of a few senators, but in the end it was easily passed. The act provided that, except for diplomats, tourists, merchants, men of science, and students, all Chinese entering Canada had to pay $50 on arrival. Vessels bringing Chinese to Canada were permitted to land only one immigrant for every fifty tons of ship's weight. Chinese residents wishing to leave the country and return later were exempted from the tax only if they obtained a re-entry permit before leaving.[22] Thus Macdonald had stalled restrictive legislation until the conclusion of railway construction was in sight, when both he and Parliament willingly yielded to west coast demands. Some parliamentarians strongly approved of such a policy and most of the rest readily acquiesced. Only a small minority were opposed. Quite likely the great majority of members accepted the image of John Chinaman which most British Columbians shared.

A further stimulus to hostility came late in 1885. Once the Pacific railway was virtually completed, thousands of Chinese were suddenly out of work. A fortunate minority used their savings to return home to China while others may have left British Columbia for the United States. Most of those who remained were unable to find new jobs. Some huddled together in small interior camps while more than 2,000 others descended on Victoria (a city of 8,500), destitute and hungry. Their plight alarmed whites in several provincial centres. Having lost sixty chickens and twenty-five pigs to a nearby camp of starving Chinese, Port Hammond residents feared an outbreak of serious violence.[23] In Victoria the city council and several prominent Chinese merchants took pity on the unfortunates and established a soup kitchen.[24] But the city's vociferous Sinophobes demanded more than mere palliatives. "There is but one remedy," Duval told the ACU, and "that is sending them back to the land from whence they came, and taking very good care that they are not provided with any certificates to return."[25]

After the worst of the destitution had passed and immigration restrictions took effect, however, open protest soon subsided. Without sufficiently urgent grievances the Anti-Chinese Union fell silent. Several new barriers now confronted Chinese immigrants and no doubt this fact disarmed their antagonists. The deep hostility of recent years remained ingrained in white British Columbia, but popular agitation ceased for a time, at least in Victoria. Yet the experience of the past four years had revealed something of the complexity of the anti-Chinese impulse. For one thing it was driven by several different motives. The first was the fear of social disorder, a threat which seemed especially acute when Chinese destitution was extreme. A second could be seen in the coalfields of Nanaimo. There latent animosity expressed itself through concern for safety in the mines. Beneath this anxiety lay the belief that the Chinese imperilled the miners' own jobs, a highly stereotyped source of alarm. Ultimately, however, heavy immigration was the sharpest goad to animus, for it roused continuing fears of Chinese usurpation. The anticipation was that the Asian would first force whites out of work and then would undermine the cultural foundations of white society.

The past few years had also revealed how widely shared were the Sinophobes' sentiments. No matter where in the province there were Chinese communities, hostility prevailed among neighbouring whites. These prejudices were far from being confined to provincial workingmen. Certainly, when popular protest movements arose, they drew heavily upon working-class support. But many public spokesmen for the anti-Chinese movement were clearly of middle-class origin, and it may be reasonably assumed that many of their sympathizers were as well.

Another feature of the anti-Chinese impulse is worthy of note— the nature of its leadership. Even though pressure groups provided a focus for popular Sinophobia during the 1880s, most of the dominant figures in the anti-Chinese movement were politicians. It might be assumed that these political leaders were exploiting racialism for their own political ends. Noah Shakespeare, for example, used the movement as an instrument to gain municipal and federal office. But far from cynically trading on popular prejudices, most west coast politicians seem to have shared the fears and convictions of their constituents. Nativism found its way into the political life of British Columbia, not because low-minded politicians abused their positions as leaders of public opinion, but because it was a natural outlet for the collective hostilities, anxieties, and demands of the community. Political channels in the west coast province openly received and transmitted these racist sentiments. During the 1880s this tendency was reinforced because British Columbia lacked a mature and differentiated structure of social institutions which might otherwise have performed these functions. Thus political agencies were among the few institutions available to articulate such sentiments.

By 1885 the years of railway construction had fixed the dye of racialism upon white British Columbia. In the following decades racial animosity was easily evoked and readily expressed. A host of racial incidents, large and small, recorded the animus which remained latent in the host community. The first of these occurred in Vancouver, soon after the birth of the city.

In March 1886, even before the town was chartered, local residents met to air their antipathy toward the Chinese.[26] Perhaps this was simply the dying echo of earlier protest in Victoria; nonetheless it was a sign that this community shared the antagonism which prevailed elsewhere in the province. Vancouver was burned to the ground in June, however, and for some time thereafter it had far more pressing concerns than those posed by Chinese immigrants. But by November a new and larger city had risen from the ashes of the old, and apparently its Chinese population had grown, too, for the local Knights of Labor undertook a vigorous anti-Chinese campaign. They boycotted prominent whites who employed or patronized Chinese, painting a large black X on the sidewalk in front of each offender's place of business.[27] At the same time, in concert with the local vintners' association, they called for restrictions on Chinese immigration, their hopes pinned on winning support for workingmen's candidates in the forthcoming municipal election. The local paper agreed with the Knights. "Take warning now while there is time," it urged its readers, "grapple with the evil while it is in its infancy." If city employers did not discharge their Chinese help in favour of whites, the paper claimed, Vancouverites would soon be faced with "the permanent settlement of the Mongolian in our midst." Indeed, "so long as the Chinaman is encouraged so long will the evil grow, and if allowed to expand as it is now, will develop alarmingly and become so great that the efforts of the people will be powerless to check it."[28]

Twenty Chinese labourers arrived from Victoria early in January in the midst of this growing hostility. Brought by a city contractor to clear land on the Vancouver townsite, they were, it was rumoured, the vanguard of up to 300 more.[29] Evidently, however, many city whites deplored the prospect of a permanent Chinese minority in the district. Under the leadership of R. D. Pitt, a prominent member of the Knights, a group of the concerned resolved to nip the problem in the bud. They appointed two committees, one to meet with the Chinese and induce them to leave, the other to urge employers to replace their Chinese help with whites.[30] On January 10 a "committee" of 75, accompanied by more than 250 supporters, paraded to the Chinese camp and presented its case. Intimidated, the Chinese needed little persuasion. They quickly packed their belongings and marched down to the CPR dock, followed by the mob which had doubled in size by the time they arrived. As the mayor looked on, someone took up a collection for their fare. Then they embarked on a steamer which soon set out for Victoria, wildly applauded by the crowd. On the following day a similar scene was enacted, while a third group of Chinese quietly left town on foot for New Westminster.[31]

Not content with their early success, Vancouver's crusaders now took steps to rid the city of Chinese permanently. In the wake of the incident, at least three hundred citizens, including many businessmen, vowed to discourage Chinese from locating in the city, to refuse them employment or trade, and to boycott whites who hired them. Evidently some Sinophobes were even raising funds to buy out Chinese property-owners. By early February an anti-Chinese league had been formed. It circulated 500 display cards reading:

VANCOUVER ANTI-CHINESE PLEDGE
To appreciate freedom we must prohibit slave labor. The undersigned pledges himself not to deal directly or indirectly with Chinese or any person who encourages them by trade or otherwise.[32]

In the meantime tempers remained hot enough that when unfounded rumours were heard of fresh Chinese arrivals, a mob of 300 whites trooped down to the CPR wharf to prevent them from landing.[33]

But the vigil in Vancouver went unrewarded, for within days of the exodus some Chinese began to return. By mid-February, one Sinophobe complained, there were a hundred more in town than there had been three weeks previously.[34] Then, late in the month, when another small group disembarked to clear land, hostility boiled over again. Soon after their arrival someone posted an ill-written notice: "The Chinese have came. Mass meeting in the City Hall to-night." By eight o'clock the council chambers were filled to overflowing, and during the next two hours the eager audience cheered a succession of anti-Chinese diatribes, all of them urging immediate action. Then, as the meeting drew to a close, a voice boomed out from the back of the hall, "those in favor of turning out the Chinese to-night, say 'Aye'," and a chorus of ayes rang out. The crowd poured into the street, formed a procession, and marched the mile west to the Chinese camp on Coal Harbour. When they arrived they surrounded the Orientals, pulled down their shanties, and threw their bedding and clothing into the campfire. They seized and beat several Chinese; others escaped only by plunging into the chilly waters of the harbour. But just as the crowd was about to escort its captives down the road to New Westminster, two police officers from Vancouver appeared and forced the mob to disperse. Later that evening, back in the city, two Chinese shacks were found ablaze, their inhabitants having fled. Next day eighty-six Chinese living near False Creek were also intimidated and they hastily decamped for New Westminster.[35]

Like the previous hostile outbursts, the Vancouver incident and the agitation which preceded it were largely the work of working-class elements. But while it resembled past occurrences in this respect, the Vancouver outbreak stood apart from them in one important way which sheds a good deal of light on the nature of Sinophobia. In the past, agitation had usually been linked with heavy Chinese immigration. In Vancouver it was not. In fact, by 1887 the province's Chinese population was dwindling and outside Vancouver nativism had subsided. What inflamed hostility in Vancouver was the internal movement of Chinese within British Columbia, the sudden arrival of a group of Asiatics in a white community where only a handful had lived before. Vancouver, of course, had fallen heir to the region's anti-Chinese tradition and once the Chinese began to arrive its animus quickly sharpened. Their coming confronted whites with the prospect of permanent racial diversity in the community. In doing so it roused profound psychological fears and stirred a deep-rooted longing within the host society for a culturally homogeneous population. The nativists therefore believed that, during these vital months when the city was being formed, action was imperative. At all costs the Chinese could not be permitted to carve a permanent niche of their own in Vancouver. An unassimilable minority, they could only weaken west coast society by destroying its homogeneous condition.

During the decade which followed the Vancouver outbreak, overt antipathy abated. There were few attempts to legislate new restrictions and fewer spontaneous outbursts of collective hostility. For this the shrinking of the provincial Chinese population was largely responsible. During the later 1880s federal legislation reduced the Chinese influx to a small fraction of its pre-restriction level while economic hardship drove many to the United States or back to China. After 1890 immigration from China increased substantially once again, but at the same time the province's white population grew from 54,000 to almost 135,000, more than doubling in size. Thus over the years the Chinese presence grew less evident, and as it did, John Chinaman seemed somewhat less disturbing. Not that animosity evaporated, however. On the contrary, the province's deep reservoir of ill-will remained ready to be tapped. No new nativistic movement or institution gave enmity specific focus; no single figure crystallized white British Columbia's rancour. Yet new fears, new circumstances, and new conflicts of interest all fed west coast racialism. Even in the absence of intense hostility, antipathy remained firmly fixed in the provincial mind.

After 1887 the British Columbia legislature, which had played a prominent role in past anti-Chinese campaigns, abandoned its formerly aggressive stance. Although it remained antipathetic toward the Oriental, it was under far less pressure from public opinion. Furthermore, provincial authority to enforce restrictive measures seemed circumscribed by both the British North America Act and the Macdonald government's penchant for disallowance. Occasionally the legislature inserted clauses in incorporation acts which prevented newly formed companies from employing Chinese labour. It also forbade Chinese employment underground in coal mines. But at a time when rapid industrial growth seemed imminent, successive provincial governments were unwilling to take action which might stay the hand of economic progress. And when compared with the legislature's past enactments, these new measures were little more than gestures. Nor did Parliament extend existing discriminatory policies. Some criticism of immigration restriction was uttered in the Senate, but it had no influence on federal government policy.

Another sign of the lower level of public animosity was the sharp decline in organized anti-Oriental agitation. Occasionally concerned citizens still gathered together in protest. In the spring of 1892 another ephemeral nativistic association—the Canadian Anti-Chinese League—was founded in Vancouver.[36] Led by a curious and slightly mad man with the unlikely name of Locksley Lucas, it had but a fleeting life. Indeed, for more than a decade after the Vancouver incident, what little popular agitation there was invariably proved to be sporadic and disorganized.

If public protest had any institutional focus whatsoever during these years, it lay in British Columbia's infant labour movement. In the late 1880s, and throughout the 1890s, first the Knights of Labor and then the newer craft unions repeatedly emphasized their unrelenting hostility to Oriental immigrants. In 1889, for example, stonemasons and bricklayers in Victoria demanded that their employers replace Chinese hod carriers and bricklayers' assistants with whites.[37] At Nanaimo two tragic mine disasters in 1887 and 1888 intensified the local miners' special sense of grievance. They struck all the mines in the district and refused to work until the Chinese were removed from underground.[38] They won their point, but success was only temporary for some mine owners were soon sending Asiatics below the surface again. As a result, during the next decade miners continued to press for an end to Oriental employment in the mines. When provincial workingmen began to enter politics, they invariably built stout anti-Oriental planks into their campaign platforms.[39] Seeking a national audience, the British Columbia labour movement also took its grievance to the Dominion Trades and Labor Congress in the early 1890s.[40] There they recited the whole litany of Chinese stereotypes, not just those which singled out the Asian economic threat. Their pleas to eastern unionists fell on sympathetic ears. Since 1885 the latter had repeatedly petitioned Parliament for an end to Chinese immigration.[41]

There were several reasons why trade unionism became one of the primary vehicles of anti-Oriental sentiment during the late nineteenth century. Unions, of course, were intended to defend the economic interests of their members, interests which Asiatics had long been held to jeopardize. Thus white trade unionists logically sought to protect themselves from competitive economic pressures which, it was generally agreed, placed them at a serious disadvantage. But protection could have been achieved in two distinctly different ways, either by absorbing Asians into the union movement or by supporting discriminatory government policies which enforced various restrictions based upon race. Admittedly the great gulf between eastern and western cultures hindered labour from making common cause with the Chinese and Japanese. But quite apart from these obstacles, cooperation was seldom ventured. Instead labour invariably favoured the second available tactic, racial discrimination. That it did was a measure of its wholehearted commitment, not merely to defence against Oriental competition, but to the pattern of motives and attitudes which underlay much of white racism.

Then, too, the prewar trade union movement was relatively powerless. It was locked in an unequal contest with capital and was able to attract only a small minority of industrial workers. For a movement in this condition, anti-Orientalism was a rallying cry of broad, popular appeal. In depicting this issue as a workingman's grievance, union leaders used racism to mobilize support for the trade unionist cause.

Finally, aside from newspapers, political organizations, and nativistic societies in the province, there were few other institutions available at this time for the expression of popular racial attitudes. British Columbia was a nascent industrial society during the 1880s and 1890s. It lacked the complex structure of social institutions which it was later to develop. Consequently public opinion had few organizational outlets. One of these was the trade union movement, which for this reason as well became a major conduit for popular racism.

Outside the labour movement, white British Columbia expressed its racial animosity in many additional ways. Theatres and other public accommodations customarily discriminated in admission and seating practices.[42] Chinese children were informally discouraged from attending public school, even though their parents paid the required school taxes and no legal obstacle barred their admission.[43] On the streets of provincial cities Chinese became common targets for stone and snowball-throwing youths. Usually only the victim's dignity was bruised, but occasionally serious injury, and even death, resulted.[44] From time to time adults made similar unprovoked attacks on passing Chinese. Such incidents as these cannot be dismissed as mere pranks or irrational gestures. They happened frequently, sometimes even under the watchful eye of the police, and only occasionally did they evoke as much as a gesture of protest from whites. They formed part of a behaviour pattern characteristic of a society marked by a major racial cleavage and were bound to recur in a community which actively promoted many forms of racism. In effect they were further signs of the breadth and depth of the anti-Chinese consensus.

During the years of declining hostility, however, popular Sinophobia did take one new turn. After 1890, in particular, white British Columbia grew alarmed at the seeming threat which the Chinese posed to the public health of the province. Not that the fear was something new. Indeed, since the 1860s the Chinese had always been considered a rather unclean and unhealthy lot. In Victoria municipal officials had tried for years, with little success, to enforce local sanitary codes in Chinatown. But this was an age of expanding public knowledge about disease, its origins, and transmission. Consequently, after smallpox besieged Vancouver and Victoria during the summer of 1892, concern for civic cleanliness grew perceptibly. The initial, uninformed assumption (later verified) was that the carrier of the disease had come from China.[45] Thus the outbreak confirmed older stereotyped perceptions which depicted Orientals as diseased. Frequent contemporary news reports of a cholera epidemic in Asia further augmented these fears. And in the wake of growing public anxiety, campaigns were launched to eradicate dirt and disease in the Chinatowns of the province.

Victorians, in particular, were acutely aware that, as their city was a seaport in constant contact with the Orient, they were especially vulnerable. The city's Chinese quarter was condemned as "a reeking mass of filth" and a potential breeding ground for disease.[46] In 1893 the city sanitary inspector tried to clean the district up while the medical health officer began to vaccinate Chinese, many of them against their will. Some of the more dilapidated dwellings in Chinatown were condemned and destroyed.[47] Later the city council authorized rigorous detention and disinfection procedures, hoping to insure that Asians who entered the city were free of contagious diseases. But it seemed an uphill task. As the city health officer declared, "we have found it difficult to carry out the sanitary regulations among the Chinese, as they tried to shirk their responsibility in this matter, as it means some expense to them; but by continual watching and frequent inspection they have been compelled to carry out the rules."[48] At a later date similar complaints were made in Vancouver. According to a local doctor, "the hygienic conditions ... in Chinatown are a standing menace to the public health."[49] In Victoria the campaign to clean up Chinatown was revived in 1900, when rumours were heard that a recent outbreak of the bubonic plague had spread from Asia to Honolulu and San Francisco. On this occasion concern was such that the city council asked the provincial government for special powers to cope with the threat.[50]

Chinatown's overcrowded living conditions were a source of equal alarm. The chief danger, Victoria's health officer warned, was the ease with which disease could be spread in such conditions. He remarked that in one instance twenty-five Chinese household servants, one of them a smallpox victim, were found sleeping in a single room. That an epidemic did not sweep the city, he observed,

was nothing short of a miracle.[51] Moreover, according to their critics, the Chinese were masters of prevarication, especially over the
matter of overcrowding. As one wit observed:

> Some Chinaman
> Has found a plan
> To outwit sanitation:
> When ten you see
> Where four should be
> He makes a declaration.

> "You sabe him—
> His name Ah Sim,
> An' him, name Ah Chi Mo—
> No more one day
> Him come to stay
> Him lib in Nanaimo."[52]

In Vancouver overcrowding was still a problem during the later
1890s, largely because of a great influx of Japanese immigrants.
Periodically city health officials swooped down upon boarding
houses late at night, counting their inmates and charging their
owners if occupancy by-laws were broken.[53]

Two other facets of Chinese health and sanitation also provoked
many whites during the late nineteenth century. One constant irritant was the Chinese laundry. Long a fixture in most provincial
centres, it was frequently condemned as unsightly and unclean.
Over the years it had been subjected to increasingly stringent legislative restrictions. Nevertheless it was still often claimed that Chinese laundrymen slept in their washing and also that they damp-
ened clothes when ironing by squirting on them water which they
held in their mouths. At public insistence, municipal by-laws forbade these practices and insisted that washermen sprinkle their
clothes with "proper and cleanly appliances."[54]

The other source of concern was the apparently increased incidence of leprosy among the Chinese. While they had long been stigmatized as a leprous race, only a few authentic cases of the disease
had come to light since the gold rush era. But in 1886 a Chinese
prisoner in the provincial jail was found to be a leper. Confronted
with his presence, both provincial and municipal authorities recoiled. The province ordered the City of Victoria to remove the
unfortunate sufferer. The city, although it had cared for destitute
and disabled Chinese in the past, drew the line at lepers and asked
several local Chinese merchants to care for him. The merchants replied that they were as much afraid of the disease as anyone, and no
one could be found to wait on him. But they did agree to pay his
passage back to China, and ultimately he returned.[55]

This method of coping with leprosy was useful only as long as lepers were discovered infrequently. But by 1891 there were at least five known lepers in Victoria and vicinity, and as a result the city fathers felt compelled to make more satisfactory arrangements. On D'Arcy Island, one of the smaller, nearby Gulf Islands, they built a lazaretto, stocked it with food (and, according to rumour, opium), and committed to it the five lepers to wait out their days, remote from all other human society.[56] Late in the year they were joined by two others sent from Vancouver, and thereafter the lonely little island's population fluctuated slightly as death removed some and new sufferers were condemned to isolation. Probably no more than a dozen resided there at any one time, their only contact with the world a quarterly visit from the Victoria medical health officer who came by tug to bring fresh supplies and take back news of those who had died.

Yet one important question remains to be answered: why were Asians singled out as a special threat to public health? The answer reveals much about the nature of west coast xenophobia. For one thing, a good deal of this concern was not at all misplaced. Major epidemics did sweep China during the late nineteenth century and therefore Chinese immigrants were potential disease bearers. Furthermore, by western standards Chinatowns were usually overcrowded and unclean. Behind their solid brick façades, those in Vancouver and Victoria were little more than conglomerations of wooden shacks and precarious stairways, plank sidewalks, and open sewers. But public concern over health and sanitation was much more than just a reasoned response to a pressing social problem. After all, Chinatown was not the only run-down district in most provincial towns and Chinese immigrants were not the only carriers of disease. Ultimately this obsession with Chinese threats to health and sanitation was an extension of west coast Sinophobia. One traditional stereotype which permeated Western thought was that of the diseased and dirty Chinaman. As stereotypes do, this one predicted a common characteristic of the Chinese immigrant, one which the British Columbian experience seemed to confirm. And once confirmed, it was given fresh life. Thus prevailing forms of racial perception made whites especially sensitive to the issue of health and cleanliness. At bottom, it was this that accounted for their concern for sanitation and their tendency to condemn the Chinese in entirety as bearers of disease.

4

THE VANCOUVER RIOT

Between 1885 and 1914 west coast society was transformed. During these thirty years British Columbia matured as an industrial and commercial society. The province's three major resource industries— fishing, mining, and lumbering—each put down firm foundations. The new port of Vancouver, Pacific terminus of the CPR, grew rapidly after 1885 and within ten years became the premier urban community in the province. At the same time rapid population growth arrived in tandem with urban and industrial development. Over these three decades British Columbia's population more than quadrupled in size, reaching well over 400,000 by the outbreak of World War I. The greater part of this gain accrued from migration rather than natural increase, for the province profited greatly from both the westward trek within Canada and the transatlantic migrations of the early twentieth century. Of the two, however, immigration was by far the more important source of population growth; while many reached the western coast from central and eastern Canada, the majority were newcomers to the country, preponderantly from the British Isles. The weight of these profound demographic and economic changes was felt for years to come, for together they pressed the west coast community into a mould which preserved its essential shape for the next two generations. By 1914 urban, industrial, and Anglo-Canadian influences already predominated in British Columbian society. Thereafter they increasingly prevailed.

When compared with the total number of immigrants who entered Canada during these years, Orientals were of little numerical significance. Between 1885 and 1914 more than 3.5 million newcomers were admitted to the country, but only slightly more than 3 per cent of them were from Asia (in part because of the restrictions imposed on incoming Orientals). Although most of the latter lingered in British Columbia, even there they formed a small minority of the thousands who settled in the province. Furthermore, as sojourners many Asians did not remain long in the west coast community, and the province's Oriental population was continually diminished by the large outflow of migrants returning to their homelands. Consequently, with comparatively small numbers of arrivals and significant rates of return migration, the Asian communities in British Columbia grew far more slowly than did the white.[1] (See table 2, p. 171.) In 1901 almost 11 per cent of the provincial population was Oriental; by 1911 the proportion had shrunk to less than 8 per cent. Thus, regardless of its continued growth, in relative terms the Asian population of the west coast province constantly shrank in size and significance.

Despite their obvious social import, however, these fundamental changes in the demography of British Columbia had little impact on white perceptions of Asian immigrants. The image of John Chinaman remained largely intact, and during the 1890s and early 1900s, when Japanese and then East Indian immigrants began to arrive in numbers, negative stereotyped attitudes quickly evolved toward them as well. In fact, one measure of the strength of the anti-Oriental consensus was the extreme ease with which it extended its influence over immigrant Occidentals. Hostility toward Asiatics was so pervasive on the Pacific coast that newcomers, even though they far outnumbered native-born whites, apparently absorbed it readily. One reason why even far-reaching social change failed to alter this pattern of racial awareness was that its content was ultimately founded not so much on shifting socio-economic circumstances as on the white community's continuing psychological tendency to cling to the ideal of the homogeneous society. The extreme social fluidity of these years may have made this need imperative. Certainly the dawning industrial age offered new opportunities for racial confrontation of a kind rooted in genuine economic tension. Furthermore, the growing institutional complexity of an expanding, maturing society produced new interest groups and organizations with an economic stake in the Oriental question. Nevertheless, whatever the occasions for nativistic outburst, and whoever were the parties that raised the outcry, the rhetoric and motivation of west coast racialism remained largely unaltered.

At the mass level, anti-Orientalism in British Columbia was highly volatile during the two decades which straddled the turn of the century. But while numerous outbursts of popular nativism erupted, none prior to 1907 was intense, sustained, or widespread, at least when judged by the standards of the mid-1880s. In fact, as had previously been the case, the chief campaigners against Asian immigrants were provincial legislators, presumably seeking to curry public favour for themselves. For more than a decade after 1895 they methodically sought to broaden the scope of existing anti-Oriental legislation. Soon after Japanese immigrants began to arrive in numbers, during the early 1890s, the legislature acknowledged that the newcomers simply added a new dimension to a longstanding social problem. After the turn of the century the first East Indian immigrants extended the problem further. Consequently the House tried to apply most existing Chinese disabilities to each of these incoming groups in turn. In particular, all naturalized and Canadian-born Asiatics were stripped of the franchise, and thereby rendered politically impotent.[2]

The main thrust of this new legislative attack was toward additional curbs on Oriental employment. In years past the House had attempted to prevent Chinese from working underground in coal mines. Government contracts had customarily been let on the proviso that contractors employ no Chinese. But until 1897 no systematic attempts had been made to circumscribe employment opportunities for Asians. In that year, however, the legislature approved the Alien Labor Act, the most comprehensive piece of restrictive legislation yet passed in the province. It banned Chinese and Japanese employment on a wide variety of private works conducted under the provincial government's charter, including railways, roads, telegraph and telephone lines, harbours, canals, and dams. But the act never took effect; instead it was nullified by the federal government.[3] Undaunted, the legislature pressed its case. It re-enacted the measure one year later, changing only its name to the Labor Regulation Act. Knowing the likely fate of the bill, however, and anxious to insure that its objectives would be met, the House took the added precaution of including restrictive employment clauses in a large number of private bills passed during the session, most of which chartered railway companies. The federal government of Sir Wilfrid Laurier opposed disallowance and would have preferred not to alienate west coast opinion. But it also was pressed by Japanese consular officials and British Colonial Secretary Joseph Chamberlain to avoid overt discrimination and therefore, after a lengthy delay, it again struck down the omnibus employment restriction bill.[4]

While the Laurier government temporized in the face of growing west coast pressure, an unprecedented tide of Oriental immigrants suddenly flooded into the province. In 1899 and 1900 almost 20,000 Asians entered British Columbia, more than half of them during the first six months of 1900. Many were Japanese recruited for work in Honolulu who, because of an outbreak of plague in Hawaii, were first diverted to California and then to British Columbia after American immigration restrictions were enforced. This substantial new influx tapped the fears and prejudices latent in west coast society. White British Columbia's ideal of the homogeneous community once more seemed in peril, and the province loosed another shrill xenophobic outcry. "If we allow this Asiatic deluge to continue much longer," one correspondent told the *Colonist*, "even our law courts and legislature will be given over to the 'heathen Chinee' and the 'little brown men'." He asked, "are we to have this great big province—a land virtually flowing with milk and honey—conserved for the best interests of the white British subject—English, Scotch, Irish, Welsh, etc.—or must it be given over entirely to the yellow and brown hordes of China and Japan?"[5] Petitions were passed around protesting the high rate of immigration. The daily press called for measures to prevent the province from being overrun. Meanwhile labour journals were equally agitated. "Is nothing to be done to stop the influx of mongols into this province?" the *Industrial World* queried. "What is in store for us as an Anglo-Saxon community? With the mongols in our mines, workshops, forests, and on railroads, and tilling our farms, what is to become of our white labourers, miners and mechanics?" "The workers of British Columbia," it muttered, "may be forced to give the government to understand, once for all, that they intend this community shall remain Anglo-Saxon."[6]

Most provincial politicians shared the growing public alarm. Furthermore, few of them failed to recognize the political utility of prejudice. In the spring of 1900, when immigration from the Orient was at its height, a provincial election was called. In the ensuing campaign many candidates raised the call for immediate restrictive legislation. Premier Joseph Martin promised to re-enact anti-Oriental immigration laws as frequently as they were disallowed. But no other candidate could possibly make as grand a gesture as opposition leader James Dunsmuir, heir to his father's coal-mining interests. In a card to the electors of South Nanaimo he promised to replace all of his Chinese employees with whites. Labour candidates also demanded stringent restrictive measures. The swelling tide of hostility swept much of the province before it. "There is almost complete unanimity of sentiment on the question of Oriental immigration, so far as the people of British Columbia are concerned," the *Colonist* observed. "If a candidate should declare himself favorable to the unrestricted immigration of Chinese and Japanese, he could not save his deposit in any constituency in this province."[7]

Soon after the election the new premier, Dunsmuir, honoured his campaign promise and began to dismiss his Chinese employees; when the legislature met in an early fall sitting, it approved a broad anti-Oriental program. Hoping to counter federal objections to past legislation, it applied the principle of the Natal formula, a language test, to the two key bills, a practice once recommended by Joseph Chamberlain. The first made unlawful the immigration of anyone unable to write and sign "in the characters of some language of Europe" a prescribed form. The second, yet another Labor Regulation Act, forbade persons or corporations who received property, rights, or privileges by provincial statute to employ those who could not read the act itself in a European language.[8] Like many of his predecessors, Dunsmuir was not at all certain that provincial authority was broad enough to enforce this legislation, but he remained convinced of the need for sweeping measures and argued his case in a lengthy letter to Laurier. The problem confronting British Columbia, he explained, was that in the face of "an indiscriminate and unrestricted immigration of Mongolians ... without lowering the general standard of living necessary to meet the decrease in wages, it is not possible for white labor to exist in the face of a system that has grown up under conditions entirely foreign to Anglo-Saxon communities, wholly inapplicable in this country, and out of harmony with our institutions." The only satisfactory way in which to solve the problem, he suggested, was to increase the per capita immigration tax to a prohibitive level and to restrict Oriental employment in Canada. Like many British Columbians, he felt that the federal government's recent Chinese head tax increase, from $50 to $100, did not suffice. He also believed that, while the province's powers of remedy were unclear, those of the Dominion were not. Therefore he urged Laurier to provide the relief which British Columbia sought. The alternative, he warned, was continued provincial legislation.[9]

Again the Laurier government, itself soon to face the electorate, for the time being ignored both the province's legislation and the accompanying Japanese protests. As a result, on January 1, 1901, the Immigration Act came into effect and was rigorously enforced during the succeeding months. Japanese who could meet the act's requirements were permitted to land; those who could not were not. Disallowance did not come until the following September. When it did, provincial authorities were more angered than dismayed, especially as they considered the Immigration Act a great success. In reply the legislature again re-enacted the two statutes.[10] No doubt, by this time members expected that the bills would once more be struck down, but they probably believed as well that their gesture would signify their protest, goad the federal government, and insure at least another round of temporary restriction. The House also approved an act which avoided overt discrimination by burying it in the bureaucratic process: a proviso was included whereby no provincial subsidies would be awarded to any concern until the recipients made an agreement with the province regarding the employment of labour on their projects.[11] For the same reason the Executive Council passed two orders in council which stipulated that employment restrictions be incorporated in many leases, licenses, and contracts let by the government.[12] Once more federal officials struck down the offending acts, but on this occasion the orders in council were beyond federal review. And during the six months between enactment and disallowance the legislation once more restricted Japanese immigration and Oriental activities in the province.

Although subsequent provincial administrations found their attempts to solve the Oriental problem continually thwarted, they insistently pressed their case on the Laurier government, repeatedly reintroducing the forbidden proposals. As Dunsmuir's successor, E. G. Prior, informed the prime minister in 1903, "any government of British Columbia will feel compelled to re-enact that legislation, which so far as it has been allowed to operate has been very efficient in carrying out what was desired. So far as this present government is concerned it feels impelled to the course not as an attitude of threat or as an act of hostility to the Dominion government, but as an assertion of its rights to self-protection."[13] These measures were regularly enacted and disallowed until 1908. If nothing else, the practice provided temporary restrictions and satisfied west coast whites that their provincial government was attempting to solve the problem of Oriental immigration.

Despite its intransigent response to provincial legislation, the federal government also felt the weight of growing west coast pressure. Increasingly since 1896 Laurier's Liberal friends in British Columbia had urged him to adopt a more restrictive immigration policy for Asians. Immediately after he took office, politicians and labour leaders in the larger provincial centres got up a petitioning movement with that very object in mind. Laurier at first seemed receptive to the idea. Personally he had little sympathy for the Oriental immigrant. "For my part," he told one correspondent privately, "I have very little hope of any good coming to this country from Asiatic immigration of any kind. I doubt if the Japanese will amalgamate with our people, and, if the amalgamation were to take place, would prove beneficial."[14] But he was also confronted with counter-vailing pressures. The CPR, whose steamship line earned a healthy income from the transpacific passenger trade, protested that it would suffer serious losses if new restrictions were imposed.[15] In addition, the government had been repeatedly pressed by Joseph Chamberlain at the Colonial Office to take no steps, and permit no provincial action, which might jeopardize imperial relations with Japan. Since the late 1890s Great Britain had actively cultivated amicable relations with Japan, and early in 1902 the two nations signed a diplomatic alliance. While Laurier was by no means an unswervingly loyal imperialist, in this instance he readily yielded to Chamberlain's requests. Moreover, although the prime minister was no friend of the Oriental, neither was he a nativist. Discrimina-tory legislation he regarded with distaste.[16] Consequently these various influences all predisposed him to avoid further restrictive measures.

But by 1900 the intensity of west coast opinion forced the Liberal government to yield to demands for curbs on Asian immigration. However strong Laurier's scruples were, they were easily overcome by the weight of British Columbian concern. Nevertheless in the case of the Japanese he was most reluctant to act. The government refused to entertain a measure based upon the Natal Act, he told the Commons, because nothing should be done which might im-peril Canada's good relations with Japan, especially now that Bri-tain was at war in South Africa. At the same time he did recognize that Japanese immigration remained a serious grievance in British Columbia, and therefore he proposed a royal commission on the question. As for Chinese immigration, his distaste for discrimina-tion was a far less effective deterrent, nor did national and imperial policy limit the scope of Canadian action. The government there-fore doubled the Chinese entry tax to $100 and, buying further time while offering the appearance of positive action, called another royal commission to investigate the Oriental problem once again.[17]

In British Columbia the increase in the entry tax was regarded with derision. Public feeling was so aroused that, with an election in the offing, west coast Liberals feared for their political necks if the Laurier government did not enforce more stringent restrictions. To meet his critics part way, Laurier chose the opening day of the federal campaign to announce the appointment of the new royal commission. R. C. Clute, a Toronto barrister, was named its chair-man. Its two other members, who represented segments of the com-munity vitally interested in the question, were D. J. Munn, a can-ner from New Westminster, and Christopher Foley, a miner and labour leader from Rossland.[18] The commission's public sittings commenced in Victoria in March 1901, and during the next three months it visited various parts of the province, hearing evidence from more than 335 witnesses.

Early in 1902 the commissioners placed their report before Parliament. In great detail it examined the impact of Oriental immigration upon the economy of British Columbia and analysed the role of the Chinese and Japanese in the province's major industries. In their summation the commissioners emphasized the deleterious effect which Oriental competition had had on the white worker and admitted that, despite the Asian's utility in several industries, on the whole his presence had proved detrimental. It also underlined the point which white British Columbia had long made: Asians were unassimilable and therefore they barred the path which led to the racially homogeneous society. The Chinese, the report concluded,

come from southern China, drawn from the poorer classes, reared in poverty where a few cents a day represent the earnings which must suffice for a family; accustomed to crowd together in small tenements or huts, close, unhealthy, and filthy; with customs, habits and modes of life fixed and unalterable, resulting from an ancient and effete civilization, with no desire to conform to western ideas. They form, on their arrival, a community within a community, separate and apart, a foreign substance within, but not of our body politic, with no love for our laws and institutions; a people that will not assimilate or become an integral part of our race and nation. With their habits of overcrowding, and an utter disregard of all sanitary laws, they are a continual menace to health. From a moral and social point of view, living as they do without home life, schools or churches, and so nearly approaching a servile class, their effect upon the rest of the community is bad. They pay no fair proportion of the taxes of the country. They keep out immigrants who would become permanent citizens, and create conditions inimical to labour and dangerous to the industrial peace of the community where they come. They spend little of their earnings in the country and trade chiefly with their own people. They fill the places that ought to be occupied by permanent citizens, many of whom leave the country on their account. They are unfit for full citizenship, and are permitted to take no part in municipal or provincial government. Upon this point there was entire unanimity. They are not and will not become citizens in any sense of the term as we understand it. They are so nearly allied to a servile class that they are obnoxious to a free community and dangerous to the state.[19]

As their presence was so injurious, and as abundant cheap labour was readily available, the commissioners urged that further Chinese immigration be effectively prohibited by raising the entry tax to $500.[20]

Japanese immigrants, the commissioners concluded, were less objectionable in some respects than were the Chinese. But in others they were an even more serious menace. "The consensus of opinion of the people of British Columbia," they reported, "is that they do not and cannot assimilate with white people, and that while in some respects they are less undesirable than the Chinese, in that they adopt more readily our habits of life and spend more of their earnings in the country, yet in all that goes to make for the permanent settlement of the country they are quite as serious a menace as the Chinese and keener competitors against the working man, and as they have more energy, push and independence, more dangerous in this regard than the Chinese."[21] But the commissioners were content that, as long as the government of Japan willingly restricted the emigration of its nationals (a practice which it had followed since the fall of 1900), no further restrictive action was necessary. If large numbers of Japanese labourers were again permitted to emigrate to Canada, however, effective immigration restriction policies based upon the Natal formula would become imperative.[22]

During the session of 1903 Parliament acted on the commissioners' recommendations and raised the Chinese entry tax to $500. The measure drew scattered protests. The CPR displayed a tender regard for its own financial interests as did a number of small employers for theirs. Perhaps the most interesting response came from a Vancouver housewife. "We are wholly dependent on Chinese as household servants," she informed Laurier. "We cannot get woman servants for love or money. For two weeks I have been trying to get a woman to help in the house by the day but there is only one really reliable woman in Van[couver] and she is so much in demand one has to wait a month before she can give them even one day." "If your bill passes," she warned, "it will mean the breaking up of homes and families flocking to hotels and boarding houses as they have been obliged to do in San Francisco."[23] But objections were few and far between. On the whole west coast whites seemed satisfied with the new tax. And it had the desired results. The number of Chinese who paid the entry fee dropped from 4,719 to 8 in the fiscal year after the act took effect. Ottawa had once more met British Columbia's nativistic demands, at least as far as imperial and national interests would permit.

The decade which spanned the turn of the century was also marked by recurrent outbursts of popular nativism in British Columbia. On the whole these were local incidents, and they probably reflected the persistence of latent racial animus rather than a general increase in the level of racial tension. At the same time, however, their scattered geographic pattern offered further proof that racialist sentiments were broadly shared across the province.

In Victoria school segregation became an issue early in 1901. Despite informal attempts to discourage them, a handful of Chinese children had begun to attend the city's public schools in the later 1890s. Although the exact number of students remains unknown, it could only have been small, for most Chinese children attended classes run by Protestant missionaries or by the city's private Chinese school. Nevertheless even a few Chinese pupils were far too many for some city whites. Residents of the Rock Bay district petitioned the local school board in February 1901, demanding the segregation of Chinese students and, failing that, their complete exclusion from school.[24] Although nothing came of the petition, within a year the local Trades and Labor Council had taken up the issue. According to spokesman T. H. Twigg, Oriental children, because of their peculiar mode of life, counteracted the school's uplifting influence. "It is regrettable indeed," he declared, "that it should be found necessary to separate at the public schools the children of one portion of the inhabitants from the other for the preservation of the Anglo-Saxon standard of moral and ethical culture. But it will only be carrying into the schools what already exists in every other institution of society—the branding of Chinese as Ishmaelites."[25] Later, after the question had been aired in public, Twigg unearthed further justification for the proposed move. "Lack of cleanliness is one reason," he observed. "Another reason is the aptness of Chinese to use words, without knowing their meaning, and disregard for decency in giving expression in English to their lascivious thoughts."[26]

When the council pressed the school board for total segregation, the trustees heard their petition with sympathy. But when the trustees took this demand to the provincial superintendent of education, they were told that "no public schools in British Columbia can be established on the grounds of colour, creed or nationality."[27] Nevertheless the TLC presssed forward with its case. In October it called a public meeting to discuss the question further. C. H. Lugrin, a local author and lawyer, spoke his fears before the crowd. "The line must be drawn somewhere," he urged. "The Mongolianization of British Columbia must be prevented at all hazards. . . . We cannot have them in equal citizenship." Although only twenty Chinese pupils were then enrolled in the city's five schools, Lugrin predicted that, "unless separate schools were established, the time was speedily coming when there would be more Chinese scholars in some of the ward schools than whites."[28] Subsequently the city council applauded a proposal to create a new school district in Chinatown, thus effectively segregating the Chinese without infringing upon provincial regulations. Shortly thereafter the trustees decided to segregate Chinese students, even though both the city's superintendent of schools and its teaching staff denied that they disrupted work in the classroom.[29]

Segregation came, but only after further delay. In January 1904 the Victoria School Board rented a special classroom space for the city's Chinese public school pupils and, pleading that this was just a temporary expedient to reduce overcrowding in other schools, opened a special school for Chinese. In June 1905, however, the school was closed for lack of students.[30] Apparently Chinese parents would not send their children to a segregated school. But during the summer of 1907 the problem arose again when the number of Chinese children wishing to enter public school increased dramatically. These were months in which nativism reached a new peak in Victoria and Vancouver. With growing racial tension in the air, the trustees decided not to approve any application unless the prospective student spoke English well enough to take the ordinary course of studies.[31] Meanwhile white students themselves mirrored the community's racial hostility: gangs of them assaulted Chinese youths several times during the fall. The *Victoria Times* reported that

complaints have been made that white boys have made an organized attempt to prevent Chinese pupils from attending the Rock Bay and Central schools. It seems that gangs of enthusiastic youthful exclusion league sympathizers have been congregating at the corner of Herald and Douglas streets and also at some point between Chinatown and Rock Bay school and not allowing Chinese pupils to pass them on their way to school. On several occasions the lads have been assaulted and in some cases prevented from going to school at all.[32]

The issue came to a head in the following March when a sixteen year-old Chinese boy was caught drawing obscene pictures in the notebooks of younger white pupils. He was quickly expelled from school but the incident prompted fresh demands for segregation. According to one local editor, the incident illustrated "the danger of allowing Chinese youths to attend the classes with white children."[33] Deluged with complaints, the board again rented a schoolroom in Chinatown and opened it to Oriental pupils in the lower grades. The city's few senior Chinese students, however, were allowed to remain in the schools they already attended.[34] Meanwhile in Vancouver the school board reversed the Victoria policy; it segregated the older Asian students and left the younger ones in integrated classrooms.[35]

In one sense the drive for school segregation, like many manifestations of anti-Oriental sentiment, had some justification. Chinese adolescents with little schooling in English had occasionally been taught in the company of young white children and thus there were social grounds for segregating older students from younger. Furthermore, there were pedagogical reasons for segregating those whose knowledge of English was slight. But behind these considerations lay a far more significant factor—the deep racial gulf which divided west coast society. Many white children and their parents strongly objected to racial intermingling in schools. Fundamentally, demands for segregation sprang from these strong racist sentiments. Segregation would have alleviated no economic threat nor discouraged any future Oriental immigration. In fact, it would have done very little to relieve the distress which, according to west coast nativists, the Oriental presence had long caused in British Columbia. Demands for segregation were not calculated proposals for the solution of educational or social problems. They were the hostile cries of a people unsettled and angered by the alien in their midst.

In addition to school segregation, between 1898 and 1906 four separate outbursts of vigilante activity flared up at different points in the province. Despite their scattered nature they too testified to white British Columbia's popular sense of racial grievance. First in the Slocan Valley, then at Atlin in the northwest, next at Salmo in the Kootenays, and finally in Penticton, mobs of irate whites forced Oriental newcomers out of town. Each incident followed the same basic pattern, one similar to the events in Vancouver in 1887. A small number of Chinese or Japanese arrived in a new and previously all-white community, most of them brought in to work as labourers. Their advent roused latent prejudices among local whites. In all four instances a mob gathered and ran the newcomers out of town, and on every occasion but one the mob's victory was complete: the community rid itself of the Oriental intruder. Only in Salmo did the Asians return, and then only under police protection demanded by their employers. The absence of effective police forces certainly made these incidents possible. But the real source of each lay in the latent nativism of the west coast province, which the presence of even small numbers of Asians could arouse. Like Vancouverites before them, whites in each of these communities feared an impending threat to their jobs (in Salmo, at least, a well-founded fear). And what was equally important, they wished for racial homogeneity in the towns where they lived.[36]

The years of sporadic racial incidents before and after the turn of the century were followed by a period of mounting racial tensions in British Columbia. They flourished especially in Vancouver, by then the home of the largest concentration of Orientals in the province. What loosed resurgent feeling in this instance was another sharp rise in immigration from Asia. First signs of the increase could be seen in the summer of 1906, when several hundred East Indians (or Hindoos as British Columbians erroneously called them, most of them being Sikhs) suddenly arrived in the city. East Indian immigrants were not new to the province. Small groups had been trickling in since at least the turn of the century but, because there were so few of them, for the most part they went unnoticed. In 1906, however, they began to arrive in visible numbers, and their conduct on arrival further increased their visibility. Often destitute upon landing and unable to find work, many begged for food and money while roaming the streets in bands. Their appearance and conduct frightened and worried many city residents, whose traditional racial phobias by now were easily aroused.[37] Public meetings and newspaper editors quickly renewed the old call for a white Canada. The mayor of Vancouver forced the CPR to detain all East Indian immigrants on board the company's ships until City Council could be sure they would not become public charges.[38] In response to popular pressure, federal officials sought out East Indians to deport under the Immigration Act, but only one was discovered and he was too ill to be moved.[39] The agitation finally did subside, but only when the rate of immigration dropped during the winter months.

Spring renewed the stream of immigrants moving eastward across the Pacific. Then, in July 1907, the number of Asians entering the country suddenly surged upward. While East Indian immigration had not yet reached the previous years' level, arrivals from China grew significantly for the first time since 1903, when the head tax had last been raised. But the most startling increase, by far, was in the number of Japanese newcomers. In July alone, over 2,300 arrived in the province, more than double the number of entrants in any month since the first of the year, and far more than were ever anticipated under the voluntary emigration restriction plan to which the Japanese government had formerly agreed. Several factors had combined to produce the influx. First, because of a misunderstanding, Japanese officials had abandoned voluntary emigration restrictions once Canada had adhered to the Anglo-Japanese Treaty in January 1907. Second, more than a third of the year's arrivals came by way of Hawaii, and therefore were beyond the control of the Japanese government. Third, several emigration agencies in Vancouver accepted contracts to supply Japanese labour for large Canadian corporations and their efforts also stimu-

lated immigration.[40] When these factors combined in the summer of
1907, Japanese immigration to British Columbia swelled to unprecedented levels.

Meanwhile increasing numbers of west coast whites were growing convinced that the Japanese had become the most serious Oriental threat in the province. Like the Chinese, they had always
seemed unassimilable since the day they first set foot in British
Columbia. But Japan's recent victory over Russia, and the dawning
recognition of her new military might, suddenly added a new dimension to the Japanese image. From this time onward white British Columbia increasingly tended to view the Japanese immigrant
as aggressive, loyal to Japan, and anxious to further her expansionist designs.[41]

Signs of growing popular consternation soon began to appear on
the west coast and Vancouver quickly became the focus of public
protest. Throughout July the urban press featured daily comment
on the "invasion," reports which grew more sensational with every
passing week. Soon the Vancouver Trades and Labor Council was
spurred to action. It pressed local political leaders to demand measures which would stem the rising immigrant tide; then it formed
the Asiatic Exclusion League to promote agitation.[42] The Liberal
MP for Vancouver, R. G. Macpherson, was particularly alarmed.
He began to prod Prime Minister Laurier, hoping to stir the federal
government into action. Macpherson blamed the Japanese government for encouraging the exodus to Canada and predicted that "in
a very short time our Province will be Asiatic." "The trouble is," he
observed, "that the people of the East think we are all agitators over
this matter. It is the last thing I want to be, but I can see without
any difficulty the Province of British Columbia slipping into the
hands of Asiatics and this part of Western Canada no longer a part
and parcel of the Dominion." Furthermore, he warned, failure to
enforce rigorous restrictions would jeopardize the Liberals' fortunes
in the province. "I would like very much to keep this country
White and I would also like to keep it Liberal," he told Laurier,
"but it is impossible to keep [it] either one of the two unless the Japs
are preemptorily [*sic*] told that they must carry out their understanding with your government [to limit emigration voluntarily]."[43]
According to the minister of the interior, Frank Oliver, who was
travelling in British Columbia during mid-August, alarm at the
Japanese influx was almost hysterical. Although some employers
favoured immigration from Asia, he reported, "there is a panicky
feeling among the inhabitants generally that they do not know
what is behind the movement. They are not in a frame of mind to

reason the matter on the generally economic side. They fear that it is a preconcerted movement; that there is a responsibility behind it, some sort of mysterious responsibility that they do not understand, and do not know the limits of."[44]

Laurier, however, was not to be stampeded. He chastised Macpherson for exaggerating the Oriental threat and urged him to moderate his language. Late in August he told the Vancouver member that

conditions, with regard to the Asiatic question, are not the same as they were twenty years or even ten years ago. Up to that time, the Asiatic, when he came to white countries, could be treated with contempt and kicked. This continues to be true for all classes of the yellow race, with the exception of the Japanese. The Japanese has adopted European civilization, has shown that he can whip European soldiers, has a navy equal man for man to the best afloat, and will not submit to be kicked and treated with contempt, as his brother from China still meekly submits to.

It was in the interests of British Columbia and Canada as well as the Empire to treat the Japanese with respect, he explained; for one thing the Japanese fleet was much closer to British Columbia than it was to Great Britain. Furthermore, if Canada's trade relations with Japan were to flourish there were "unavoidably some disadvantages to be expected, along with the profits."[45] With these considerations in mind, Laurier moved slowly in reducing the inflow of Asian immigrants.

In the meantime, however, the Asiatic Exclusion League had cut all ties with the Trades and Labor Council and had embarked upon an independent program of public agitation. From the outset, despite its trade union roots, it was more than a workingman's organization. It soon attracted support from middle-class whites, among them political leaders from both major parties.[46] But while the league held frequent meetings, passed insistent resolutions, and dispatched delegations to meet with various government officials, it did not win the mass support for which its leaders had hoped. Attendance at league meetings remained disappointingly low, perhaps because of its narrowly based trade union origins. In an attempt to attract more popular interest, the executive organized a mammoth anti-Asiatic parade for September 7, complete with a brass band. Fraternal organizations, ex-servicemen, and the city's fifty-eight trade unions all promised their support.[47]

On the evening of the seventh Saturday night crowds thronged Vancouver's streets. It had been a hot, sticky day. The air was heavy with rumours that another boatload of unwanted immigrants was soon to arrive. Two days previously a mob of whites had driven several hundred East Indians out of Bellingham, Washington, nearby; the victims fled north across the border, and reports of the disturbance heightened the atmosphere of racial tension. The league's parade set out, seven or eight hundred strong, just after 7 p.m. As planned, a brass band serenaded the procession with patriotic airs while the marchers waved banners proclaiming "Stand for a White Canada" and "What shall we do to be saved." They also flaunted an effigy of Lieutenant-Governor Dunsmuir to be burned in front of City Hall. Dunsmuir had recently reserved the latest immigration restriction act passed by the legislature; some suspected he had done so to ensure a supply of cheap labour for his own collieries. As the procession wound through the city streets hundreds stepped from the sidewalks and fell in line. By the time it reached City Hall the parade had swollen to eight or nine thousand. There the crowd cheered as someone put the torch to Dunsmuir's effigy. Then 2,000 jammed the hall for the protest meeting which followed while the remainder loitered restlessly outside.

In the hall, before a packed and noisy audience, a succession of speakers denounced the Oriental influx. A. W. Von Rhein, a leading member of the league and vice-president of the Vancouver TLC, presided. Speakers for the evening included two local clergymen, Rev. Dr. G. Fraser and Rev. G. H. Wilson; Harry Cowan, a prominent figure in Liberal labour circles; A. E. Fowler, secretary of the Japanese and Korean Exclusion League in Seattle; C. M. Woodworth, president of the Vancouver Conservative Association; J. E. Wilson, a recent arrival from New Zealand; and W. A. Young, an organizer for the American Federation of Labor. Enthusiastic applause greeted each of the speakers' tirades, in particular Wilson's account of how New Zealand and Australia had grappled with the Oriental menace. Then the assembly endorsed a series of resolutions which demanded an immediate end to all immigration from Asia.

At the same time, unable to get in, thousands clustered on the sidewalks outside City Hall and listened to speakers who from time to time left the meeting to address them. According to one witness, the Seattle exclusionist, A. E. Fowler, gave a particularly inflammatory address and thoroughly agitated the assemblage.[48] Soon after nine o'clock part of the crowd drifted into Chinatown, less than a block away, and within minutes a riot was in progress. The outburst was precipitated when a youngster threw a brick through the window of a Chinese store. Within seconds the air was filled with sticks, stones, bricks, and bottles aimed at every window in sight. Minutes later another mob swept through the Japanese quarter on Powell Street, leaving a second trail of broken glass in its wake. Most of the property damage was done during the riot's early minutes, but during the evening clusters of men circled the vicinity, looking for a chance to do more mischief. The Japanese themselves vigorously repulsed a second attack. Confronted with broken bottles, the sound of shots, and an angry mob shouting "Banzai," their opponents quickly lost heart. But it took Vancouver's police force four hours to control the crowd in Chinatown, which left behind it a few minor injuries, thousands of dollars of property damage, and thousands of Chinese and Japanese quivering with rage and fear.[49]

The riot was neither planned nor was it (as some have since suggested) largely the work of American agitators.[50] It was simply a spontaneous outburst, one which asserted west coast racialism in a clear and emphatic way. But despite this obvious sponteneity, the origins of the outbreak were rather more complex. In fact, its primary roots lay in the longstanding racial cleavage which rent west coast society and the psychological tensions —especially the fear of racial heterogeneity—which this condition induced. Given the region's long history of strained race relations, the upsurge of Asian immigration in the summer of 1907 had three important effects. It stimulated racial tensions always latent in west coast society, it raised again the question of the province's cultural destiny, and it demonstrated the inadequacy of previous solutions to the Oriental problem. Furthermore, federal recalcitrance and provincial impotence had led many whites to conclude that there was no political agency which would now cope with the sudden immigrant threat. Thus the historic structure of race relations in British Columbia combined with the absence of political channels receptive to public protest to make the AEL momentarily the focus of popular hostility and alarm. The league's parade and meeting provided an occasion for the collective expression of fears and animosities that were broadly shared in Vancouver. The riot vented racial tensions which had been building up for several weeks. The outbreak itself was leaderless, precipitated by a single brick thrown in a highly charged atmosphere. But though the mob acted spontaneously and lacked any disciplined organization, it was far from blind, for it selected its targets carefully. It broke the windows in buildings which Orientals occupied, but with one or two slight exceptions left those of neighbouring, white-owned businesses untouched. Moreover, from the outset property was the mob's only target. While most Chinese and Japanese fled from the first onslaught, some mingled in the crowd unmolested, at least during the early part of the evening. The great majority of injuries were inflicted during the brawl which occurred when the Japanese sprang to their own defence in the face of a second attack.

While some professed shock at the riot and condemned it as a disgrace, criticism had no deterrent effect on the anti-Oriental crusade. During the following weeks the league flourished as never before. Meanwhile in Vancouver racial tension remained acute for days after the incident. There were minor disturbances in Chinatown on the night after the riot and on Monday evening unsuccessful attempts were made to burn the Japanese school. The press made new demands that the province remain a white man's country and city streets blossomed with pedestrians sporting "White Canada" ribbons. On their part Orientals armed themselves until police forbade city merchants to sell them knives and guns. Along Powell and Hastings streets store fronts were boarded up for a week while occupants braced themselves for another assault. W. L. Mackenzie King, then federal deputy minister of labour, described the state of public opinion when he arrived early in October.

The feeling in this city, and in the other parts of the Province wherever I have been, is very generally strongly anti-Japanese. I believe it is no longer merely a labour, but has become a race agitation. In the first place, the people have become alarmed lest by a continuance of the augmentation of the Japanese population in the Province by such large numbers as have come in during the present year the proportion of these people to the white population will become preponderantly great, while the fact that the Japanese have proven themselves the equal of the white man in so many ways has caused people of all classes to fear their competition. Nothing has surprised me more than to find, in conversation with persons who have every reason to wish for an increase in the available supply of labour a very decided opinion that other than Japanese labourers must be sought.[51]

In such an atmosphere the Exclusion League thrived. On September 12 a crowd of 300 packed the Labor Hall to elect the league's executive, approve its constitution, and pay the annual membership fee of 50 cents. New members flocked to join at later meetings and by October more than 2,000 had signed the rolls. Financially the league prospered; through donations and membership dues it soon gathered $5,000. T. R. E. McInnes, a Vancouver lawyer who infiltrated its upper ranks and informed Ottawa of its activities, reported that at least fifteen per cent of its supporters were merchants and professionals, among them some of the city's leading men.[52]

Riding the crest of public support, the league lost little time in pressing its views upon influential politicians and civil servants. Soon after the riot W. D. Scott, federal superintendent of immigration, received a league delegation at a stormy meeting when he

Grocery shop of Nishimura Masuya, Powell Street, Vancouver, after the 1907 riot. Damage and business losses $139.

arrived in Vancouver to investigate the recent Asian influx. Another group met with Robert Borden, leader of the federal Conservative Party, when he visited the city late in September.[53] The exclusionists attacked Premier McBride, whom they strongly suspected of having connived at the reservation of the latest immigration act. They also importuned Laurier with requests for exclusion and sent an observer to all sessions of the latest Royal Commission

Vancouver's Chinatown after the riot, September 1907.

on Oriental immigration, called in the wake of the Vancouver incident. In addition, offshoots of the league were founded in other
provincial centres. Early in October a crowded meeting in Victoria,
chaired by the mayor, agreed to form a branch. Soon another was
formed in New Westminster. Others quickly sprang up in Nicola,
Rossland, and Cedar Cove, a suburb of Vancouver.[54] An attempt
to found a branch in Nanaimo failed only when Ralph Smith, the
popular member of Parliament for the city, defended the Liberal
government's Oriental policies at the organizational meeting. And
for the rest of 1907 the Vancouver exclusionists, always the driving
force in the movement, held frequent, well-attended meetings.
They listened to endless speeches on the Oriental menace, approved numerous resolutions, and condemned all politicians who
seemed to oppose them. Some league leaders even flirted briefly
with thoughts of independent political action, though in the end
nothing came of the proposal.

After the New Year, however, public interest in the league began
to wane. By mid-February 1908 its active membership had shrunk
to 900.[55] Federal restrictions and winter's onset had reduced Asiatic
immigration to a mere trickle, and once more the issue lost much of
its sense of urgency. Furthermore, the league's leadership was now
badly split. One faction wished to cooperate with American exclusionists who, anxious to make theirs an international movement,
were zealously cultivating Canadian support. The other wanted to
avoid such entanglements and worked hard to evade the American
embrace. If McInnes can be believed, he became an *agent provoca-
teur* and increasingly aggravated the discord.[56] Consequently,
divided within and lacking something of its former *raison d'être*, the
league fell upon evil days. It met periodically throughout the spring
and summer, but for the most part it attracted steadily dwindling
audiences. On the first anniversary of the riot City Hall was barely
half full for the league's commemorative rally, and when the annual
dues were called for half of the audience rose and left.[57] Racial
tension had once more ebbed and shortly thereafter the AEL disappeared from public view.

The riot placed the Laurier government in a rather awkward
position. It was forced to placate both Japan and British Columbia
simultaneously. While the Japanese submitted only a mild note of
protest, the prime minister's continued concern for friendly relations with Japan, as well as the niceties of diplomacy between two
treaty signatories, made reparation imperative. On the other hand,
anti-Oriental demands from British Columbia had never been more
insistent. During the weeks which followed the outbreak, Laurier

was deluged with petitions demanding that immigration from Asia be halted. In October the publisher of the Vancouver *World*, the only Liberal paper in the city, threatened to withdraw his paper's support unless restrictive measures were soon forthcoming.[58] Caught in a cleft stick, Laurier first expressed the nation's official regrets and then sent Rodolphe Lemieux, postmaster-general and minister of labour, to Tokyo, entrusted with the delicate task of urging Japanese officials to enforce stricter emigration controls. Simultaneously, Lemieux's deputy minister, Mackenzie King, was named royal commissioner to settle Japanese claims in Vancouver. While Laurier felt compelled to reimburse the Japanese for their losses, however, he felt no similar need to meet Chinese claims. Evidently China's lack of international prestige, her less aggressive efforts to protect the welfare of her citizens overseas, and her more distant relations with Canada and the Empire led him to conclude that the Chinese could be treated with less solicitude. It was not until the following year, after two entreaties from Imperial officials who hoped to settle similar claims for Britons in China, that King was requested to assess Chinese losses too.[59]

King went to Vancouver in October and after a series of hearings awarded Japanese riot victims a total of $9,000 in compensation. The Chinese, who sustained more damage, were later given $26,000. Immediately after settling the Japanese claims, King was instructed to examine the origins of the Oriental influx. In mid-November he seized the documents of several immigration companies and held a second set of hearings, during which he examined more than a hundred witnesses, most of them Asiatic. His report, which dwelt at length on Japanese immigration, attributed the riot largely to fear of numbers rather than racial prejudice or economic conflict. It exonerated the government of Japan from any major responsibility for the problem. Instead it singled out high immigration from Hawaii and the activities of immigration companies located in Canada. The most satisfactory way to solve the problem, King concluded, was to prohibit immigration by way of Hawaii, to forbid the practice of importing contract labour, and to limit carefully the remaining number of Japanese arrivals.[60] King made no recommendations concerning Chinese immigration. But he did suggest that East Indians had frequently been lured to Canada by the inducements of steamship companies, ticket agents, and individuals who sought to exploit them. Their sojourn in British Columbia had been a hardship for themselves and had caused unrest in the province. As a result, King implied, immigration from India should also be discouraged.[61]

While King was probing the sources of the recent Japanese in-rush, Lemieux was in Tokyo discussing the problem with Japanese officials. After a month of negotiations the two sides concluded an agreement whereby Japan would voluntarily restrict emigration and permit only previous residents, domestic servants employed by Japanese, and contract labourers approved by the Canadian government to leave for Canada. The latter two categories of migrants were limited to 400 yearly.[62] Lemieux justified the need for restriction by adopting the stance of west coast exclusionists. He argued that "Orientals belong to a civilization developed through the centuries, along lines totally and radically divergent from ours," and that "there is a well nigh impassable gulf between the two." Certainly, he continued, they were "formidable competitors in the field of labour," but

be that as it may, the fact remains that British Columbians object to a vast alien Colony, exclusive, inscrutable, unassimilative, with fewer wants and a lower standard of living than themselves, maintaining intact their peculiar customs and characteristics, ideals of home and family life, with neither the wish nor the capacity to amalgamate, which gradually by the mere pressure of numbers may undermine the very foundations of *their province*.

They have to safeguard the future and the distinctiveness of their race and civilization, and in their passionate and unalterable conviction, they cannot be protected unless the free ingress of Orientals is restricted and regulated.[63]

Meanwhile during the fall of 1907 both political pressure and popular opinion were forcing the federal government toward a more rigorous policy of Oriental exclusion. From British Columbia came biting attacks by Richard McBride, the Conservative premier of the province. At the same time federal Tories began to court the exclusionists. Touring the province late in September, when popular racialism was at its height, Robert Borden remarked that "the Conservative party ... will ever maintain one supreme consideration to which all material considerations must give way; and it is this: British Columbia must remain a British and Canadian province, inhabited and dominated by men in whose veins runs the blood of those great pioneering races which built up and developed not only Western, but Eastern Canada."[64] Even Laurier's west coast supporters were adamant. As federal and provincial Conservatives snapped at his heels, five Liberal members from British Columbia stood in the Commons and demanded immediate restrictions upon Oriental immigration.[65]

Soon after Lemieux had concluded his negotiations, the cabinet bowed before the winds of west coast protest and approved an order in council which placed new restrictions upon the entry of

Japanese and East Indian migrants. After January 8, 1908, all immigrants were prohibited from entering Canada unless they came from the country of their birth or citizenship by "a continuous journey and on through tickets" purchased in their home country.[66] While the order applied indiscriminately to all immigrants to Canada, in reality it was aimed only at East Indians and Japanese who came from Hawaii. There being no direct steamship line from India, virtually all Indian immigration was thus eliminated. At the same time the door was shut on the Hawaiian route for Japanese immigrants. The order provided effective restriction while avoiding the distasteful and increasingly unacceptable practice of indicating undesirable immigrants by race or nationality. Henceforth this order and the Lemieux agreement, together with the Chinese Immigration Act, formed the new foundations of the Liberal government's Oriental immigration restriction policy.[67]

But if these restrictions appeased British Columbia's Liberals, they certainly fell far short of the expectations of other west coast residents. Provincial Conservatives heaped criticism on the new immigration policy. By the time the federal election was called, for October 1908, the Tories had taken a popular stand against further immigration from Asia. The issue played a central role in the party's election campaign in the province. And in the end the election proved a major setback for provincial Liberals. They lost five of their seven seats, including that of William Templeman in Victoria, the only defeated cabinet minister in the government. The party's share of the popular vote dropped almost 14 per cent in British Columbia. But Liberal losses were not the result of the immigration issue alone. Both internal party divisions and a strong opposition campaign were in some lesser measure responsible.[68] Yet by 1908 many British Columbians believed that the Laurier government was not willing to meet their demands and enforce more stringent immigration restrictions. The Tories, meanwhile, had openly courted provincial nativists. Two years of growing racial tension and the absence of resolute government action had cost the Liberals dearly in the Pacific province. The election results were one more indication of the racism ingrained in west coast society.

PART TWO

EAST INDIAN INTERLUDE

5

THE KOMAGATA MARU INCIDENT

The first East Indians to arrive in Canada had come late in the nineteenth century. Initially their numbers were very small, but by 1905 enough had entered British Columbia to attract at least brief notice. Then, in 1906 and 1907, a sudden surge had brought 4,700 to the west coast province, just as migration from China and Japan reached one of its periodic peaks. The resulting eruption of white nativism had led to the riot of 1907. In the wake of the incident, federal immigration restrictions sharply curtailed the East Indian influx. During the next seven years, therefore, fewer than 125 Indians were permitted to land. In all, between 1905 (when statistics first were recorded) and 1914, just under 5,300 East Indians entered the country, a minuscule proportion of the 2,500,000 immigrants who came to Canada during these years.

Once they arrived in the country, however, very few Indian immigrants moved east from British Columbia. The majority lingered on the coast, for the most part in the Vancouver area. Moreover, a substantial number of those who arrived did not remain for long. Perhaps as many as 1,500 soon moved south across the American border. Others apparently stayed only a short while and then returned to India. At no time could the East Indian population of British Columbia have stood at more than 4,000, a peak perhaps reached in 1907 when immigration was at its height. Thereafter the province's East Indian population dwindled perceptibly. Quite likely not even 2,000 remained on the eve of World War I. A small but visible minority, they comprised less than half of one per cent of the provincial population.[1]

Although their numbers included a handful of Muslims and Hindus, virtually all of the Indian immigrants were Sikhs. The majority came from Hoshiarpur and Jullundur, two districts in the northeastern region of the Punjab, where the Sikhs were especially numerous. The remainder were from several centres scattered throughout the Punjab. Hoshiarpur and Jullundur were wheat-

growing districts, and consequently most of the Sikhs in British
Columbia were steeped in the peasant farming traditions of the
Punjab's subsistence wheat economy. Perhaps a thousand were
former soldiers and had once had some military training as well.[2]

Why did East Indian immigrants come to Canada? Previous explanations have emphasized forces external to Punjab society.
Mackenzie King, for example, concluded in 1907 that they had
frequently been lured to British Columbia by glowing propaganda
from steamship lines, ticket agents, and fellow-countrymen who
sought to exploit them.[3] But strong imperatives toward male emigration were also rooted in Punjabi life. The regions from which
most emigrants came suffered intense and growing population pressures during the late nineteenth and early twentieth centuries. In
1904 the population density of Hoshiarpur was 867 persons per
square mile of arable land; that of Jullundur was only marginally
lower. Both were among the most densely peopled areas in the Punjab. Wage rates for labour were low in these districts, a problem
aggravated by sharp inflation in land and staple commodity prices
during the 1880s and 1890s. Furthermore, by the end of the century, in these regions migration had become a common solution for
economic problems.[4] The overwhelming majority of emigrants were
male. They commonly represented a landowning family group, one
which could spare a labourer and which often mortgaged its holdings to send the emigrant abroad. He, in return, sent his savings
back to his family, which used the income to advance the family's
interests, typically through purchasing land or improving housing.
Because it produced additional income, migration thus benefited
the family. In the Jullundur village of Vilyatpur, during the early
twentieth century, those families which sent emigrants abroad
gradually expanded their landholdings at the expense of those who
did not. Often emigration was permanent and in many cases the
emigrant did not even marry. By seeking work in a foreign land, he
was usually making a great sacrifice for the common good of his
family.[5] For these reasons East Indians in Canada were almost exclusively male sojourners. Perhaps even more than their Chinese
counterparts, their chief object was to earn surplus wealth and remit it to family members across the Pacific.

Once they arrived in British Columbia, about two-thirds of the
East Indians settled in Vancouver, New Westminster, and vicinity.
The remainder scattered themselves in several centres throughout
the province. For the most part they sought work as common labourers. Many found it in sawmills, lumber camps, and on railway
construction gangs, while land clearing and seasonal farm work

engaged others. With few exceptions, East Indians were not employed on a contract labour basis and in consequence they were absorbed into the existing provincial labour force. Unemployment remained a serious problem for many of the migrants; as most East Indians were casual labourers, they were especially prey to the vagaries of provincial demands for labour. Within a short time, however, at least a small number acquired land holdings while another handful established themselves as independent businessmen and realtors.[6] In this way the East Indian community somewhat broadened its economic base. While wage rates for East Indians varied considerably, they were close to those paid to both Chinese and Japanese. Generally East Indian workers, like other Asians, earned one half to two-thirds of the wages paid whites for similar sorts of work. Like their Chinese counterparts, East Indian immigrants accepted arduous, short-term, low-paying jobs and intermittent unemployment. As sojourners, their primary concern was to earn surplus income and send it to India. All other considerations were subordinate to this task.

Like the Chinese before them, the East Indians in British Columbia were only marginally integrated into west coast society. To some extent, of course, work and commerce bound whites and Indians in a network of formal, impersonal relationships. At the same time segregated housing never divided the two races as much as it had whites and Chinese, there being no Indian equivalent of Chinatown. But these exceptions aside, hosts and guests shared no significant social bonds. Soon after they arrived the East Indians began to found their own religious, social, and political organizations. First among them was the Khalsa Diwan Society, formed in Vancouver in 1907 to meet the Sikhs' religious, educational, and philanthropic needs. In addition, faced with white hostility and legislative discrimination, the Indians quickly organized to protect their mutual interests. They also took a growing interest in Indian politics and by 1908 radicals within the community were calling for national revolution in India. The Sikh Temple became a centre of political activity and over the next several years the immigrants formed a series of societies committed to two goals: self-defence in Canada and Indian nationalism. Internally, however, the community was far from united. On the contrary, it was marked by several cleavages, the deepest being that which divided radical from moderate nationalists.[7] But whatever its internal structure, it stood well apart from the host society, clearly distinguished by separate social, cultural, and political institutions. Moreover, as sojourners, the East Indians had no incentive to assimilate. Consequently, like the Chinese, they formed a small, distinctive segment within west coast society. In doing so they reinforced its structurally plural condition.

That white British Columbia objected to pluralism its long history of Sinophobia clearly indicated. And after 1900 the East Indian segment within west coast society stirred the same concern for racial homogeneity that the Chinese presence had long aroused. But how, precisely, did antipathy toward the Chinese (and, increasingly, Japanese immigrants too) affect evolving white attitudes toward East Indians? These related prejudices were not simply additive. Yet when they arrived, Indian migrants entered a community of heightened racial awareness, enduring racial cleavage, and recurring racial tension. Consequently white perceptions of East Indians were framed by the community's fixed assumptions about previous Asian immigrants. The entire history of west coast race relations left its mark upon the East Indian image, for in one sense the new arrivals seemed merely another dimension of the province's longstanding Oriental problem. Nevertheless in themselves these older conceptions of Asians could not determine in detail the various East Indian stereotypes. When numbers of Indians began to come to British Columbia, they quickly aroused a series of new objections. Consequently a distinct Indian image soon formed in the minds of west coast whites. It was neither as complex nor as elaborate as that of the Chinese. But certainly it expressed as much hostility.

Popular conceptions of India preceded Indian immigrants to North American shores just as those of China had once arrived in advance of the Chinese. The India which they depicted was a land of teeming millions, of filth and squalor, of exotic, peculiar customs. The Indians seemed a lesser breed of men, given to weakness, servility, and in some cases villainy. Most likely these ideas, part of the western image of India, were widely shared in Canada when the first large group of East Indian immigrants arrived in 1906.[8] Furthermore, contact between the newcomers and whites soon began to flesh out the bare bones of these stereotypes. Many of the Indians were destitute when they landed. As they frequently seemed penniless and ill-prepared against the weather, many whites concluded that these newcomers from tropical or semitropical regions were quite unsuited for life in British Columbia's more rigorous climate. W. D. Scott, federal superintendent of immigration, who investigated the sudden influx in the fall of 1906, declared that, "the transfer of any people from a tropical climate to a northern one, which for months in winter is damp and cold, must of necessity result in much physical suffering and danger to health, not only on account of non-acclimatization, but also on account of ignorance in the matter of housing, food and clothing."[9] His views soon were commonplace in west coast communities. Consequently the suggestion often was made that the immigration of East Indians should be prevented out of charity to themselves. Mackenzie King took this stand in his report on Indian immigration in 1908. "It was clearly recognized in regard to emigration from India to Canada," he concluded, "that the native of India is not a person suited to this country, that, accustomed as many of them are to the conditions of a tropical climate, and possessing manners and customs so unlike those of our own people, their inability to readily adapt themselves to surroundings entirely different could not do other than entail an amount of privation and suffering which render a discontinuance of such immigration most desirable in the interests of the Indians themselves."[10]

Some well-established Oriental stereotypes were also applied to East Indians. Like all Asians they often were seen as unclean, diseased, and a threat to public health. "The country from which they come ... has long been recognized as a hotbed of the most virulent and loathsome diseases such as Bubonic plague, Smallpox, Asiatic Cholera and the worst forms of Venereal diseases," one critic claimed, "and however strict the medical examination at our ports may be—there is a constant danger of these people being the means of transmission of diseases to our people."[11] Health officials constantly reiterated the charge that they lived in disgustingly filthy and overcrowded conditions.

The fear that East Indians threatened the livelihood of the white working man also derived from older perceptions of Oriental immigrants. Trade union spokesmen often objected that Indian immigration was again flooding the province with cheap Asiatic labour. The Victoria Trades and Labor Council, labour's most insistent anti-Indian voice, demanded vigorous federal action to stem the inrushing tide. Unless this was done, it predicted, "the introduction of this class of Cheap Labour will be the means of excluding the very class of labour that is most essential for the progress and prosperity of the country—i.e., white workers, who if paid a fair living wage could settle here, maintain homes and rear families and thoroughly fulfill the duties of citizenship."[12]

In addition, like other Asians before them, the Indians prompted fears for British Columbia's white destiny. According to their detractors, their caste system, their mode of dress, and their many peculiar social customs set them outside the mainstream of life in the province. "They are a case more apart even than the Chinese," the *Colonist* declared. "Their habits of life are unsatisfactory. They do not bring their wives with them, and will not make homes and rear families. They are totally unfitted for a white man's country.... For the Sikh in his home we have every respect; for the Sikh in Canada there is no proper place, and it is a great unkindness to a well-meaning people to bring him here."[13]

These fears for the province's racial destiny were strengthened by the common assumption that, like other Asiatics, East Indians could not be assimilated. As the secretary of the Victoria TLC explained:

The people of India, in common with all Asiatic races, are reared and nurtured in and under the influence of civilization and environments that seem to be, in principle, totally opposed to the civilization and environments under which we of the Western civilization are born and reared. In practice they certainly are found to be both unwilling and incapable of assimilating with the people of the western races who have settled and developed this country, and who, for very justifiable reasons, aspire to control the future destiny of this broad and fair land, with the hope that civilization in the best and truest sense may advance and develop to a fuller degree than has yet been achieved. But the invitation or admission of these people, the Hindus, would threaten and even make impossible the realization of such hopes.[14]

R. G. Macpherson, the Liberal member of Parliament for Vancouver and a vigorous opponent of all Oriental immigration, agreed. In the fall of 1906 he told the cheering audience at a meeting held to protest Indian immigration:

It is not enough to call it a question of cheap labour; it is not enough to raise the question of colour, race or creed. To be a Canadian citizen, at the beginning of this twentieth century, is no small thing. The men who built up this country, who hewed homes out of the forest, were men of first class, A 1 stock, and the responsibility they left us is great. The sentiment expressed in the proud phrase, *Civis Romanus sum*, becomes the citizen of Canada as well as it became the citizen of Rome. A race of men who cannot appreciate our mode of life, our mode of education, all that goes to make up Canadian citizenship, are not fit immigrants of this country. On the broad grounds of Canadian citizenship I attack this question.[15]

In affirming a positive sense of Canadian nationality Macpherson had placed East Indians beyond the pale. As British subjects they had a special claim on entry into Canada, and since India, like all Asia, was seen as a land of swarming masses, this raised the prospect of an unending stream of unassimilable immigrants. Fundamentally, then, East Indian immigrants touched the nativist's central fear that their presence would imbed an alien minority in the social foundations of British Columbia, thus preventing the creation of a homogeneous society.

As was true in the case of the Chinese, there were some British Columbians who stood outside the consensus. East Indians evoked a greater measure of white sympathy than either the Chinese or

Japanese. Among their employers, admittedly, opinion was divided. Some found Indians slow to learn but competent when they were trained, while others considered them unsatisfactory workers and hired them only because of the current labour shortage.[16] Within the larger community the newcomers enjoyed scattered support. Several advocates reasoned that imperial citizenship and past military service entitled these immigrants to special consideration. "It seems to me," argued one staunch champion, "that these Punjabis are entitled to official recognition and protection. Hundreds of these men have been soldiers in our Army and wear medals for their services in the field. They are subjects of our Empire, and are yet denied the rights of citizenship by a large proportion of their fellow subjects."[17] Their future immigration should be prevented, he admitted, but those already in the country should not have to endure any discrimination.

Occasionally Protestant church and social reform organizations, virtually all of them outside the west coast province, also took the side of the East Indian immigrant. They responded most readily to Indian complaints, recurrent after East Indian immigration was virtually prohibited, that their wives and children were not permitted to join them in Canada. In reality immigration law placed no special limitation upon the entry of Indian women and children; existing regulations applied to all, regardless of age or sex. Yet when Indian leaders charged that they were specifically denied the consolations of family life, some sympathetic whites took them at their word.[18] Moreover, unlike the leaders of other Asian immigrant communities, a few prominent East Indians actively promoted the Indian cause among white Canadians. Dr. Sunder Singh, a graduate of Oxford and leading spokesman of the Indian community's moderate nationalist minority, cultivated support in both British Columbia and eastern Canada. At his urging the Canada India Committee was founded in Toronto to work toward better interracial understanding as well as the elimination of all racial discrimination.[19] Ultimately, however, only a small number of whites in British Columbia actively advocated fair play for East Indians, and their attempts to publicize the Indian cause came to very little. By and large west coast whites remained firm in their racist convictions.

In the decade before World War I successive outbursts of racial animus marked relations between East Indians and whites in British Columbia. Predisposed to racial hostility by their fear of racial pluralism, whites emphatically rejected the East Indian immigrant.

The first outburst occurred in Vancouver during the summer of 1906, the torrent loosed by the sudden arrival of several hundred immigrants. Once again west coast nativists called for a white Canada while civic officals did what they could to discourage immigration. Later in the year, as the rate of immigration fell, agitation ceased.[20] In 1907, however, heavy Asian immigration and resurgent racial tension once more raised the question of migration from India. While Oriental immigration had long troubled Ottawa, that of East Indians caused particular embarrassment. Most British Columbians objected to Indians as much as they did other Asiatics, and in the wake of the Vancouver riot further immigration restrictions seemed necessary, if only to prevent renewed violence. Yet Canadians and East Indians were both British subjects and, in order to preserve strong imperial ties as well as to prevent unrest in India, overt discrimination was to be avoided. Canadian, British, and Indian officials shared this desire equally.[21] The task, however, was not an easy one. Laurier considered the Indian problem more serious than that of either the Chinese or the Japanese. "Frankly," he told the governor general, "I see no solution for it except quietly checking the exodus from India."[22]

The continuous passage rule, adopted in January 1908, virtually eliminated all opportunity for East Indian migration to Canada. Shortly thereafter Mackenzie King went to Britain to discuss the question further with senior officials in the Colonial, Foreign, and India Offices. Placing Canada's case before them, he urged that restrictions were needed to prevent further unrest, to avoid unseemly legislation, and to protect the Indians themselves. His argument was well received. In the end the Indian government promised to discourage prospective emigrants to Canada, although it did refuse to impose its own legislative restrictions. King was also assured that neither India nor Great Britain would take exception to Canadian restrictions should they ever become necessary. In addition, he discovered, Indian law already prevented the emigration of contract labour to Canada. Therefore existing law in India and Canada was sufficient to bar East Indian immigration to British Columbia. The Canadian regulation which required all immigrants to possess $25 upon landing was, in King's eyes, a necessity for the Indians' own protection and the amount could be increased if necessary.[23]

While these restrictions immediately reduced Indian immigration to a trickle they did nothing to solve the problem of those immigrants already in the country. As a result, federal officials cast about for ways of encouraging them to leave. Late in the summer of

1908 the minister of the interior's private secretary, J. B. Harkin, visited Vancouver and discussed with several East Indian leaders the possibility that the immigrants might accept indentured labour in the West Indies if the Canadian government provided transportation. Indian leaders showed signs of interest and in October two of their number accompanied Harkin to British Honduras to see if it might make a suitable home for East Indians living in Canada. Harkin later explained that "the steps taken in this connection were designed to prevent the possibility of hundreds of Hindus, (using this term to include Hindus proper, Sikhs and Mohammedans) becoming a burden upon Vancouver and vicinity; to offer as an alternative to the necessity of wholesale deportation to India a measure of opportunity in a country climatically better suited to them, and one in which they would be able to compete more successfully with other labour than they are in British Columbia."[24] While the party was in Honduras Harkin became convinced that the Indian delegates were satisfied with the prospects the colony offered; he believed that 1,000 would accept the opportunity to move. But the delegates thought otherwise, and when the mission returned, one declared that he had been offered a bribe to report favourably upon the proposal.[25] Instead he denounced the plan before a meeting of his countrymen, and in the ensuing commotion the entire project collapsed.

One reason federal officials promoted the Honduras proposal was that, even after migration from India had virtually ceased, anti-East Indian feeling remained strong on Canada's west coast. As one trade union leader observed in Victoria in 1911, "the working people of this City regard all the Native tribes of India in the same light as any other Oriental Nation. The light in which the working people of this City view Oriental immigration and their well-known attitude on that question is one of persistent and unequivocal opposition."[26] As long as such feeling persisted, so did the possibility of another racial outburst. Consequently, in November 1913, hostility swelled again when a group of three dozen East Indian immigrants were admitted to the province. Before the Supreme Court of British Columbia they had successfully challenged the legality of federal immigration restrictions, thereby opening the gate for any others who wished to follow.[27] But on this occasion the mere prospect of renewed migration from India prodded the nativists into life. Soon after the judgement was handed down they deluged Conservative Prime Minister Robert Borden with a flood of protests. In response the cabinet hastily erected a new barrier to Indian immigration. On December 8 it approved an order in council which, citing the overcrowded state of British Columbia's labour market, temporarily prohibited labourers and artisans from entering the province.[28] Then, early in 1914, the formerly illegal regulations were proclaimed again, this time free of legal flaws.

On May 23, in the face of these obstacles, the *Komagata Maru* arrived in Vancouver harbour with 376 prospective East Indian immigrants on board. The ship was under charter to Gurdit Singh, a wealthy Sikh merchant and contractor from Hong Kong. Why he had chartered the craft and recruited its passengers is not entirely clear. At least three plausible explanations of his motives have been offered. According to one suggestion, Gurdit Singh considered Canadian immigration restrictions an affront to all Indians and he therefore wished to break them down by forcing entry into the country. Another explanation is that, as a fervent Indian nationalist, he hoped to foment unrest in India if the immigrants' entry was prevented. A third interpretation, perhaps a more likely one than the others, is that he stood to gain substantial financial profits if the enterprise was successful and the immigrants were permitted to land. It may even be that he hoped to develop a regular passenger traffic between India and British Columbia.[29] But whatever were his motives, in Canada they seemed nothing more than a direct challenge to the policy of East Indian exclusion. This single belief governed all responses in Canada to the ship and her immigrant cargo.

From the moment the Borden government first heard of the ship's departure from Hong Kong, it declared its intention to enforce the recent immigration regulations with vigour. When the ship arrived in Vancouver, Ottawa reaffirmed its determination.[30] But far from departing immediately, the *Komagata Maru* remained anchored in Vancouver's harbour, a few hundred yards from shore, for two months before it left. During the first weeks Dominion immigration officials examined each prospective immigrant individually. They permitted twenty who were previous residents to land and declared another ninety medically unfit for entry. Then the legality of the federal exclusion order was challenged in provincial courts, another time-consuming process. In all, seven weeks passed before the provincial Supreme Court upheld the order, removing the last legal obstacle to the ship's departure.[31]

In Vancouver the arrival of the *Komagata Maru* provoked an outburst as intense as that of 1907. By now the city had clearly become the geographic focus of west coast racialism, in part, at least, because of her highly visible Asian minorities. Vancouver's

Above, the *Komagata Maru*, HMCS *Rainbow*, and sightseers' craft in Vancouver harbour, July 1914. *Below*, Sikhs on board the *Komagata Maru*, Vancouver, 1914.

nativistic tradition sustained persistent racial tensions in the community, even though it was only infrequently that they grew acute. In recent years the climate of white opinion had grown antagonistic toward East Indians, perhaps more so than toward other Asiatics. Consequently Gurdit Singh's apparent challenge to the policy of exclusion, and even more the possible success of his challenge (a prospect which seemed credible as a similar one had succeeded six months earlier), revived the racial fears and animosities which were latent in west coast society. The result was an outpouring of racist rhetoric directed at the Indians, whose arrival prompted objection, and also at the federal government, whose power it was to grant or refuse the Indians' request for entry. Two themes dominated the cries of the nativists: fear of inundation by hordes of Asian immigrants and concern for the unassimilable nature of the Indian.

After the ship dropped anchor the Borden government was assailed with petitions which supported the government's resolve to exclude the new arrivals and urged greater efforts to prevent them from landing.[32] Provincial journalists swelled the growing chorus. "It is not a question [of] whether this particular group of Hindus shall be allowed to land," the *Vancouver News-Advertiser* claimed, reviving once more a cluster of popular negative stereotypes.

There are 300,000,000 natives of India behind them, who have the same rights as these. If a million were accepted the remaining 299,000,000 would have the same claim. Every one of them would have the same grievance if he were excluded as this comparatively small group, and the additional grievance that he is subject to an invidious discrimination. The question before the people of Canada is whether the country is to be thrown open to all the people of India or closed to all.[33]

It was the Indians' inability to assimilate that prompted another editor's objections. "It is impossible 'to make Canadians out of immigrants whose customs, traditions and habits forms an insurmountable barrier between them and the Canadianization.' [*sic*]." "East Indians are good men," he declared. "In Canada they are in the wrong place. That is all. Unfortunately for the East Indians it is also everything."[34] According to a local Methodist monthly, the economic aspect of the problem was serious,

but the social and moral aspects are much more serious to contemplate. It is not mere unreasoned prejudice that influences Western feeling; it is not that the Asiatics are inferior; it is that they are different, so different that the two races are really incompatible, and such an attempt to fuse them as a common people is useless and would inevitably result in a lowered standard of civilization, which would hardly look attractive to even the ardent advocate of Hindu rights to unrestricted immigration on the plea of the brotherhood of man and fellow-British citizenship. Surely it is utter nonsense to argue from this basis when it is evident that each race is better off in its own natural environment, and when, too, the unrestrained mixing of the races on this Coast would lead to economic disaster and ethical demoralisation.[35]

Meanwhile Premier Richard McBride pressed the federal government to stand firm against entry.[36]

In Vancouver the outburst reached a peak on June 23 at a public meeting of worried citizens called by Mayor T. S. Baxter. The ship had been anchored off shore for a month and no sign of its imminent departure could yet be seen. On the contrary, many city residents seemed to believe that the immigrants would soon land, through subterfuge if through no other means. Long before the meeting opened, 1,500 people had packed the hall while twice that number milled about on the street outside its entrance. "A noticeable feature of the large audience," the *News-Advertiser* observed, "was the solid character of the type of citizen represented, and in the crowded street outside the panama hat was prominent in appearance rather than the cheaper kinds of headgear."[37] After speakers had addressed the crowds both indoors and out, the meeting demanded the immediate deportation of all the ship's passengers and legislation to prevent similar incidents in the future.

The highlight of the evening was a stirring address by H. H. Stevens, Conservative member of Parliament for Vancouver and now the city's leading anti-Oriental spokesman. In his remarks, which were repeatedly interrupted by enthusiastic applause, Stevens voiced the central concern of west coast nativists, the belief that unassimilable Asian immigrants threatened the province's cultural homogeneity. Canada was a nation of but seven and one-half millions, Stevens told the gathering, but "in the Orient—at our doors—there are 800 millions of Asiatics," millions which at "the very least tremor ... would unquestionably swamp us by weight of numbers." "What would have happened if immigration from Asia had been allowed through all these years to come through the Western portals into British Columbia?" he asked. "Canada today would have been swamped with Orientals and there would be left today practically not a vestige of the civilization of which we are so proud." Stevens believed that, fundamentally, Asiatic immigration threatened the nation's destiny. "Very briefly," he assured his attentive audience,

what we face in British Columbia and in Canada today is this—whether or no the civilization which finds its highest exemplification in Anglo-Saxon British rule shall or shall not prevail in the Dominion of Canada.... I am absolutely convinced after the most searching inquiry, that we cannot allow indiscriminate immigration from the Orient and hope to build up a Nation in Canada on the foundations upon which we have commenced our national life (applause). In laying down that principle I cast no aspersions upon the civilization of Asia, but I impress upon you this solemn fact, that these two civilizations are entirely distinct in every important feature.... The question is will that civilization or will those brought up through centuries under that civilization assimilate in a satisfactory manner with the people of this country. That is the great problem facing us today, and I hold that no immigration is or can be successful where it is impossible to assimilate and readily assimilate the immigrant (prolonged applause). This is the absolutely fundamental principle of all systems of immigration, and must necessarily be so.[38]

Although no more protest meetings were held in Vancouver, a similar one took place in New Westminster one week later,[39] and so long as the ship was in harbour, the entire community remained on edge. Tension increased when, on the eve of their expected deportation, the Indians seized control of the ship and repulsed a midnight boarding raid of 150 policemen and immigration officers. Negotiations followed and Martin Burrell, British Columbia's representative in the Borden cabinet, intervened. Meanwhile HMCS *Rainbow* stood by to prevent further unrest. Finally, under the watchful eyes of thousands, many of whom stood on the city's rooftops to witness the concluding act of the drama, the *Komagata Maru* weighed anchor and set out through the straits for Hong Kong. Then, and only then, did public concern subside.

When compared with the numbers of immigrants who annually entered the province, the 376 on board the *Komagata Maru* in 1914 were of very little significance. Furthermore, aside from a handful of previous residents, none of the prospective immigrants landed. Yet while the ship lingered in port, racial tensions in Vancouver remained high, as high, indeed, as they had been in 1887 and 1907. Why was this so? The answer cannot be found in direct economic or social conflict, for the Indians remained on board and confrontation was avoided. Perhaps an element of feared or anticipated conflict provided one motive force. But far more important was the generalized fear of Asian immigration engendered by the west coast drive for cultural homogeneity. That a deep and permanent racial cleavage divided British Columbia its white residents were well aware. In assessing the origins of this racial division, however, they could largely ignore the native Indian population for it had long since been pushed aside and seemed to languish in decay. The Asian community, on the other hand, was a dynamic, growing segment in west coast society. Its continued expansion promised only to broaden the racial fissures which already fragmented this society.

Cultural pluralism, then, was unacceptable to the white community. Within it the plural condition generated profound, irrational racial fears. Pluralism stirred a deep longing for the social cohesion

which could only be achieved, it seemed, by attaining racial homogeneity. R. E. Gosnell, a prominent journalist, historian, and public
servant, charted the province's course when he declared in 1908:

This vast and in some respects still unknown country has possibilities in store for it
not yet, perhaps, dreamed of. It has without peradventure, great possibilities as the
home for the British emigrant and as a field for the investor; possibilities as the
point of convergence of trade and commerce along the All Red Line to the utmost
development of which the statesmen of the Empire are pledged; possibilities as an
educational centre as famous as any in Europe; possibilities of great industrial
wealth; possibilities in short as a greater Britain on the Pacific, where British arts
and institutions will expand under fresh impetus, 'where the British flag will
forever fly, where British laws and justice will be respected and enforced, and
where British men and women will be bred equal to the best traditions of the
race.'[40]

Gosnell's remarks were merely a personal statement, made without
reference to the racial question. Nonetheless they offer at least a
glimpse of the communal purpose, the social aspirations, and the
cultural self-image shared by many west coast whites. It was a
vision that admitted no Asian presence.

Yet the hostile outburst of 1914 differed in one significant respect
from that of 1907: there was no rioting, even though public feeling
was as aggravated as it earlier had been. This was so because by
1914 the federal government appeared sympathetic to white British
Columbia's demands for exclusion. In 1907 the Laurier government had seemed deaf to all such pleas, but evidently the Borden
government was ready to listen and to act. It was this willingness to
turn the East Indians back that ultimately prevented an outbreak
of racial violence.

PART THREE

THE RISE OF ANTI-JAPANESE FEELING

6

JAPS

When Japanese immigrants arrived in British Columbia they were usually called simply "the Japs." This was not just an innocent nickname. Like the label "John Chinaman," it was a term of derision and contempt. In the minds of those who used it, it conjured up a cluster of racist assumptions, a disparaging image of all Japanese, in Canada and abroad. Moreover, these stereotypes were extremely influential. From the 1890s to the 1940s they dominated white British Columbia's perceptions of Japanese immigrant society. Broadly diffused throughout the province, they profoundly shaped the course of race relations in the community.

British Columbia's image of the Japanese immigrant, like those of his Chinese and East Indian counterparts, was drawn from two separate sources: popular beliefs about Japan and direct contact with the immigrants themselves. In the first instance, nineteenth-century western perceptions of Asia commonly included a few generalized notions about Japan and her people. By and large these beliefs were based upon little but fleeting observations, rumours, and second-hand accounts, at least before mid-century, for Japan was largely veiled from western eyes until 1853, when Commodore Perry forced her to accept commercial relations with the United States. But thereafter successive merchants, missionaries, diplomats, travellers, and journalists visited Japan and reported their impressions to an increasingly interested West. Newspapers, periodicals, school books, and popular literature spread these ideas to a vast audience on both sides of the Atlantic. Consequently, by the turn of the twentieth century Europe and North America possessed a fuller, though perhaps no more accurate, portrait of Japan than ever before, and these ideas helped shape whatever initial understanding of Japanese immigrants most Canadians possessed.

During the first half of the nineteenth century western thought tended to blur the many distinctions between China and Japan. Usually Japan was closely identified with China and both were considered part of the larger Asian whole, a mysterious, over-crowded, and backward society when judged by western standards. Initially this was most likely the result of the limited knowledge of Japan shared throughout the West. Nevertheless after 1853 even the spread of information about Japan did not dispel these impressions; in some respects, to western eyes, the nation always appeared indistinguishable from the rest of Asian society. The Yellow Peril, for example, seemed a single Oriental threat to the West, one of which Japan was merely a part.[1]

But after mid-century a distinctive image of Japan gradually formed in western thought. The Japan of *The Mikado*—Gilbert and Sullivan's operetta, first produced in 1885—was mysterious, quaint, irrational, and capriciously cruel as well. That of the Italian composer Giacomo Puccini, writing twenty years later, was rather more exotic. He set *Madama Butterfly* in a land of silks and lacquered ware, of paper fans and flowers. Both works obviously drew heavily upon impressions of Japan widely held in the West.[2]

Of far more significance was the fact that from 1870 onward western observations of Japan increasingly emphasized Japanese progressiveness. Whereas the nation's seclusion had formerly been a sign of backwardness, once her isolation had ended, her rapid modernization attracted growing attention. Industrial expansion and technological development, two basic measures by which the West gauged other societies, forcefully impressed many outside observers of Japan. Western comment similarly emphasized her educational, bureaucratic, and political reforms.[3] As one widely used Canadian public school geography observed in 1876, "within the last few years, no country in the world has made such rapid progress as Japan. Railways and steamships have been built, education has been greatly encouraged, and European institutions generally adopted."[4] In the eyes of foreign observers Japan still fell short of the western goals toward which, it was assumed, she was earnestly striving. By implication, moreover, as long as this was so she remained an inferior nation. Yet this judgement notwithstanding, during the late nineteenth century "westernization" seemed one of Japan's most salient characteristics. The resultant image of the Japanese was a curious blend of the traditional and the progressive, with emphasis increasingly placed upon the latter themes and perceptions.

Japan's growing military strength was an aspect of her progress which first interested, then concerned, and ultimately obsessed many western onlookers. During the late nineteenth century Japanese military growth was generally considered one facet of the modernization experience, further proof that Japan wished to emulate the West. Indeed there were westerners who initially found much to praise in Japanese militarism. According to one American Methodist missionary, the Sino-Japanese War of 1894-95 was one in which "the ideas and methods of the Western nations [were] in conflict with the worn-out civilization of the Orient." In his mind "the conduct of the war on the part of the Japanese was highly creditable. It was the first instance of war carried on by an Asiatic nation in accordance with the high ideals of the Red Cross Society."[5] And as long as Japan's military energies were vented on backward China—simultaneously being victimized by western imperial expansion—her militarism was viewed in a favourable light.

But after Japan's victory over Russia in 1905 a rising note of alarm replaced this former praise. The thought that Asians had defeated Europeans in battle proved a sobering one in the West and it quickly prompted a reassessment of recent Japanese history. No longer an antique empire in the earliest stage of development, Japan suddenly seemed a modern, aggressive, expansionist power, driven by avarice, overpopulation, and desire for international prestige.[6] She now appeared to challenge the military might of western nations and therefore posed a threat to western dominance in Asia. Some observers even believed that she had set her sights on ascendancy throughout the entire north Pacific basin. Backward Japan was obviously not so backward after all, and this realization sent eddies of alarm across the surface of western thought.

In British Columbia attitudes toward Japan underwent the same fundamental shift. There too her progressive image took on a new, negative meaning. "Japan is wide awake, with every nerve a-tingle; with its eyes steadfastly fixed on a fair horizon," observed the editor of *Westward Ho! Magazine*, a Vancouver literary monthly, in 1908. "Its policy has been decided on, its course is mapped out, its mission is in the word of one of its greatest statesmen, 'To lead Asia'.... The ambition of Japan is to stand on International equality with the white races. It admits no point of inferiority, and is straining every nerve to gain and maintain its forces."[7] In 1912 one British Columbian, worried about the new Anglo-Japanese treaty, warned that it would "give to Japan ... an exclusive and ominous ascendancy over the industrial, commercial and political affairs of Asia and the British-Pacific colonies. And the day Japanese Asiatic and Pacific supremacy is an accomplished fact, the day the changeless millions of China become a tool of Japan, Japan is mistress of the world, and the white man's dream will have become a nightmare, and a new meaning will be involved in the 'White Man's Burden'."[8]

Once fixed in the west coast mind, the image of an aggressive, militaristic Japan was not to be dislodged. For one thing it became a recurring, if minor, theme in local fiction. One elaborate account — "The Pacific War of 1910" — published serially in 1909 and 1910, depicted a well-planned, unprovoked Japanese attack on British Columbia. Victory for the defenders occurred when

the mighty armies of Japan were hurled back, and the Yellow Peril, which during the previous decade unceasingly menaced the prosperity of the American continent, had been broken forever, by the patriotic bravery of the men of British Columbia, by the scientific skill of her sons, and the loyal devotion to the motherland which had inspired even young boys to prove that the daring hearts of their forefathers — hardy pioneers of the past — were still dominating the character of the newer generation.[9]

In a similar vein, a short story of the same period described a vicious Oriental attack on a Canadian ship off the Pacific coast. The timely arrival of the British North Pacific Fleet saved not only the ship but Vancouver as well. As the tale concluded:

> And saved it might be, for ever from thee,
> Thou sly tawny Jap, thou slimy Chinee.
> From Mr. Sam Slick who prevails to the South.
> From envious hordes who with wide gaping mouth
> Stare now at our treasures, our riches untold;
> Our fruit and farmlands; our silver and gold;
> Our copper and coal, and our forests sublime;
> Our wealth all abounding for now and all time;
> Our Ports and our Harbours that greatness afford —
> Protection to Commerce, defense to the sword.
> Ye Chinese who grovel and snivel and leer
> Get rich on your hoarding and then disappear;
> Make off helter-skelter in double quick run,
> With the wealth of our soil to the Land of the Sun.
> Ye Japanese clad with equipments of war
> Whose armies and navies and Juggernaut car
> Would crush, if they dare, and claim as their own
> What belongs to the white man — the white man alone.
> Avaunt ye whom envy and malice propel
> To usurp all our splendour by tactics of Hell![10]

The sense of a Japanese military threat to the province could scarcely be made more explicit. Similarly, another fictional account of Japanese aggression, Hilda Glynn-Ward's racist novel *The Writing on the Wall* (1921), described a Pearl Harbor-like aerial attack on Victoria, Vancouver, and Nanaimo, one carefully coordinated with extensive fifth column activity.[11]

During the 1920s and 1930s these assumptions about Japanese militarism persisted in the United States and Canada, particularly

Yellow journalism, *The Sunday Sun*, August 7, 1921.

along the Pacific coast. It was generally believed that Japan not only had designs upon western North America but had the military strength to achieve them.[12] In Canada students of public affairs, both xenophobes and others, were alarmed by Japanese expansionism.[13] The image of Japanese aggression was a persistent theme in west coast popular thought. As the Vancouver *Sunday Sun*, one of the more alarmist of provincial newspapers, observed in 1921:

Japan is no longer thousands of miles away across the Pacific Ocean. The fighting power of Japan is not far removed from the great cities on the Pacific coast, or from inland cities, or from Atlantic coast cities. Thanks to the flying machine, every nation at every moment is within striking distance of every other. As easily as a hawk can strike at a chicken yard ten miles from its nest, so easily can Japan, if she chooses and when she chooses, strike across the Pacific. Flying machines are sent, knocked down, wings detached in great freight ships or on warships. They could be assembled, loaded with machine guns, high explosives and deadly gasses, at the rate of a hundred in an hour from a fleet of apparently innocent merchant ships, approaching without warning and anchoring fifty or a hundred miles off shore.[14]

Such claims were commonplace during the interwar years.[15]

The second major source of western Canada's Japanese image was the interracial contact which followed Japanese immigration. If western perceptions of Japan made an imprint on the beliefs of British Columbia's whites, Japanese immigrants in the province left an even clearer mark. As growing numbers arrived in the west coast community, several new negative assumptions were formed and then clustered about the well-established popular image of Japan. To a limited extent these impressions were based on direct observation. Once provincial whites encountered Japanese immigrants at close quarters, they could form their own opinions about these strangers in their midst. But on the whole British Columbians knew no more about Japanese immigrants than they did about the Chinese. By and large their racial assumptions were formed not through interracial contact but through the self-perpetuating tendency of racial stereotypes.[16] Popular attitudes, more than any other single influence, shaped the Japanese image held by west coast whites.

Nevertheless a distinctive Japanse image was slow to form in provincial thought for, initially, whites did not clearly differentiate the Chinese and Japanese. Consequently, during the 1890s and early 1900s, the image drew heavily upon older Chinese stereotypes and generalized assumptions about the nature of Asian society. This could be traced to the fact that nineteenth-century western images of Asia often failed to distinguish clearly among its component parts and also to the similar physical appearance and socio-economic status of the two immigrant groups. Gradually, however, a distinctive Japanese image began to emerge in the west coast mind, as hundreds and then thousands of migrants from Japan arrived in British Columbia. But it was not until after Japan defeated Russia that the image finally came into focus. That single, dramatic event fused western impressions of Japan with evolving west coast assumptions about the immigrants themselves. The result was a bold, threatening image of the newcomers.

Perhaps the most durable of all Japanese stereotypes was the belief that they jeopardized the economic interests of white British Columbia. Formed soon after the Japanese first arrived in the province, this impression was quickly fixed in west coast racial thought. Because they accepted low pay, long work days, and low standards of living, Japanese immigrants seemed a threat to the white workingman. Obviously this attitude owed much to older assumptions about the Chinese. In fact, once Japanese migration commenced, nativists frequently described the two peoples as one, engaged in relentlessly driving white labour out of work. On the other hand, some critics clearly distinguished between the two. Those who did usually argued that, compared with the Chinese, the Japanese were more aggressive competitors and therefore were even more dangerous.[17]

During the 1890s, when immigrants from Japan were comparatively few, their competition generally appeared to affect only individuals or small groups of white workingmen. But after the turn of the century, as they arrived in growing numbers, this rivalry began to appear rather more alarming. Among whites the conviction grew that Japanese immigrants were gaining control of entire industries in the province. The west coast fisheries seemed a clear case in point. From the early 1890s to the early 1920s the number of licensed fishermen in coastal waters increased markedly and, as it did, the proportion of them who were Japanese increased steadily, too. By 1902 more fishermen were Japanese than were either white or Indian, although at no time were the Japanese actually in the majority. To many white fishermen and other observers as well, it seemed that the Japanese were striving for full control of the industry; some believed that they had already achieved it.[18] Similar claims were made after 1910 as growing numbers of Japanese took up fruit and berry farming in the Okanagan and Fraser River valleys.[19] Some industrial employers, of course, dissented from this view. Nevertheless from the time of their arrival the theme of Japanese economic penetration persisted in British Columbian thought.

This belief was intertwined with the equally common assumption that aggression was intrinsic to the Japanese character. The economic acitivities of the Japanese immigrant seemed convincing proof of the point. According to R. G. MacBeth, a Presbyterian clergyman and former resident of Vancouver, Japanese immigrants aroused the same objections as did the Chinese.

In addition, it ought to be said, that the Japanese, while remaining here in large measure unassimilated, are more vain and aggressive. They are not content to do the lower and, in some senses, the more menial work as the Chinese are: they will not be hewers of wood and drawers of water; they push themselves into every avenue of business, and at the present time, for instance, they have practically pushed white men out of the extensive fishing industry of British Columbia.[20]

Two early provincial historians agreed. "The people of British Columbia," they wrote in 1914,

were slow to recognize that the Japanese is a far more dangerous antagonist than the Chinese; that his superior education, his training, and his more plastic nature fit him to compete in a far greater variety of occupations and to mould himself to the conditions of the country, and that unless restrictions are placed upon his entry every class of the community and every avocation in the province will find this enterprising yellow man slowly, but surely, elbowing his way in and taking possession.[21]

Furthermore, many whites were convinced that not merely economic but military aggressiveness typified the Japanese. From 1900 onward—especially during the depression years—Japan's expansionist foreign policy constantly reinforced this conclusion. The Japanese in their homeland seemed proud, bold, pugnacious, and anxious for hegemony over the Pacific, and these beliefs coloured white British Columbia's impressions of the immigrant Japanese. As one rural weekly observed in 1924: "Of all the people on the globe, the Japanese are perhaps the most intensely patriotic. Their idolizing of military prowess and sacrificial patriotism is extreme and this fervor, which has survived centuries of time, still burns hot in every son and daughter of Nippon no matter [in] what country they be."[22]

There were two distinct facets to this point of view. One represented the immigrants as unswerving Japanese nationalists, steadfastly loyal to the Emperor and therefore disloyal to Canada. Imbued with the aspirations of modern Japan, it was argued, these immigrants could never be woven into the social fabric of the province. Their vernacular newspapers, language schools, and other cultural institutions all reinforced this common assumption. According to one nativist writing in 1934, "There are Japanese schools conducted in Japanese in British Columbia at which all Japanese children in the neighbourhood are required to attend. At these schools the principles of Japanese nationalism are taught. It is impressed upon these budding Canadians that Japan and her people are superior to the white race and will some day rule the Pacific with a rod of iron."[23]

The other facet seemed more disquieting: in the eyes of some whites, Japanese immigrants threatened the military security of west coast society. Not surprisingly, one of the first to raise the question was an intelligence officer in the Canadian militia who noted in 1908 that, even though no evidence warranted his suspicions, he considered the Japanese dangerous.

Although an admirer of the Jap I cannot but regard his presence in Canada as a menace to the Country and to the Empire. Their aggressive patriotism renders it out of the question that they can ever populate the country as Canadians, but they are certainly ta[k]ing possession of it as Japanese. From a military point of view their manner of occupying the country is I think dangerous in the extreme. They are established all the way up the coast and throughout the interior in a manner that enables them to obtain the fullest information of the country.[24]

According to alarmists, the potential menace took two different forms: espionage and (in the event of war) fifth column activity. In fact, suspicion of Japanese spies and fear of possible wartime treachery recurred in west coast racial thought, both north and south of the international border, from 1905 to the eve of Pearl Harbor.[25] The paternalism of the Japanese consulate in defence of immigrant interests, and the well-known fact that the laws of Japan conferred dual citizenship upon naturalized Japanese Canadians, combined to reinforce even further this prevailing cast of mind.

Coupled with these assumptions were two other popular beliefs. One was the persistent notion, common long before the outbreak of World War II, that many Japanese were illegal immigrants. Not surprisingly, this idea came to the fore after 1931 when a major immigration fraud was uncovered in Vancouver. This in turn gave added credence to the repeated rumours that Japanese military officers were infiltrating the country.[26] The other was a rising sense of alarm that the high birth-rate among Japanese immigrants seriously threatened the whiteness of white British Columbia. The Japanese were breeding so quickly, it seemed, that their growth rate was outstripping that of provincial whites. "How many Yellow men are there in this vast, fertile and immensely rich Province today," asked one alarmed resident. "Nobody knows. Statistics become useless in the face of Oriental cunning. All that is known for certain is that the Japanese birth rate is more than double that of the White population. *All that is certain is that, with an imperfect count of the Oriental equation, in the last ten years the ratio of Japanese to Whites has changed from 1 in 253, to 1 in 13.*"[27] What this implied for the future seemed all too clear.

The idea that Japanese land acquisition also threatened the white community was another common belief. From the early 1900s, when the first few Japanese immigrants began to purchase land, the extension of Japanese landholding was a cause of continued concern. For one thing, it was claimed, the process would entrench Japanese colonies in the province. For another, it drove white farmers from the land because the Japanese, with their low standard of living, were unfair competitors. As a labour paper reported in 1914, fruit farmers near New Westminster were being forced out of business: "Where a short time ago the small fruit industry was in the hands of white people, furnishing them with a comfortable living, now the Japanese are in possession of many tracts of valuable land and it will not be long before the caucasian will be swept away by the invading yellow horde."[28] In the Okanagan local whites expressed similar fears after World War I, when Orientals began to buy land in the valley. "Is Summerland to continue to be the home of British peoples, or is it to become a settlement for Orientals?" asked one interior newspaper after a Japanese purchased an orchard plot in the community.

Individually a number of the Japanese we have among us are fine, clean young men. Unfortunately there is such a wide difference between the two races the settling here of Orientals can mean nothing but two distinct colonies for which there is not sufficient room. If all our land is occupied by white people we can have a strong, thriving and prosperous community. Every orchard held by an Oriental makes that much less room for the needed white population. If the sales to Orientals continue social life will be narrowed by reduced white population, thus making others more inclined to sell out and move elsewhere. Fortunately we have only made the beginning in a movement in this direction and such a calamity may yet be averted.[29]

Of all the familiar assumptions about Japanese immigrants, however, none proved more pervasive, none more durable, than the belief that they could never be assimilated. White British Columbians were convinced that, like the Chinese, the Japanese would never be absorbed into west coast society. Any thoughts of intermarriage as a possible solution to this problem were quickly discarded. Popular mythology had it that miscegenation could only lead to racial deterioration.[30] A few whites agreed that the Japanese were more likely to become acculturated than were the Chinese. Indeed, to some of them this was further cause for alarm. But generally it was assumed that, socially and racially, the Japanese could never be assimilated. "My principal objection to them," a Vancouver workingman testified in 1902, "is that they do not assimilate, cannot assimilate, with our race, and that our country should be for men of our own race, instead of being overrun by an alien race."[31] More than any other, this was the constant refrain of west coast nativists, for many British Columbians did not wish a permanent, alien minority to be lodged in their province. To them, it was the gravest threat which the Japanese immigrants posed. As a widely endorsed petition to Laurier argued in 1906, Oriental immigration precluded a homogeneous Canadian citizenship, and in doing so imperilled the nation's very existence.[32]

In sum, at the core of the Japanese image lay a single central belief: the concept of peaceful penetration. Peaceful penetration implied the quiet, relentless, and insidious infiltration of Japanese immigrants into west coast society. Moreover, the concept emitted unmistakable overtones of fifth column activity.[33] In one way or another, most popular views of the Japanese were coupled with this assumption. The public mind commonly ascribed aggressiveness, unassimilability, expanding economic control, high birth-rates, illegal immigration, and a potential for subversion to newcomers from Japan. The idea of peaceful penetration fused western impressions of Japan with those stereotyped traits so widely attributed to Japanese immigrants. Here too the components of the image neatly interlocked. The overwhelming impression created was that immigrants from Japan gravely threatened white British Columbia.

It is impossible to tell precisely how many whites held these beliefs. In the absence of opinion polls and other quantitative assessments, any observations about the extent of the consensus can only be impressionistic and general. Nevertheless all available evidence strongly suggests that this image was broadly shared by white British Columbians. Perhaps the most convincing sign was that these attitudes dominated public discussion about the Japanese for more than half a century. In virtually every forum where white opinion was uttered, these beliefs recurred time and again. Dissent was extremely uncommon. The dissenters were few and isolated—a handful of ministers and university professors, scarcely men of sufficient influence to mould mass opinion. The great majority of British Columbians, of course, left no records of their thoughts. In this instance, however, silence implied acquiescence in, if not consent to, prevailing attitudes. Certainly, when racial tension arose, as it did after Pearl Harbor, this opinion was easily mobilized.

Nor was acceptance of these attitudes related to any clear social cleavage within the white community. Aside from the few dissenters and a small number of employers who praised Japanese working-men (usually on economic rather than egalitarian grounds), these ideas transcended existing social bounds. Undoubtedly whites in coastal communities, where the great majority of Japanese congregated, clung more tightly to their prejudices than did those in the interior. But many interior residents shared these racial sentiments and they did not hesitate to voice them whenever the occasion arose. As far as can be judged, then, the articulate among white nativists spoke for most British Columbians. Of course, not everyone in the province shared a single cast of mind. Nonetheless, from the 1890s to the 1940s this generalized, negative image was widely diffused throughout the province.

The Japanese image, like that of the Chinese, remained relatively static. For the first decade or so after the immigrants began to arrive, it had no clear structure. But after the turn of the twentieth century its central ideas jelled, and henceforth the Japanese image changed relatively little. During the 1930s it emphasized Japanese militarism and potential subversion more than it had previously. Yet, in spite of this, these ideas remained largely fixed. As self-fulfilling prophecies, racial stereotypes have the capacity to regenerate themselves, and these were no exception. Fed by such persistence as well as by social, economic, and psychological strains, this hostile image of the Japanese flourished for more than half a century in west coast popular thought.

If this is how Japanese immigrant society appeared to white contemporaries, was it the actuality of Japanese life in Canada? How accurate was this unflattering image of "the Japs"? The answer to these questions can only be found in a general description of the immigrant community.

When the first Japanese came to British Columbia is not at all clear, for no systematic records of their entry were kept until 1905. But during the late 1880s a small number annually fished on the Fraser during the summer salmon run, and in the next decade their numbers grew substantially. By the mid-1890s about 900 were engaged in the fisheries (probably the great majority of the Japanese in the province) and by the turn of the century this figure had more than quadrupled. In 1901 the federal census recorded more than 4,500 Japanese then resident in British Columbia.[34] Thereafter the community's rate of growth fluctuated markedly. Until 1921, when its numbers reached 15,000, it almost doubled in size each decade. During the next ten years growth continued, but at a much slower rate. In the depression years it ceased entirely, the community remaining the same size throughout the decade. On the eve of Pearl Harbor about 22,000 Japanese lived in the west coast province. A small but visible minority, they constituted less than 3 per cent of the provincial population.

Before World War I the Japanese population grew largely through immigration rather than natural increase. For the most part the early immigrants were male sojourners, some of whom crossed the Pacific annually on a seasonal basis. During these years there were two peaks of migration. One introduced perhaps 11,000 Japanese immigrants between July 1899 and August 1900, most of whom were apparently bound for the United States and soon left the province.[35] The other, in 1906 and 1907, brought in an equal number, but in this instance the majority remained in British Columbia. These years aside, the annual rate of Japanese immigration was relatively low. Furthermore, because of increasingly tight emigration controls exercised by Japan at Canada's request, it continually declined. On the average, 666 entered Canada each year from 1908 to 1921, 380 annually until 1931, and 82 a year thereafter until war with Japan broke out.[36] In addition, immigration was partially counterbalanced by steady return migration. One estimate in the late 1930s placed the number of those who had returned to Japan at 12,000 or 13,000.[37] Obviously the Japanese community of British Columbia was in a constant state of flux.

During the interwar years, however, there was an extremely significant change in this pattern of population growth. Initially both the Japanese and Chinese communities expanded almost entirely through migration, but the former, unlike the latter, soon began growing through natural increase. While the vast majority of Chinese immigrants remained male sojourners, a significant number of Japanese migrants were women joining their husbands in British Columbia which they intended to make their permanent home. As early as 1911 the ratio of Japanese men to women in British Columbia was about 5 to 1. Within ten years it had shrunk to 2 to 1 and thereafter it was reduced even further.[38] During the period from 1910 to 1930, in particular, women comprised the majority of all Japanese who entered the country. This sharp increase in the number and proportion of female Japanese immigrants was largely because of the migration of "picture brides," married by proxy in Japan to husbands who lived in Canada.

But it was not until the later 1920s that the full significance of female Japanese migration was realized. Then nativists discovered the high birth-rate which prevailed within the Japanese immigrant community. The annual Japanese birth rate during the Twenties and early Thirties was two to four times that of norms in British Columbia while their yearly rate of natural increase was from 3½ to 10 times that of the provincial average. In large part this was attributable to the peculiar demographic structure of the immigrant community. Most of the migrant women were of child-bearing age and their husbands were likewise relatively young and virile.[39] But whatever the cause, the result was the birth of a second generation of Japanese Canadians—the Nisei—whose commitments were to life in Canada. Indeed, by 1941 almost 30 per cent of the Japanese community had been born in Canada.[40] Some sojourners still remained within the Japanese community, but far more quickly than other Asian immigrants the Japanese had put down roots in west coast society.

As yet little is known about the precise origins, character, and motives of the Japanese who came to British Columbia. One survey taken in 1934 indicated that almost half came from four scattered prefectures in Japan: Hiroshima, Wakayama, Shiga, and Kagoshima. The remainder were drawn from thirty-two of the forty-four other prefectures on the islands. Hiroshima included a major urban industrial centre and Wakayama, a coastal prefecture, supported a fishing industry. With these exceptions, the economy of each of the four prefectures was founded upon rice agriculture. The great majority of those immigrants surveyed were either farmers, fishermen, or common labourers in Japan, although a small number were craftsmen as well.[41] Three-quarters of the men who came were between the ages of 15 and 30 when they arrived, while the average age of immigrant women was slightly over 25 years.[42] Rural poverty, population pressure, and tales of opportunity abroad were probably the major motive forces underlying Japanese emigration, just as they were for the Chinese and East Indians. To the limited extent that this can be ascertained, the migrants apparently were drawn not from among the very poor but from the ranks of those who, despite a modest income, were faced with a ceaseless struggle to preserve themselves from that state. Often attracted to Canada by the chain migration process, they came in order to improve their economic condition.[43]

During the 1890s and early 1900s Japanese immigrants most often found work in the fisheries of the province. In particular they were drawn down to the Fraser River where by the turn of the century more than 4,000 were engaged at the height of the annual salmon run. By then a further 500 were employed in provincial sawmills where they had begun to replace Chinese as unskilled labourers.[44] Most likely some lumber workers were fishermen who had sought alternate work out of season. Aside from these major forms of employment the Japanese initially took jobs where they could find them, most of them arduous and requiring little skill.

As the years passed and the immigrant population grew, patterns of Japanese employment changed significantly. The numbers of Japanese engaged in the fisheries continued to increase until by 1919 they held almost half of the fishing licenses issued. But under pressure from white fishermen, the federal government systematically reduced the number of Japanese fishermen throughout the 1920s. Simultaneously a growing number of Japanese found work in the provincial forest industry. During World War I numbers of Asians entered this sector of the industrial work force, largely because of the growing labour shortage in British Columbia. By the end of the war more than a third of the province's 16,000 forest workers were Oriental, over 2,000 of them Japanese. Throughout the early 1920s their numbers grew further although, with the great postwar expansion of the industry, they actually constituted a lower proportion of the total labour force.[45] Toward the end of the decade their numbers began to shrink, in part because of a provincial minimum wage law intended to drive them from the industry. During the depression years, of course, they declined even further.

The greatest changes in employment patterns among the Japanese, however, took place outside these primary industries. Between 1910 and 1930 the occupational base of the Japanese community broadened remarkably. Agriculture attracted the single largest number, especially to mixed farms and soft fruit farms. Although forbidden by law to acquire crown lands, all Asians were free to buy property privately. By 1931, 20 per cent of all employed Japanese were farmers or farm labourers. Many others took up commercial and service occupations, as shopkeepers, clerks, cooks, and domestic servants. A small but significant number achieved professional vocations.[46] In short, on the eve of World War II, Japanese could be found employed in virtually all occupational categories, though they did remain heavily concentrated in a small number of them.

The Japanese had several motives for seeking out new occupations. In part they were driven by increasing legal restrictions upon their previous areas of work, as well as the more informal pressures of popular prejudice. On the other hand this search for new employment was also a measure of rising aspirations. As they left behind their sojourner years, the Japanese commenced an assimilative drive for upward social and economic mobility. Like most immigrants who enter new societies at the bottom of the economic scale, the west coast Japanese sought higher incomes and improved living standards. For this reason many soon abandoned the seasonal, low-paid work which they had performed on arrival. They preferred the greater stability of less seasonal occupations or the prospect of higher profit from a self-owned enterprise.

What did Japanese workers earn? Unfortunately the answer to this question is not at all clear, although a few general observations about wages and incomes can be made. The earnings of Japanese fishermen were in proportion to their catch. Canners paid all fishermen, regardless of race, a fixed sum per salmon, the rate usually varying within a single fishing season as well as from year to year. There was no discriminatory wage policy in the fishing industry. The incomes of Japanese fishermen, like those of whites and Indians, depended primarily upon the size of the salmon run, the prevailing price offered for salmon, and the fisherman's luck and industriousness. The incomes of farmers and small businessmen were similarly governed by fortune, hard work, and the marketplace. Japanese in these occupations functioned in open, competitive markets. What their earnings as a group were there is no way of knowing. But many undoubtedly found these callings profitable, as the growing number of Japanese engaged in them testifies. On the other hand, in some industries—the mining and forest industries in particular—wage discrimination was the norm. In 1902, for example, Japanese sawmill employees were paid $.90 to $1.00 daily while whites earned $1.50. Similarly, in 1905 Japanese mine labourers earned $1.37 to the $2.75 per day paid whites for the same work.[47] On the whole, Japanese workers, like their Chinese counterparts, earned one-half to two-thirds of what whites were paid for equivalent work. Their incomes, too, were affected by market conditions, but they were competitors on the lower fringe of the labour market, one composed largely of Asian immigrants.

Like the Chinese and the East Indians, Japanese immigrants to Canada quickly erected a complex social structure within their own community. Some social institutions they imported from Japan, others they adapted or created in Canada. The family—the basic unit within Japanese society—was one transplanted institution. Intensely patriarchal, it bound family members together in an extended network of kinship relations. In doing so it tied the Issei, the first generation of immigrants, to their relatives in Japan and thus reinforced their transpacific orientation. This kinship system and its associated values set Japanese immigrants apart from their hosts in west coast society, where the nuclear family was the norm. But during the interwar years, which were marked by extensive acculturation among the second generation, the traditional Japanese family began to crumble. The children of Japanese immigrants increasingly rejected its paternalism and embraced the more egalitarian Canadian family instead.[48]

The Buddhist church was another traditional institution brought from Japan. It entered a community in which Christian ideals and institutions were firmly fixed and because of their powerful influence Buddhism, like the Japanese family structure, was soon substantially transformed. From the outset it was faced with strong Christian competition, much of it generated from within the immigrant community itself. Long before a Buddhist temple was founded in British Columbia, evangelical Protestantism, preached by devoted Japanese converts, had gained a faithful audience in Japanese Canadian society.[49] By 1931 about one-third of the Japanese had become professing Christians. The Nisei, in particular, were drawn to the Gospel. During the mid-1930s approximately equal numbers among them were Christian and Buddhist. Their widespread acceptance of Canadian religious practice was yet another sign of their extensive acculturation. Moreover, as Buddhism accommodated itself to west coast society, it began to absorb elements of Christianity, if for no other reason than to prevent the further erosion of the faithful. It adopted Christian organizational techniques and in some instances even borrowed Christian forms of worship. Japanese children, for example, regularly sang "Buddha loves me, this I know" during weekly Sunday School meetings at the local temple.[50] Not only was Buddhism altered by the migration process, but a significant minority rejected it completely. For them it had lost its central meaning and offered only an impediment to acculturation.

The Japanese community in British Columbia also generated a wide range of voluntary associations, many patterned upon similar institutions in Japan and others designed to cope with problems unique to an immigrant minority. By the 1930s the immigrants had established at least 230 religious and secular organizations to serve their various interests. Some, including trade unions and businessmen's associations, performed essentially economic functions; others met social, educational, and philanthropic needs. A small number also provided political leadership, acting as spokesmen for group interests as well as intermediaries between the immigrant community and the host society. But whatever the purposes of these associations, most of them focused the life of the community in upon itself and in doing so heightened its sense of self-consciousness as an immigrant minority.[51]

Patterns of settlement did much to sustain this sense of community, for from the earliest years of migration the immigrants tended to live in separate enclaves. Between 1900 and 1940 they congregated on the coast near the canneries and sawmills where many of them worked. In 1931 almost three-quarters of them were located in greater Vancouver and the nearby delta region while small groups lived in several centres on Vancouver Island, near Prince Rupert, and in the Okanagan Valley. The fishing village of Steveston at the mouth of the Fraser River became the province's largest Japanese centre outside Vancouver itself. Meanwhile growing numbers of Japanese farms dotted the Fraser delta area. Vancouver remained the home of the largest concentration of Japanese, the majority of whom clustered in the Powell Street area east of the city's business district. Lesser numbers gathered south of False Creek on the fringes of an industrial belt.[52]

Although its extent cannot accurately be measured, acculturation proceeded more rapidly among Japanese immigrants than it did within the Chinese and East Indian communities. While in many respects the other Asian minorities tended to remain sojourners in west coast society, the Japanese increasingly absorbed the customs, norms, and values which prevailed in the province. The Issei—in particular those who married and settled in British Columbia—took the first hesitant steps in this direction. Among the second generation, exposed to the schools and playgrounds of the province, the process was greatly advanced. By the 1930s the Nisei had abandoned much of the culture of their parents and absorbed that of west coast society instead.

Yet, while extensive acculturation characterized Japanese immigrants in Canada, they were only marginally integrated into the west coast community. Together with the Chinese and East Indians, they constituted a separate segment within the British Columbian population. Physiognomy, social institutions, and physical segregation set the Japanese apart from white society. These factors were mutually reinforcing and each in turn was further reinforced by white racialism. Even the Nisei were rebuffed, despite their growing absorption of western culture. In sum, both the orientation of the Japanese immigrant community and the closed nature of British Columbian society barred the path to racial integration. Consequently Japanese immigration further buttressed the structurally plural condition of west coast society.

To the limited extent that integration was achieved, it was through common participation in shared economic institutions. Whites and Japanese often enjoyed the fraternity of the workplace, although more often than not they met as supervisors and subordinates respectively. Commercial dealings offered another avenue of interracial contact, but here again the relationship was formal and impersonal. Consequently economic forces did little to bridge the gap between hosts and immigrants. On the contrary, often they further widened the existing racial cleavage.

West coast nativists commonly claimed that economic relations between whites and Orientals were essentially competitive. They ascribed white prejudice toward Asian immigrants to the latter's unfair competition within the marketplace, and subsequent commentators have generally taken them at their word. There is no doubt that interracial economic competition did exist; the Japanese, for example, rivalled whites in salmon fishing and berry farming, among other pursuits. But the precise nature and extent of these competitive pressures were not clear at the time and they remain clouded today. Nor can a detailed analysis of white–Japanese competition be offered here. There are, however, four observations about the Japanese role in the provincial labour force which do shed some light upon the relationship between economic competition and west coast racialism.

First, popular thought commonly attributed unfair Oriental economic competition, including that of the Japanese, to the low standard of living of immigrants from the Orient. Accustomed by debased conditions in Asia to a life of mere subsistence, Chinese, Japanese, and East Indians could therefore work for less than west coast whites, and thus drive down the wages of the white workingman. But low living standards were not intrinsic to the Asian character as was commonly implied. On the one hand, they were inherent in the sojourner condition. Because many Asians in Canada supported families at home, they economized scrupulously in order to accumulate cash savings. For this reason even those who enjoyed the same income levels as whites accepted lower standards of living. At the same time the sojourners constituted a pool of labour which would accept low wage rates. As long as Asian immigrants placed cash savings before all other economic goals, they willingly lowered their living standards and wage demands as well. In doing so they ultimately created a labour market for extremely low paid labour, one in which Orientals came to be concentrated whether they wished it or not. Permanent migrants, on the other hand, were not as willing to accept low wages and low standards of living. Japanese residents, in particular, worked hard to better both their incomes and their living standards.[53]

In the second place, economic rivalry between whites and Japanese could be generated as much by rapid Japanese penetration of a few enterprises as it was by direct wage and price competition.

Salmon fishing and berry farming were two cases in point; the Japanese entered both in such numbers that by the 1920s they controlled a substantial proportion of one and dominated the other. In both instances it appears likely that Japanese competition lowered commodity prices. But Japanese expansiveness seems to have been at least an equal source of tension in both activities, for as Japanese influence grew in each that of whites declined.

Third, by and large Japanese were employed in unskilled occupations, although a small number held positions requiring some skills. One consequence was that, in industries which incorporated a hierarchy of skills, work was stratified upon racial lines as well. For example, in many companies within the forest industry unskilled work was largely done by Asians, while with few exceptions skilled and semi-skilled work remained the preserve of whites. This pattern of work organization reduced interracial economic conflict. Indeed, in such cases the races served complementary economic functions, for Orientals took jobs which whites generally would not perform, at least at wage rates employers were willing to pay. It is even probable, although not capable of proof, that Asian labour, by driving a wedge of low-paid workers into the bottom stratum, may have forced at least some whites upward into higher skill and income categories.

Finally, even though the Japanese dispersed themselves throughout the labour force, they remained concentrated in a few occupations, salmon fishing, berry farming, lumber manufacturing, and pulp and paper production in particular. Even as small businessmen the Japanese specialized heavily. In Vancouver the largest number ran rooming houses, dry cleaning establishments, grocery and candy stores, and dressmaking shops.[54] Compared with whites, Japanese were disproportionately represented in all but rooming house keeping. Outside these enterprises Orientals were seldom either numerous or concentrated in specific business activities.[55] Therefore, whatever the competitive pressures created by the Japanese presence in industry, agriculture, and commerce, they were sharply circumscribed by these specialized patterns of work. Despite the real, and sometimes intense, economic rivalry between the two races, competition was severely limited in these important ways.

By and large, then, the white image of Japanese immigrants had little basis in fact. Some stereotypes—for instance those of economic competitiveness and the high birth-rate—contained more than a kernel of truth. But generally such truths were only partial and misshapen. The stereotype of Japanese economic competition characterized the acts of specific groups of Japanese as those of the entire community. Similarly, that of the high Japanese birth-rate neglected those demographic factors which largely explained the phenomenon. Consequently even beliefs which were rooted in fact usually were serious distortions of reality. Others, like that of the Japanese subversive threat, were nothing more than fictions.

Thus, in the case of the Japanese, appearance and reality were no more at one than they were in that of the Chinese. Despite this incongruity, the dissonance lasted for at least half a century, and this fact raises the fundamental question, why did these beliefs persist despite their insubstantial foundations? Much of the answer lies in the impact which racial pluralism had upon west coast society. Japanese immigration introduced a new element into the social structure of British Columbia and thus reinforced its structurally plural nature.[56] Separated from each of the other segments by sharply drawn social boundaries, the Japanese immigrant community remained socially, economically, and politically subordinate to the dominant white population. It shared with the Chinese an intermediate rank on that scale of race which prevailed in British Columbia. The presence of Japanese immigrants, like that of the Chinese before them, raised the level of racial awareness in west coast society and therefore encouraged the acceptance of negative racial stereotypes. In the minds of whites, the Japanese (like all Oriental immigrants) blunted the communal drive for a homogenous society, one of the fundamental collective goals of west coast whites. At bottom this was a deeply irrational yearning, a fact which made it the more fixed and immutable. As no Asian immigrant group was considered assimilable, all appeared to bar the path to racial and social homogeneity—that condition which nativists meant by the phrase "white British Columbia." As much as was true of Sinophobia, this remained the basis of anti-Japanese sentiment.

But in contrast to anti-Chinese prejudice, that aimed at the Japanese was augmented by an important supplementary factor: white British Columbia's tendency to identify Japanese immigrants and their children with the expansionist foreign policy of Japan. The aggressive militarism of Japan, which western perceptions increasingly emphasized after World War I, was easily combined with those vivid impressions of Japanese immigrants generated in the western province. The result was a far more threatening image than was ever attributed to the Chinese. The peaceful penetration of the aggressive "Japs," it seemed, heralded a far graver menace in the event of war on the Pacific. Consequently, when racial outbursts did occur, such as that which followed Pearl Harbor, they assumed an intensity unprecedented in the history of west coast race relations.

7

EXCLUSION

From 1914 to 1939 the dominant patterns of social and economic growth, established in British Columbia over the previous three decades, were further reinforced. These years saw the continued expansion of the province's major primary industries, lumbering, mining, and fishing. In addition, a significant secondary manufacturing sector emerged, much of which processed products drawn from the existing resource base, while major commercial development paralleled this pattern of industrial growth. Meanwhile the provincial population continued to increase rapidly, doubling in size during this quarter-century. Two aspects of its expansion are especially worthy of note. First, growth was exceptionally dynamic in the Vancouver region. Before the first war one-third of the province's residents lived in the metropolitan area; by the time of the second world conflict almost one-half did so. Vancouver had clearly become the preeminent city in the province. Second, the Anglo-Canadian predominance in British Columbia was further heightened during these years, particularly in Vancouver where 87 per cent of the population was British or Canadian-born by 1941.[1]

While this was a period of significant social and economic expansion, it was also one of serious socio-economic dislocation. Twice the provincial economy oscillated sharply between prosperity and recession, with peaks from 1916 to 1918 and 1925 to 1929, and troughs from 1919 to 1922 and 1930 to 1935. These cycles were broadly in rhythm with those of the national, if not North American economy. At the same time they were amplified by the dominance of export-oriented resource industries in the economic life of the province. High unemployment characterized both depressions and in each case other factors further aggravated this condition. In 1919 demobilization released thousands of men from military service just at the onset of recession. Furthermore, ill, disabled, and unemployed veterans from other parts of the country descended on Vancouver, attracted by prospects of work or the city's salubrious maritime climate. Ten years later the phenomenon recurred as thousands of single, unemployed transients arrived to seek work and shelter on the coast. In both instances the result was further social and economic strain.

Meanwhile the proportion of Asians in the province continued its steady fall.[2] Restrictions increasingly choked off the flow of immigrants, sojourners returned home to their families, and imbalanced sex ratios limited opportunities for expansion through natural increase. Consequently the population growth rate of the Asian minority as a whole was relatively low. Only the Japanese community expanded significantly over this quarter-century. In fact, during the 1930s the number of Orientals in British Columbia dropped by 17 per cent.

But white British Columbia's images of Asians were virtually untouched by these sweeping changes. Those few, new racial stereotypes which emerged after the turn of the century served only to re-emphasize the strong negative impressions ingrained in older perceptions. In other words, these racial beliefs persisted largely independent of social and economic circumstance, a fact which once again suggests that this pattern of racial awareness was ultimately grounded much more in psychological tensions than socioeconomic ones. These psychological tensions derived from white society's desire for racial homogeneity, a drive continually stimulated by the racially plural condition. The enduring nature of these beliefs also emphasized that, once these images took root in the culture of the province, they assumed a life of their own. Given the self-perpetuating tendency of racial stereotypes, they needed little reinforcement to keep themselves alive. British Columbia offered them far more than the necessary minimum.

These images continued to shape the course of British Columbian race relations throughout the interwar years, just as they had ever since the Fraser River gold rush. In particular, they established a climate of popular opinion amongst west coast whites which was permanently conducive to outbursts of racial hostility. This being so, many kinds of incidents could rouse popular prejudice and provoke a racial incident. The interwar years would reaffirm this fact conclusively. One clear example of the impact which popular stereotypes had on patterns of race relations can be seen in the Pacific coast fisheries. There the interplay of economic and psychological factors promoted an antipathy toward the Japanese which prevailed for half a century.

When the first Japanese sojourners arrived in British Columbia most found seasonal work in the province's salmon fisheries. A small handful fished on the Fraser River in the later 1880s and during the next few years their numbers grew appreciably. By 1893 they held 20 per cent of the 1,174 gill-net licenses issued on the river. Thereafter the fishing industry expanded rapidly, and as it did their numbers grew at an even greater rate. At the turn of the century they had become the most numerous of the three races—Japanese, Indians, and whites—in the fishing fleet, not just on the Fraser but along the entire British Columbian coast. Never an absolute majority, they usually held between 40 per cent and 50 per cent of the gill-net licenses issued annually, a position which they occupied until the early 1920s.[3]

During these years the industry was in a state of flux. Expansion, rationalization, and mechanization all transformed the canning sector, increasing government regulation enforced conservation practices in the fisheries, and recurrent labour unrest spread among white fishermen. Further instability derived from the cyclical production patterns characteristic of the industry and the fluctuating international market for canned Pacific salmon. One of the very few constants in the industry was interracial tension. From the early 1890s onward, persistent friction dominated the relations between white and Japanese fishermen. It surfaced first in 1893, when white contract fishermen formed a union and held a short-lived, unsuccessful strike for higher fish prices. The fishermen's primary goals were clearly economic, but they were also alarmed by growing Japanese influence in the fisheries. They singled out the latter as a major source of their ills. Not only were Japanese fishermen driving others off the river, whites claimed, but they obtained their fishing licenses by fraud. Therefore they should be kept out of the fisheries altogether. Feeling was so intense during the strike that, although they claimed Japanese support, white fishermen first barred them from the union and then refused to help them form their own.[4]

For the next seven years racial tension in the industry remained largely quiescent even though, from time to time, white fishermen called for an end to Japanese competition. In 1900, however, growing labour unrest once more raised the level of interracial strain. Two new fishermen's unions were formed in the spring, one in Vancouver and the other in New Westminster, as fishermen sought to defend their interests in the face of the growing strength of the canners. Although the Vancouver union attempted briefly to sign up Japanese, ultimately none were admitted to either organization. Perhaps some union leaders saw advantage in cooperation, but rank-and-file hostility precluded the possibility. The Japanese fishermen, in turn, formed their own benevolent society, for they too sought the strength which comes from collective action.[5] But when the unions and Japanese struck the canneries as the sockeye season opened on the first of July, the Fraser River fishermen were obviously far from united.

The strikers demanded a guarantee of twenty-five cents a fish, five cents more than the canners had offered. Initially both white and Japanese fishermen agreed on this objective. But solidarity did not last. Within a week many Japanese, willing to accept the canners' offer, were out on the river. White union men replied with intimidation to force them back on shore and for a short while their efforts were successful. On July 22, however, the Japanese accepted an offer from the canners, one which white fishermen had emphatically rejected, and immediately began to fish. Two days later the militia was called out at Steveston in response to pleas from the canners, and it enforced an uneasy peace in the fishing community. After another week most white fishermen came to terms as well.[6] The strike thus ended in victory for the canners. Whatever its impact on labour relations in the fisheries, its influence on race relations was abundantly clear. It had pitted white and Japanese fishermen against one another in open confrontation and in doing so had seriously inflamed race relations on the Fraser. According to E. P. Bremner, a Dominion labour commissioner in the province, "there is no doubt that the imbittered feeling against the Japanese, stood largely in the way of a settlement and I am of the opinion their presence in such numbers, is the real if not the exciting cause for all or most of the dissatisfaction on the river."[7] It may even be, as has since been argued, that competition with the Japanese was the compelling force behind the unionization movement.[8] In any event, henceforth whites and Japanese were acknowledged rivals in the fisheries.

In 1901 the two races clashed once more when striking whites condemned the Japanese for returning to fish while they remained out. And during the next two decades white fishermen repeatedly complained about competition. "I fished down below [at the mouth of the Fraser] for 10 or 12 years," one fisherman commented bitterly in 1905, "and then the Japs drove me to fishing up the river, and now they are going to close that down. It looks as if the river was closed to a white man altogether." "The Japs has it altogether their own way," he declared. "Eleven years ago there was somewheres between two and three thousand white men fishing on the river, now there's not more than seven or eight hundred if there's that."[9] In 1914 New Westminster fishermen formed an association to protect themselves from Japanese competition.[10] Because of continued protests from white fishermen and their supporters, in 1912 the federal Department of Fisheries began to restrict the number of commercial fishing licenses issued to Japanese.[11] These restrictions were slight and only marginally affected the Japanese fishing community; nevertheless they were a sign of what lay ahead.

In 1919 Japanese fishermen received half of the 4,600 salmon gill-net licenses issued in British Columbia, more than they had had in any previous year. At the end of the season, for reasons largely unrelated to this study, the Department of Fisheries proposed to remove all license restrictions on salmon canning and fishing in British Columbia. White fishermen generally approved of the proposal, apart from their fear that the number of Japanese competitors would grow even further.[12] When the department announced its amended regulations in December, the new policy took the fishermen's protests into account. In the forthcoming season, the department ordered, Japanese fishermen would receive no more than the number of gill-net licenses issued to them in 1919 and thereafter these would be reduced on a systematic basis.[13]

At first, however, the department did not actually order any reductions. Fewer Japanese held licenses over the next three years, but this decline was natural rather than enforced. Nonetheless renewed complaints were raised during the early 1920s, part of the latest upwelling of anti-Asian feeling in the west coast province. Fishermen, veterans' groups, and a number of politicians all demanded additional license restrictions on Japanese fishermen.[14] Under growing public pressure the department first planned a program of systematic license reductions and then appointed a commission to investigate problems within the Pacific fisheries. During its summer public hearings the commission received many complaints about Japanese fishermen. Most often they were accused of unfair and illegal practices and of driving whites out of the industry.[15] Strongly influenced by these claims, the commission report recommended even greater reductions than the department had earlier proposed. The number of fishing licenses issued to Japanese in 1923, it advised, should be 40 per cent less than in 1922.[16] The department took this advice. In 1923 only 1,200 gill-net licenses were issued to Japanese, 800 fewer than they had' held in the previous year.

Subsequently, over the protests of canners, further reductions were made. Then in 1926 the House of Commons' Standing Committee on Fisheries proposed that henceforth the number of licensed Japanese fishermen be reduced by 10 per cent a year until they were all eliminated by 1937.[17] In response the Amalgamated

Association of Japanese Fishermen contested the issue in court. The Supreme Court of Canada upheld their case in 1928 and the Privy Council sustained this judgement in the following year. Thereafter the federal government enforced existing restrictions by order in council and abandoned all plans to introduce further reductions. This stabilized the number of licenses granted to Japanese throughout the 1930s, limiting them to considerably less than half of those issued during the immediate postwar years. But in spite of this development racial tension persisted in the white fishing community.[18] It was not to be dispelled until the Japanese were forced from the industry after the outbreak of war with Japan.

Thus the Pacific coast fisheries offer a clear example of white-Asian conflict based in part upon economic competition. Japanese immigrants rapidly penetrated the industry during the 1890s, imposing on whites those competitive pressures which stemmed from their rapid expansion. There is little doubt that they were aggressive fishermen and that their presence in the industry tended to lower the rates which canners paid all fishermen, regardless of race. At the same time, however, prevailing racial attitudes conditioned white fishermen to view their relations with their Japanese counterparts as solely competitive. Cooperative action was the key to eliminating that conflict. Yet west coast racism, which was very much a part of the prewar trade union movement, precluded this possibility, despite occasional initiatives from the Japanese themselves. Consequently persistent white demands for Japanese expulsion from the fisheries was the product of competitive pressures as well as prevailing racial attitudes. Both economic and psychological forces left their mark on race relations in the fisheries.

During the early years of World War I, anti-Orientalism was dormant in British Columbia. Criticism was isolated, organized protest largely absent. But even before the armistice, white prejudice began to coalesce about two new irritants: growing Asian influence in farming and retail trading. Since at least 1908 Japanese landholding had aroused concern in some quarters and, by 1913, residents of the Okanagan Valley were sufficiently disquieted to hold public meetings on the question.[19] They bound themselves not to sell or lease land to Orientals for the next five years and requested that a permanent prohibition be enacted for the province. By 1917 farmers in the lower mainland were also complaining of land purchases by Chinese and Japanese while the advisory board of the provincial Farmers' Institutes urged that they be prevented from acquiring title to agricultural land.[20]

In 1919 the tempo of protest increased and during the next three years interested groups of whites, virtually all of them from agricultural districts in the province, campaigned against Oriental land acquisition. Support came from farm organizations (the Farmers' Institutes, the United Farmers of British Columbia, and the British Columbia Fruit Growers' Association) as well as boards of trade, veterans' leagues, town and city councils, and ratepayers' associations.[21] Late in 1919 and early in 1920 there was a pronounced flurry of agitation in the Okanagan Valley. What prompted the outcry in this case was the construction of two buildings by Chinese in Penticton. Led by the local branch of the Great War Veterans' Association, the community met to object. Similar meetings were soon held in Peachland and Kelowna under GWVA leadership and, together with fruit growers in convention at Vernon, they marshalled local opinion against Oriental land ownership.[22] The protesters repeatedly emphasized that expanding Asian land holdings jeopardized the economic future of the white farming community. But of equal importance was the fact that their rhetoric was heavily freighted with the stock claims and stereotypes of provincial nativists. A public meeting in Kelowna resolved in January 1920 that "the ownership of land in B.C. by Japanese and Chinese is continually increasing, and constitutes a peril to our ideal of a white British Columbia, as it is impossible for Japanese and Chinese to become assimilated as Canadian citizens."[23]

Meanwhile white retailers, particularly in the province's two largest cities, were mounting an independent campaign against Oriental merchants. Chinese hawkers and peddlers had long vexed the mercantile community. But complaints about Asians in business grew common only toward the end of the war. When Chinese merchants located themselves in a previously all-white business district in Vancouver, local retailers demanded that City Council restrict the process.[24] Similarly, in May 1919 Victoria businessmen vowed ceaseless vigilance in the defence of the city's new early closing by-law, in order to protect themselves from Asian competition.[25] By 1920 the provincial board of the Retail Merchants' Association of Canada had endorsed Oriental exclusion, a measure which they continued to advocate for several years.[26] The Vancouver Board of Trade and the Victoria Chamber of Commerce also joined the chorus and called, not just for exclusion, but for school segregation and curbs on Asian property ownership as well.[27] In the spring of 1922 retail merchants in Victoria promised support for the city's recently formed Asiatic Exclusion League, while in Vancouver their counterparts planned to found a similar organization.[28] By the following

KEEP PENTICTON
WHITE

A Public Meeting of the Citizens of Penticton
will be held in

STEWARD'S HALL
On Friday Evening, Jan. 2nd
at 8 o'clock.

This meeting is called under the auspices of
the Penticton Branch of the Great War Veterans
of Canada.

Its object is to consider ways and means of
making our town unattractive for the Yellow man.

The men who sacrificed so much to save the
country from one enemy, are determined that another shall not reap the benefit. Give them your
support and co-operation. Attend the meeting.

Speakers will include:

H. B. MORLEY, President of Penticton Board of Trade

T. H. WILSON, of the G.W.V.A. Executive

REV. A. H. HUNTLEY

The Reeve and Councillors and Real Estate
Dealers are especially requested to attend.

GOD SAVE THE KING

Notice of meeting, Penticton, 1920.

year they were pressing city council for segregated shopping districts.[29]

Like the province's farmers, these merchants complained of economic competition. Continued Chinese immigration, the New Westminster branch of the Retail Merchants' Association warned in 1922, would by "sheer force of numbers alone, offer a competition which no Canadian Citizen, whether he be engaged in business for himself, or as an employer of others, or in any form of agriculture, can successfully meet."[30] But like the farmers, they also drew heavily on that reservoir of racial anxiety which was stored up in the province. The threat, as they described it, was not just to the livelihood of the white mercantile community. "We strongly feel," the Vancouver Board of Trade urged in 1921 as they recommended the strict control of Oriental landholding, "that we should do everything in our power to retain British Columbia for our own people. We realize that the owners of the land must eventually control the destinies of any country, and we must urge that every precaution should be taken to preserve to us and our children this great heritage of ours."[31]

Thus the objections roused by these two new irritants closely resembled the traditional nativistic assumptions of white British Columbia, and this suggests that the hostility which they occasioned owed little to economic conflict. Chinese and Japanese immigrants were indeed moving into new sectors of the provincial economy. But given the limited extent of this activity, the actual competitive pressures on whites must have been relatively slight. While the land holdings of Orientals had grown in recent years, especially in the Fraser River valley, they were still far from extensive. In 1921 Asians owned twenty-two square miles of farmland in the province and leased an additional twenty. This represented about 5 per cent of the improved land in the province.[32] At the time of the protest in Kelowna Orientals owned a mere 112 acres in the district, more than enough to provoke concern but less than would generate significant competition.[33]

Nor should the extent of Chinese and Japanese commercial competition be overemphasized. Certainly whites and Asians were frequent business rivals. This was particularly true in Vancouver where, during the early 1920s, Orientals held more than 13 per cent of all trades licenses even though they constituted less than 8 per cent of the population.[34] Yet this imbalance was not as threatening as at first glance it might seem. For one thing many Orientals in business catered only to their own countrymen. They took part in an economy whose bounds were those of the racial minority and therefore seldom competed with the white mercantile community. For another, Asians concentrated themselves in a narrow range of enterprises. Most frequently they peddled fruits and vegetables from door to door and ran corner groceries, restaurants, rooming houses, barber shops, laundries, and dry-cleaning businesses. These were forms of petty commerce which offered services in common demand and required few skills, low capital investment, and only a modest knowledge of English. For these reasons they were easier for Asian immigrants to enter than most other forms of business. Undoubtedly, as Chinese and Japanese corner stores spread throughout Vancouver, white grocers often felt the pinch. But in reality genuine competition was confined to a very few activities. Most protest from the white mercantile community came from outside these commercial limits and was occasioned more by anticipated conflict than its pressing reality.

Of course, economic competitiveness was a central component in all Oriental images. For years white British Columbia had believed that the Asian's lower standard of living disrupted every marketplace in which he was found. Thus he continually undercut the position of whites, whether they were workers or businessmen. Essentially, however, this was a stereotype, one segment of a larger pattern of racial awareness broadly accepted by west coast whites. Like many other stereotypes it had a kernel of truth, but in this case the myth was far larger than the reality. Moreover, these and similar racist assumptions were widely shared throughout the province. In such a climate of opinion even minor social and economic strain could rouse latent anxieties and prompt hostile outbursts. Expanding Asian farm and business activity did precisely this.

Another indication of persistent white racism was the revival of the issue of school segregation. Since the early years of the century Oriental pupils in Vancouver and Victoria had been partly segregated. In Vancouver the practice was common only in schools with large numbers of Asian children and then only when their knowledge of English was deemed inadequate. If this was not done, it was commonly argued, the backward Orientals would retard their white classmates.[35] But during the anti-Oriental resurgence of the early 1920s Victoria trustees grew dissatisfied with their partial segregation program. In September 1922 the board segregated all Chinese students on the opening day of school, on the pretext that they had an insufficient grasp of English. A lengthy controversy ensued. First a group of white ratepayers, predicting a drop in their property values, objected when Chinese classrooms were located in their district. Then the Chinese boycotted the segregated schools.[36]

So intransigent were the two sides of the dispute that an impasse occurred until late in the following spring. Then the trustees relented. When school resumed in September full segregation was abandoned and the Chinese boycott was dropped.[37] Nonetheless the special classroom remained for those with imperfect English.

Land ownership, retail competition, and school segregation all were matters touching the racial sensibilities of separate interest groups of whites. Why then did agitation on these questions occur more or less simultaneously? A large part of the answer lies in the fact that during the late 1910s and early 1920s the level of generalized racism in British Columbia was on the rise again. Each of these three issues was nourished by a quickening of the longstanding conviction that immigrants from the Orient were a threat to white society. But unlike previous crests of hostility no single influence seems to have set this tide in motion. While Chinese and Japanese immigration increased in the immediate postwar years, this fact occasioned little comment in the province. Instead, what seems to have happened is this. The period from 1919 to 1922 was one of serious social and economic disruption in British Columbia. Demobilization brought thousands of returned veterans to the province while industrial production declined during the postwar recession. Unemployment rose and wage rates fell. Throughout this period war veterans' organizations and to a lesser extent the trade union movement became spokesmen for the discontented. One of the many targets of their criticism was the Asian immigrant. According to these critics, Orientals were taking jobs that rightfully belonged to whites. On behalf of the unemployed, veterans demanded that whites replace Oriental workers.[38] Labour leaders agreed and called for an end to immigration from Asia.[39] Gradually these sporadic complaints gathered momentum until in the summer of 1921 a new anti-Oriental movement was born.

In this instance if a single precipitating factor can be isolated it was a vigorous campaign launched in July by the *Vancouver Daily World*. Attempting to shore up its sagging circulation, the recently reorganized *World* saw good copy in the anti-Oriental issue. During the summer months journalist J. S. Cowper repeatedly warned against the Asian penetration of the British Columbian economy. Soon the anti-Oriental cry was heard from many quarters. The *Sun* took up the cause and in August published H. Glynn-Ward's lurid racist novel, *The Writing on the Wall*.[40] Other provincial papers seized upon the theme, in points as widely dispersed as Comox, Prince Rupert, and Penticton.[41] At the same time the Vancouver

TLC mounted yet another drive against the west coast Oriental. First they approached 150 organizations in the province, requesting support in the common cause of a white British Columbia. Then, with the aid of veterans and merchants associations, they formed a new exclusion league.[42] During the next few months, others sprang up in Nanaimo, Courtenay, and Prince Rupert.[43]

The Vancouver Asiatic Exclusion League's program had three basic goals: an end to Oriental immigration, deportation of Oriental criminals and illegal immigrants, and whatever additional steps were needed "to preserve white dominion and control."[44] But while these aspirations were shared by many west coast whites, the league was none too successful in attracting public support. In October it claimed a membership of some 20,000 but no doubt this was little more than an idle boast.[45] Its public meetings were infrequent and its organizational work was slight. Its real tasks were performed by a few executive members and they were largely concerned with publicity. Another group of nativists surfaced briefly in the fall and published several issues of a thirty-page journal called *Danger: The Anti-Asiatic Weekly*. The editors had at least one eye seemingly focused on the coming federal election and perhaps this was the reason why, when the election was over, *Danger* passed as well.

Clearly the league lacked the vigour and public appeal of many of its predecessors. Yet this was by no means because its clientele had vanished. On the contrary, nativism obviously flourished in British Columbia during the early 1920s. Previous exclusion leagues, however, had been the products of a more simply-organized society, one with fewer institutional outlets for the expression of public opinion. The earlier leagues were organizations formed about a single, central cause and they drew their membership from the community at large. But by the 1920s this institutional pattern had changed substantially and a more complex array of interest-related associations was in place in west coast society. This gave provincial whites many more vehicles for the expression of collective opinion, such as business organizations, veterans' groups, and patriotic societies, than they had previously enjoyed. Furthermore, many of these bodies represented interest groups which had their own specific anti-Oriental leanings. In short, as conduits of popular sentiment exclusion leagues had grown obsolete by the end of World War I. Their persistence was a sign of continuing popular racism, but they had lost their functional utility. Popular prejudice had found a newer, more appropriate series of channels.

Meanwhile the storm of public hostility continued unabated into 1922. The *World* launched a drive against the drug traffic in Vancouver, the result of which was a campaign to clean up Chinatown. "The feeling against the Chinese is running very high just now," reported Rev. D. A. Smith, a Presbyterian missionary at work in the city's Chinese community.

You have no doubt heard in the East about the very recent drive against the drug traffic of which we are told Vancouver is the centre. Matters in the drug line have reached a tremendous pitch and numerous mass meetings are being held every week to arouse public indignation. This as you know comes very close to certain Chinese and so, in consequence, not only has a real thorough drive been made against the oriental so far as drugs are concerned but sanitation, disease, schools, in fact everyhing in which Chinese are engaged is at present getting the "once over."

Obviously, when aroused, the public temper dictated a thorough house-cleaning of that which whites found objectionable within the Chinese community. According to Smith, ill-feeling touched the very core of Christian society. "When I tell you," he wrote, "that so many of our own Church people are in open arms against them [the Chinese], then you know what that means. One has to do battle against a whole sea of trouble. I feel, at the present time, that the biggest fight I have to put up, and those of us who are in this work, is not against the Chinese non-believer but against the narrow racial, color prejudice of our own kind which is at present aggravated by a tremendous unemployment."[46]

This latest upwelling of hostility soon left its mark on provincial politics. Ever sensitive to the ebb and flow of public opinion, and intensely nativistic by tradition, west coast politicians began again to champion a white British Columbia. In 1921 and 1922, after lengthy debate, the provincial house resumed its demands for an end to Asiatic immigration. It also called for additional constitutional powers which would allow the province to bar Orientals from any proprietary interest in land and from ownership and employment in provincial industry.[47] At the same time the legislature amended the Factory and Shop Regulation acts, largely in order to force early closing by-laws and "white" working conditions upon Orientals.[48] Meanwhile the Liberal government of John Oliver resumed the enforcement of a longstanding clause in government contracts which prevented contractors from employing Orientals. Government and management jointly sought ways to replace Asians with whites in the pulp and paper industry.[49] For his part Premier Oliver importuned the prime minister in Ottawa on the basis of the provincial Liberal party's resolute opposition to further Asian entrants.[50]

Among provincial political leaders of the moment, A. M. Manson, attorney general and minister of labour, was the leading nativist. During the spring and summer months of 1922 he campaigned energetically for exclusion, speaking before a variety of very receptive audiences. "The Oriental is not possible as a permanent citizen in British Columbia," he told the Retail Merchants' Association in Victoria, because "ethnologically they cannot assimilate with our Anglo-Saxon race." Moreover, "they labor harder and subsist on harder living conditions than the white man cares to live under, or should live under, and they are still the toiling slave they were in their own countries, with a pittance for wages and long hours of labor. They have no desire for the luxury and ease which the white man finds increasingly necessary to his existence."[51] As a senior minister in the government, Manson took the initiative in arguing the case with employers, urging them to replace Asian labour with white on the railways and in the pulpmills of the province.[52]

But despite their heartfelt commitment to racial discrimination, provincial legislators had little power yet unused to mould prejudice into policy. They could tighten existing laws which affected Orientals, but by the early 1920s the British Columbia government had more or less exhausted the possibilities of legislation. Past experience had shown that they had only limited legal authority to curb an Asian's civil rights and none whatsoever to prevent his immigration. By and large these powers lay with the federal government. Thus much of the thrust of west coast nativism was necessarily aimed at Ottawa.

Leaders on this front of the campaign were members of Parliament from British Columbia, notably H. H. Stevens, a Vancouver Conservative, and Unionist W. G. McQuarrie, who represented New Westminster. Stevens had been a prominent nativist since long before the war, and during the latest upsurge of racial animus he resumed his old crusade. McQuarrie and others soon joined him and together they took to the platform in defence of a white Canada, campaigning across the province for an end to all Asiatic immigration.[53] In Ottawa they first placed pressure on the Department of Immigration and Colonization. During April 1921 a group of them led by Stevens demanded more rigorous administration of the Chinese Immigration Act and as a result of their demands the act was tightened up.[54] But still far from satisfied, and spurred on by a recent increase in Chinese arrivals, in 1922 the province's members launched a concerted drive in Parliament for Asiatic exclusion. On May 8 McQuarrie moved that the government "take immediate action with a view to securing the exclusion of future [Oriental] immigration."[55] There followed a day-long debate in which British Columbia members from both sides of the House put forward the province's case. Far from spontaneous, this was a well-orchestrated, nonpartisan move on the part of the province's parliamentarians, all of whom spoke at length and in favour of the motion. Ultimately the resolution was passed, although not before an amendment substituted the words "effective restriction" for "exclusion," thus overcoming Prime Minister King's concern at giving offence to the nations affected.

Within the Department of Immigration and Colonization senior officials had realized for years that existing exclusion policy was in some ways a failure. In particular, the Chinese head tax had not reduced immigration to the extent that had long been desired.[56] From time to time, therefore, in an effort to lower the immigration rate, the department had amended its regulations. Usually public pressure was what prodded them into action. Early in 1919, for example, growing racial unrest in Vancouver began to give concern to immigration officials. Equally alarmed, the resident Chinese consul feared that more arrivals in the near future might precipitate a riot.[57] With both parties agreed on the need for further restriction, steps were quickly taken to achieve this end. Steamship companies were asked to transport only merchants and Chinese who were returning to Canada. At the same time the department also refused to accept the head tax on any immigrant over the age of fifteen.[58] Thus new immigrants were barred from entry, at least for the time being.

Such amendments by no means satisfied nativistic opinion, and the persistent discontent of the westernmost province continued to disturb department officers, who were, moreover, growing increasingly dissatisfied with the Chinese Immigration Act as an administrative instrument. In February 1922, with popular anti-Orientalism ascendant both in British Columbia and in Parliament, the department added its voice to those which were urging a major revision of Chinese immigration policy. A. L. Jolliffe, the controller of Chinese immigration, proposed that the head tax be abolished and that henceforth Chinese immigration be strictly limited to diplomats, merchants, and students. This could be done, Jolliffe suggested, by diplomatic agreement with China, by amendment to the general Immigration Act, or by substitution of a new exclusion act for existing legislation. Of the three possibilities, he recommended the last.[59]

On its part the King government was far from inured to pressures such as these, especially when they came from Parliament. This was particularly clear in King's ready acceptance of the

McQuarrie resolution, a motion which enjoyed broad-based support within the House. It was a clear indication that the government would willingly enforce far more stringent immigration restrictions if this seemed expedient. In July the minister of the interior went west to make a study of public opinion on the immigration question. Soon after, on the initiative of the government of China, itself anxious for relief from the humiliating entry tax, King began to negotiate with the Chinese consul general. The Chinese sought a diplomatic understanding similar to the Gentleman's Agreement with Japan. They requested control over the migration of Chinese labourers to Canada and agreed to accept any restriction on numbers which the government of Canada specified. Under such an agreement students, clergymen, and an annual quota of merchants would also be permitted free entry. King's first response was favourable; he agreed to such proposals as long as effective restriction was fully guaranteed.[60]

Meanwhile the government prepared the necessary enabling legislation. But when the measure was finally introduced in February 1923, despite the previous negotiations and much to the surprise of the Chinese consul, it made no mention of any diplomatic agreement.[61] Instead the old Chinese Immigration Act was repealed and replaced by a far more restrictive measure. Under the new legislation the entry of Chinese into Canada was confined to four classes of immigrants: representatives of the Chinese government and their staffs, Chinese children born in Canada, students coming to a university or college, and such merchants as were permitted under regulations prescribed by the minister responsible for immigration.[62] Thus the head tax was abolished and in its place stood a law which imposed virtual exclusion. The King government had succumbed to west coast opinion. One goal of the nativists had finally been achieved.

At the time, however, King saw it all rather differently. "What the Government has aimed at," he told Newton Rowell, who had written of his misgivings,

is to get rid of the highly objectionable head tax and to substitute therefor a passport system similar to the one which is applicable in the case of the Japanese. The immigration authorities are adamant in their view as to the necessity of the strictest kind of regulation to prevent fraud. The door has been left open for the Minister to go much farther in the admission of immigrants than the Act on the face of it appears to admit....

...My own impression is that we have a Bill which, everything considered, ought to go far toward solving a critical situation in British Columbia, and at the same time substituting good-will for ill-will as between the people of China and ourselves.[63]

But if the door still seemed ajar in the eyes of the prime minister, this was merely to be an illusion. During the next quarter-century only a handful of Chinese crept through the narrowest of cracks that remained.

Yet even though they had finally achieved the long-sought goal of Chinese exclusion, white nativists in British Columbia remained far from satisfied. For one thing Japanese immigrants were still permitted limited entry. For another, Asian influence in the province seemed ever more pervasive. As a result the anti-Oriental outpouring persisted throughout the decade, even though its intensity somewhat abated. In some respects, however, the character of racism differed after the exclusionist victory. Of course the nativists quickly reoriented their goals. While still anxious for total exclusion of all Orientals, they pressed much more insistently than before for restrictions on Asian residents. But at the same time a new extremist tone crept into racist rhetoric, and the demands of some vocal whites became greatly exaggerated. Terms like "confiscation" and "repatriation" were heard for the first time. Far from quieting the public outcry of the white supremacists, it seems that exclusion had merely diverted their prejudice into adjacent channels.

Farmers and merchants in the province continued to make their protests. At frequent meetings and annual conventions, farm organizations regularly reaffirmed their opposition to Oriental landholding, and peppered Victoria and Ottawa with their repeated demands. By the end of the decade some farmers were suggesting that Asian property be expropriated and the Asians themselves be removed from the country.[64] The provincial government's *Report on Oriental Activities Within the Province*, published in 1927, gave the farmers added encouragement, for it seemed to reaffirm what they had argued all along—that Asian landholdings had grown alarmingly. In some communities growers formed cooperatives to defend themselves against Oriental competition.[65] Meanwhile whites accused Asian farmers of misdeeds ranging from price cutting and evasion of marketing legislation to unsanitary growing practices.

From Vancouver merchants as well came complaints of Asiatic encroachment. They repeatedly condemned the movement of Oriental shops into white business districts.[66] Early in 1928 a group of provincial businessmen, most of them from Vancouver, petitioned the government in Victoria for trades licensing legislation which would enable municipal governments to limit the number of shops controlled and owned by Orientals. Ultimately, they hoped, these businesses would be eliminated entirely.[67] Soon afterward A B.C.

Group, a loosely knit, short-lived association of Vancouver businessmen, was formed "to give active support to all proper anti-Oriental measures, and to those who put them into effect." The guiding hand behind this movement was that of T. R. E. McInnes. Long a student of British Columbia's Oriental problem, and of late an outspoken white Canada advocate, his *Oriental Occupation of British Columbia*, an intensely nativistic collection of recent newspaper columns, had been published by the *Sun* in 1927. The group drew support from major sectors of the city's commercial life: shopkeepers, wholesalers, printers, chain grocers, department store owners, and one or two real estate and investment brokers as well. It also had the backing of the Retail Merchants' Association and the local council of the United Commercial Travellers of America.[68] Although McInnes' group proved ephemeral it was not without influence. The provincial government's Trades Licences Act, passed in the spring of 1928, bore the stamp of the businessmen's demands.

Intermittently other opponents of the Asian also broadcast their grievances, and these too were touched with a growing sense of extremism. Veterans' groups called for an end to Japanese immigration and by 1927 were urging confiscation of property and immediate deportation for all Chinese in Canada.[69] In February of the same year, the Ku Klux Klan briefly emerged in Vancouver, citing the "grave danger" of "other racial stocks" to the standards of Anglo-Saxon Canada, claiming that "these people cannot be assimilated into our Canadian Nation," and demanding the exclusion, expropriation, and repatriation of all Asiatics.[70] At the same time two major Vancouver dailies, the *Province* and the *Morning Star*, increased their anti-Oriental publicity, most notably through McInnes' alarmist columns and subsequent book. In addition, the papers heavily publicized the government's report on Oriental activities, a statistical compendium which purported to reveal the great inroads which Asians had made into the social and economic life of the west coast community.

Four new anti-Oriental leagues were also formed in the province during the later 1920s. The first and shortest-lived was founded in Vancouver early in 1925 under the auspices of the Native Sons of Canada. But despite initial support from thirty-four organizations (including the older, moribund AEL) it could not maintain its early momentum and soon disappeared from public view.[71] The second emerged in Victoria, again under the patronage of the local Native Sons. In this instance representatives from eighty associations and societies first met in March 1925 to discuss the Oriental problem.

During the spring they held a succession of well-attended public meetings at which they debated various anti-Oriental strategies. They endorsed exclusion, minimum wage legislation (in order to eliminate unfair Asian competition), and then organized a group of white vegetable peddlers intended to compete with itinerant Chinese vendors.[72] Finally they too formed an Oriental Exclusion League in yet another attempt to marshal public opinion. In this instance the league lingered on into the new year and embraced the principle of Chinese repatriation before it too vanished.[73] A third league was founded in Vancouver in 1928; it played no public role except that of enrolling a membership.[74]

The White Canada Association, the fourth and longest-lived of these various organizations, was formed in Vancouver late in 1929.[75] At its founding meeting it brought together representatives from a broad range of institutions throughout the Lower Mainland, among them municipal governments, ratepayers' associations, farm organizations, businessmen's groups, and patriotic societies. Trade union support, however, was absent save for a representative of the British Columbia Fishermen's Association. In fact, by now labour was split on the Oriental question. The WCA was intended to foster "legislation which will prevent further Oriental penetration in British Columbia, and reduce the present menace to our national life." It lost no time in placing its case before the provincial government, its first demand a measure to limit Asian land control.[76]

As was often true of similar, earlier societies, one man was the driving force behind the WCA: Charles E. Hope, the organization's secretary. A resident of British Columbia since the later 1880s, Hope was an engineer, businessman, and part-time farmer. Although he was only one of several who founded the association, soon the others fell away and he was left on his own, the sole remaining active member. In 1930 and 1931, and to a lesser extent throughout the decade, Hope carried on a personal campaign on behalf of the WCA. He published a pamphlet, wrote magazine articles, presented briefs, sent letters to editors, and maintained an extensive correspondence with federal and provincial officials.[77] He scrutinized, warned, urged, and demanded, all in the name of a white British Columbia. His frequent assertions to the contrary, after 1930 Hope represented no one but himself, even though he claimed to speak for the WCA. Yet in another sense he typified much of white public opinion for his concerns were those which for years had lain at the heart of west coast racialism. "Can an Oriental ever be assimilated by absorption into the Canadian race and nation?" he asked in 1931.

We must remember we are trying to evolve a Canadian race as well as a Canadian nation and no nation can ever arrive at a peaceful and homogeneous condition of stability if it contains two entirely separate races so widely different as the Eastern Asiatic and the Western European—in other words, the Oriental and white races—which will never come together by absorption methods voluntarily. A few people, I understand, profess to believe that if given time they will. The answer is—when they do is the proper time to admit them to full citizenship.

Alien and unabsorbable races should be welcomed to Canada for international trade and cultural purposes, but for internal trade and settlement to the displacement of the white race—never![78]

The formation of these four associations was yet another sign of persistent, deep-seated racial animosity in British Columbia. This being so, what accounts for their obvious lack of success in attracting and preserving public support? Two factors seem paramount. In the first place, like their counterparts of the early 1920s, these leagues were obsolescent institutions. As has already been suggested, other organizations, most of which represented specific interest groups, had largely usurped their basic function, the mobilization of public opinion. Second, and more important, was the cyclical nature of mass opinion. Once popular racialism had reached a crest in the early 1920s, it began to subside and over the next decade and a half, while far from quiescent, lacked its former dynamism. During these years no events of sufficient magnitude occurred to congeal white hostility and precipitate a new racial crisis. Lacking an aroused public, exclusion leagues had no adequate base on which to build popular support. Consequently they remained ineffective despite the constant presence of prejudice in the minds of the province's whites.

Meanwhile, throughout the mid and late 1920s, provincial politicians continued their own anti-Oriental campaign. No session of the legislature lacked debate on the question, and invariably the House took a firm nativistic stand. It stiffened its resolve to exclude all Asians from the country, flirted with the idea of repatriation,[79] and imposed additional curbs upon Oriental residents. These new laws, however, were rather more covert than past legislation had been. None of them designated Oriental immigrants by name but instead imposed restrictions by indirect means. The minimum wage law enacted in 1926 was intended to enforce a basic wage in selected industries; if this were done it would eliminate that competitive edge which Orientals enjoyed. When the measure was introduced in the lumber industry, it was hoped that if employers were forced to pay the same base rate to every worker, they would soon dismiss their cheaper Asian employees and hire whites instead.[80] The Trades Licences Board Act, passed in 1928, was of similar inspiration. It authorized the creation of municipal licensing boards with extensive regulatory powers. The hope of those who supported the bill was that the boards would halt the spread of Oriental commerce.[81] By contrast, several openly discriminatory measures which were proposed during these years all failed, in every instance because they were considered beyond the competence of the House.

From the mid-1920s onward, the nativists continued to urge their case in Ottawa, even though, in British Columbia, hostility had begun to decline. On this front provincial members of Parliament were most active in the cause, chief among them A. W. Neill, the independent member for Comox-Alberni on Vancouver Island. During the middle years of the decade Neill doggedly pressed the government for Japanese exclusion. What he wished was a policy identical to that embodied in the Chinese Immigration Act. Most of Neill's provincial colleagues joined him in the campaign. In the House as well as in private, both severally and in concert, they persistently attacked the continuance of Asiatic immigration.[82]

For its part the King government, sensitive to this pressure and sympathetic to its aims, resumed discussions with Japan on the subject of immigration in April 1925.[83] The negotiations, however, proved difficult and protracted. Canada demanded a further revision of the Gentleman's Agreement, one which permitted a maximum of 150 entrants each year and also put an end to picture bride migration. But the Japanese were loath to yield, and as the King government remained equally intransigent negotiations were prolonged until early 1928. Meanwhile the government of British Columbia, more convinced than ever of the growing Oriental menace, began anew to petition for further restrictive measures. As Premier Oliver told the prime minister in January 1927:

The situation has reached a point at which, it seems to me, it is the duty of the Dominion Government to grapple with it. The longer the facing the issue is postponed, the more difficult will it be to deal with. The stopping of Oriental immigration entirely is urgently necessary, but that in itself will not suffice, since it leaves us with our present large Oriental population and their prolific birth rate. Our Government feels that the Dominion Government should go further, and by deportation or other legitimate means, seek to bring about the reduction and final elimination of this menace to the well being of the white population of this Province.[84]

Its resolve thus stiffened, the King government persisted, and in the end the Japanese yielded. Late in May 1928 they agreed to limit the number of emigrants destined for Canada to 150 per annum, and also to end the migration of picture brides.[85] Although not total exclusion, this was sufficiently restrictive to satisfy west coast demands, at least for the time being. Thus by the late 1920s British Columbian nativists had virtually reached a long-sought objective. Oriental immigration had been reduced to a trickle.[86]

Until the later 1930s anti-Orientalism in British Columbia remained at low ebb, which strongly suggests once again that the primary roots of racism were not economic. Not once during these years, even in the depths of the depression, did west coast whites launch a concerted drive against the Asian. From time to time isolated criticism still was heard,[87] but no general upsurge of popular racism ensued. For the time being, at least, British Columbia's nativistic energy had been largely dissipated. In fact, for the first time in the history of west coast race relations, a few whites began to promote the Asian cause in public. Their numbers were very small and their influence of little weight, at least when compared with the strength of the nativistic consensus. Nonetheless theirs was a gesture of some significance for it marked the first sharp departure from past practice in the province.

For years, of course, Asian immigrants had had the occasional white defender, especially among the Protestant clergy. But seldom had church leaders confronted racism openly. They usually confined their advocacy to private representation.[88] Furthermore, Canadian Protestantism was far from at one on the Oriental question. In British Columbia, particularly, nativism permeated the church, and clergymen sometimes supported exclusionist groups. Moreover, the mission movement among Asian immigrants was founded upon an intense assimilationist drive. Even the missionaries, despite their professed sympathy for the Orientals, believed in the need for rigorous immigration restrictions.[89] The Protestant Church's response to the Asian immigrant was thus an amalgam of ethnocentrism and evangelical humanitarianism.[90]

Outside the Church white support for Asiatics was very seldom broadcast, at least before 1930. At no time had the anti-Oriental movement an opposing counterpart. For the most part those who harboured more liberal views must have kept them to themselves. One of the very few proponents of more generous treatment for Asians was Dr. T. H. Boggs, a professor of economics at the University of British Columbia and chairman of the local section of an American sociological survey of Pacific coast race relations. Boggs accepted the need for stringent immigration restriction. "So long as racial assimilation through intermarriage is not feasible," he declared, "exclusion must be recommended."[91] At the same time, however, he urged that all naturalized Orientals be granted full civil rights. For one thing this was necessary to avoid future "misunderstanding and mutual recriminations." For another it would promote cultural assimilation. "A permanent denial of full citizenship privileges to naturalized Orientals," he concluded, "cannot be justified on high grounds of justice or on the dubious grounds of expediency,"[92] Yet, whatever his somewhat more broad-minded beliefs, Boggs stood virtually alone. Perhaps this was one reason why he made so little attempt to publicize his views.[93]

During the early 1930s, however, a small but growing number of whites espoused the cause which Boggs had abandoned. Increasingly their interest centred on the question of the franchise. Of course Chinese, Japanese, and East Indians in British Columbia had been disenfranchised provincially and federally since long before World War I. After the war the Vancouver Great War Veterans' Association had requested the vote for Japanese veterans, and initially the provincial government had agreed. When faced with a barrage of protest, however, Premier Oliver hastily retreated and rescinded the proposal before it became law.[94] Throughout the rest of the decade suggestions that Asians be given the vote usually evoked a similar response.[95] Not until 1931 did the province finally yield, and then only a minim. On this occasion, at the behest of the Canadian Legion, the House voted by a margin of one to grant the vote to eighty surviving Japanese war veterans.[96]

To a handful of liberals like H. F. Angus, another economist at UBC, this gesture seemed quite insufficient. As did his colleague Boggs, Angus accepted the need for immigration restriction. But he too objected to the various disabilities imposed on British Columbia's Orientals. The franchise restriction Angus considered especially invidious.[97] In 1934 he began to campaign, in the press and on the platform, for the enfranchisement of second-generation Oriental Canadians.[98] From time to time the *Canadian Forum* also published similar sentiments.

Formed in 1933, the new Co-operative Commonwealth Federation soon took up the cause as well, an indication of the left's growing interest in civil liberties. Signs of this shift had been visible throughout the 1920s as the trade union movement, while still strongly nativistic, ceased to play a central role in anti-Oriental campaigns. Then the Trades and Labor Congress, at its convention in Vancouver in 1931, altered its position on Asiatic immigrants. Under pressure from an affiliated Japanese union, the congress dropped the exclusionist plank it had stood on for more than thirty years; at the same time it called for equal franchise rights for all native-born Canadians.[99] In addition, J. S. Woodsworth, the new party's leader, had traditionally taken a strong civil libertarian stand.[100] Consequently the CCF was from the outset predisposed toward liberal views on the franchise question.

Woodsworth publicly endorsed the vote for second-generation Orientals late in 1934. In the following September the party reaffirmed its stand and in British Columbia the issue became contentious during the fall federal election campaign. Angus MacInnis, one of the province's three CCF members, raised the question in Parliament in 1936.[101] Yet the party as a whole was by no means an active campaigner for the cause of Asian enfranchisement. The question was so unpopular and divisive that expediency soon tempered its earlier idealism. By 1938 the president of the British Columbia section had promised that the CCF would hold a plebiscite before extending the franchise to Asians, a policy on which party councils were seriously divided.[102] The party maintained substantial political support in the province throughout the later 1930s, but its platform on civil liberties attracted little of this allegiance. On the contrary, the CCF in British Columbia muted the issue to improve its electoral chances. Its successes at the polls must be explained by other, unrelated factors.

The fact was that the supporters of Oriental enfranchisement had prodded a hornet's nest. Nativists condemned Angus when he began to speak in public, and at least one of his critics demanded his dismissal from the university. Meanwhile the province's Native Sons and Native Daughters recoiled at the very thought of the Oriental voter.[103] The CCF was attacked by the Liberals and Conservatives in turn, both of whom gladly belaboured the socialists with appeals to white racism.[104] Although liberal sentiments on race relations did find a voice in the 1930s, their spokesmen were few and relatively isolated. Essentially it was Angus and several CCF politicians who took the Asian's case to the public. Although their views were occasionally welcomed, more often they were met with indifference, if not open opposition. Most British Columbian whites had long since made up their minds. They opposed the very presence of the Asian immigrant.

8

EVACUATION

Between late 1937 and early 1942 resurgent nativism once more flooded white British Columbia. Three waves of anti-Orientalism swept across the province, in 1937-38, 1940, and 1941-42, each of them of several months' duration. The third was by far the greatest in magnitude. Indeed, its crest was broader and higher than that of any previous racial outburst in the history of the province. Never before had west coast whites been so intensely aroused. Never before had their protests been so vociferous. Never before had they confronted the federal government with such insistent demands. And in the end, never before had the response of Ottawa been as drastic as it was on this occasion.

The Japanese were the sole targets of these three new outbursts. While anti-Chinese sentiment found intermittent voice in British Columbia during the 1930s, mounting anti-Japanese prejudice had largely eclipsed it since the last days of Chinese immigration. During the depression years images of Japanese militarism came to dominate white attitudes toward the Japanese. To growing numbers of British Columbians, Japan seemed bent on a program of conquest which might well sweep the entire north Pacific rim. On this account the Japanese minority on the west coast appeared more threatening than ever. In the eyes of white observers, its unwillingness to abandon Japanese culture was proof of continuing loyalty to the new Japanese Empire, and even more unsettling was the inference that the Japanese immigrant community harboured subversive elements, men and women who would undermine the nation's defence efforts in the event of war with Japan. At bottom, of course, these assumptions were variations of the longstanding popular belief in Asiatic unassimilability. They had been buried in white racial thought since the Russo-Japanese war. What brought them to the fore during the early 1930s was the resumption of Japan's military adventures in Manchuria. Her subsequent attack on China in 1937 placed them in even sharper relief.

It was the invasion of China in the summer of 1937 that touched off the first of these incidents. In Canada reports of this aggression provoked the first strong outburst of anti-Oriental feeling in a decade. Much of it was directed at Japan herself. Across the nation indignant Canadians boycotted Japan's products and protested her war atrocities.[1] Meanwhile British Columbians aimed new barbs at the local Japanese. Animus was most intense in coastal centres — especially Vancouver and Victoria, and their surrounding districts — where provincial nativism traditionally had been strongest. To some extent the Japanese were made scapegoats of Japan's militarism. But many whites also saw in them another cause for concern, for the attack fused old racial antipathies with vague, new anxieties in the minds of west coast residents. Suddenly the region's long-standing fears of isolation and vulnerability were stirred to life again, and this new, tense atmosphere breathed fresh life into the community's dormant racial hostility. At the same time the menace inherent in the Japanese image was once again confirmed. Japan, it was presumed, had designs on British Columbia. Rumour had it that hundreds of illegal Japanese immigrants were present on the coast, that Japanese spies and military officers lived surreptitiously in the community, and that a potential Japanese fifth column was growing in the province. The result was a new upsurge of anti-Asian sentiment.

Archdeacon F. G. Scott, a popular Anglican wartime padre, precipitated the new outbreak in mid-November 1937, one week after the Japanese had taken Shanghai. In a widely reported interview with the *Toronto Daily Star* he suggested that Japanese officers were living, disguised, in fishing villages along the west coast.[2] A few coastal residents ridiculed Scott's claims. Others, however, vouched for their truth, and his supporters won the day for a public outcry followed in the wake of his remarks. Capt. MacGregor Macintosh, a Conservative member of the legislature, first endorsed Scott's report and then, early in 1938, raised charges of widespread illegal Japanese immigration.[3] Led by A. W. Neill, by now a perennial foe of the Oriental immigrant, provincial members of Parliament from all parties demanded a halt to Japanese immigration.[4] Simultaneously Alderman Halford Wilson urged Vancouver City Council to limit the number of licenses for Japanese merchants and to impose zoning restrictions upon them.[5] Meanwhile Vancouver's major daily newspapers launched their own anti-Japanese campaigns.[6] In Ottawa the prime minister received a flurry of protest notes while the outspoken Alderman Wilson's mail brought him letters of support.[7] The chief object of public concern was the persistent rumour that hundreds of illegal Japanese immigrants were living in the province, a tale made all the more credible by memories of serious immigration frauds which had been discovered early in the decade.

Judged in the light of previous anti-Oriental incidents, this was not a major outburst. Its central figures, Wilson and Macintosh, made no attempt to organize a protest movement. They merely spent their energies in making public demands for more restrictive legislation. Nor was popular hostility as intense as it had been in the past. Because the level of animosity was relatively low and dynamic organizational leadership was absent, this precluded the development of a major racial crisis. Nevertheless all signs pointed to increasing public tension, and the weight of this concern was soon felt in Ottawa.

Prime Minister Mackenzie King was loath to grasp such a nettle as this. King probably wished to placate British Columbia's nativists, or at least quiet them if he could. At the same time, he was subject to countervailing pressures. He was anxious not to embarrass British interests in Asia by taking any initiative which might provoke Japanese ire. Japan's renewed militarism had heightened his own inherent sense of caution. But demands from the west coast grew so insistent that ultimately he could not ignore them. Urged first by Premier T. D. Pattullo of British Columbia and then by Ian Mackenzie, the only west coast representative in the cabinet, King early in March 1938 promised a public enquiry into rumours of illegal Japanese entrants.[8]

But the mere promise of an investigation did not still demands for an end to Japanese immigration. Macintosh went even further and called for the repatriation of all Japanese residents in Canada, regardless of their citizenship.[9] On March 24 the Board of Review charged with the investigation held its first public hearing in Vancouver. During the next seven weeks it conducted a series of additional meetings in major centres throughout the province, and once the hearings commenced, popular unease appeared to dissipate. The hearings themselves put an end to scattered public protest by offering a forum to the vociferous. Furthermore, the meetings forced critics to prove their allegations or remain silent, and many chose the latter refuge. Public concern subsided to such an extent that when the board concluded, early in 1939, that rumours of illegal Japanese immigration had been greatly exaggerated, its report attracted little notice.[10]

But while hostility ebbed appreciably, it was not completely dispelled, and for the next two years the west coast Japanese remained the targets of rumour, suspicion, and criticism. Repeated calls rang out for an end to all Japanese immigration (now fallen to less than 60 per year) while the Vancouver City Council tried to restrict the number of trade licenses issued to Orientals.[11] Then, in the spring of 1940, the second wave of animosity began to well up. In this instance the anxious wartime atmosphere created by Canada's recent belligerency heightened traditional prejudices and aggravated racial tensions in west coast society. At the same time, and for the same reason, Japan's Asian military campaign again began to rouse concern. The growth of general unease once more strengthened feelings of vulnerability and insecurity in the community. Prompted by mounting anxiety, the cry went up that illegal Japanese immigrants were infiltrating the country; renewed demands were made for an end to all Japanese immigration as well as for stronger Pacific coast defences. Tales of the Japanese subversive threat also circulated freely.

It was Alderman Halford Wilson who headed this new campaign of protest. Throughout the summer of 1940 he warned of Japanese subversion and called for closer restrictions on all Japanese residents.[12] Wilson still made no attempt to organize a popular movement, but he did remain the most insistent of the Japanese community's critics. Apart from himself, it is difficult to know for whom Wilson actually spoke. Few British Columbians in 1940 were willing to follow his lead in public. Yet he was by no means the only outspoken public figure and undoubtedly there were many whites who endorsed the general thrust of his remarks, if not their specific aim. Certainly his crusade was a measure of the times for anti-Japanese nativism was once more on the rise,[13] and in Ottawa as well as Victoria this resurgence soon became a source of some concern.[14] The worry was that Wilson's comments might put the torch to public discontent and touch off racial disorder. According to C. G. Power, the minister of national defence for the air, who visited the west coast early in the fall, public feeling was "running high" and the "danger of anti-Japanese outbreaks was serious."[15]

While provincial and federal authorities grew increasingly alarmed at the prospect of racial turmoil, senior military officers in British Columbia were also concerned by the presence of Japanese on the coast. Intelligence officers had kept watch on the Japanese community since 1937 and from the outset had accepted the prevailing assumption that Japanese residents, regardless of their citizenship, would endanger national security in time of war. As early as June 1938 the Department of National Defence had explored the prospect of widespread Japanese wartime internment.[16] In 1940, during the summer's crest of popular anti-Japanese feeling, the Pacific Command's Joint Service Committee approved contingency plans to meet both an external Japanese attack and an internal Japanese insurrection. The committee also endorsed an intelligence report which warned of possible sabotage by the west coast Japanese fishing fleet. Japanese residents, it reported, "could very easily make themselves a potent force and threaten the vital industries of British Columbia." If war broke out, the committee believed, every Japanese resident in British Columbia should be considered a potential enemy.[17]

On the other hand the RCMP tended to minimize the Japanese threat. Since 1938 officers in "E" Division, stationed in Vancouver, had also kept the Japanese under surveillance. In 1940 they assigned three constables to observe the community and also employed Japanese informants. On the basis of continual investigation, the force concluded that Japanese residents posed no real threat to Canada. On the contrary, it observed what it believed to be convincing evidence of Japanese loyalty to Canada. Signs of this were especially clear in the community's strong support for Victory bond drives and Red Cross work, the Nisei desire to volunteer for military service, and the widespread Japanese wish not to arouse white antagonism. "This office," the Officer Commanding at Vancouver reported late in October 1940, "does not consider that the Japanese of British Columbia constitute a menace to the State."[18]

Was there substance to this apparent threat of Japanese subversion? The Board of Review in 1938 had found no proof of wholesale illegal immigration. Nor had the RCMP discovered any indication of serious danger, and surely this was the organization best able to judge.[19] It had scrutinized the Japanese community more carefully than had any other agency. Neither military intelligence nor popular rumour was founded on such close observation, and the claims of each should be judged accordingly. All available signs pointed in one direction only: no significant evidence of Japanese treachery could be seen at this time. Nor would any be discovered at a later date. The threat of Japanese subversion was created by the union of traditional racial attitudes and perceptions shaped by the fears and anxieties conjured up by war. Yet despite its insubstantial basis, the threat was real enough to many British Columbians, and it was the goad which stirred popular animus to life once more.

This resurgence of anti-Japanese sentiment again placed the King government in an uncomfortable position. Whatever it felt about the demands of west coast nativists, more than ever, in the summer of 1940, it wished to avoid irritating Japan as this might jeopardize British interests in the Pacific, if not induce war itself. Moreover, by this time Canada was preoccupied by the European conflict and presumably the federal government wished to avoid distractions. Therefore it hesitated as long as seemed possible before taking action. But by September 1940, when rumours first were heard that Oriental Canadians would be included in the first call for military service, the question could no longer be ignored. Just as Japan announced her alliance with the Axis powers, these reports provoked a sharp cry of protest. Bowing before the rising winds of criticism, the Cabinet War Committee omitted Asian Canadians from the first draft and then formed a special committee to investigate the question of Orientals and British Columbia's security.[20]

The committee soon confirmed that anti-Japanese feeling was high in the province and that this, rather than Japanese subversion, was the greatest potential source of danger to the community. Its major recommendations were therefore aimed at reducing public tension. In order to scotch persistent rumours of illegal Japanese immigration, it urged a new registration of all Japanese residents, both citizens and aliens alike. It also proposed the creation of a standing committee of prominent British Columbians to advise the government on problems relating to Orientals in British Columbia.[21] For their part, because of the delicate state of Anglo-Japanese relations, King and his cabinet were anxious to avoid even the threat of civil disorder in British Columbia, and they implemented the recommendations in the hope of restoring public calm. Intent on disarming British Columbia's nativists, the government included MacGregor Macintosh on the Standing Committee. And in order to reassure the Japanese, it nominated Professor H. F. Angus, the long-time champion of full civil rights for second-generation Japanese Canadians.[22]

If the King government hoped its new initiative would calm popular fears, however, it must soon have been disabused of its optimism. During the first half of 1941 the public temper remained aroused, and there were signs that some British Columbians were growing even more suspicious of the Japanese. Agitation continued, even though no credible leadership had emerged to give protest a focus. Halford Wilson kept up his one-man campaign, now repeatedly urging that in the interest of national security all Japanese fishing boats should be sequestered.[23] The state of tension remained a source of concern to federal officials who still feared a racial incident. Wilson was singled out as the chief cause for alarm, and unsuccessful efforts were made to persuade him to keep silent.[24] Meanwhile, in military circles fear of public disturbance was matched by continued suspicion of the Japanese themselves. As an intelligence report noted in July 1941, widespread Japanese sabotage was unlikely in the event of war, but it remained a possibility unless proper security precautions were taken and the Japanese themselves were protected from white provocation.[25]

In the final months before Pearl Harbor was bombed, racial tensions began to abate. Nevertheless conditions remained favourable to a new anti-Japanese outburst. Influenced by the community's xenophobia, its traditional racial cleavage, and its anxieties borne of war and isolation, white British Columbians continued to suspect their Japanese neighbours. The west coast Japanese could not be trusted. Their allegiance was in doubt. Given the opportunity, it was assumed, some among them would betray the province to the enemy. For its part the federal government, while alarmed by the Japanese problem, was ill-prepared to meet the issue head on. It feared that Japan might use a racial disturbance as a *casus belli*, but aside from forming the Standing Committee it had done very little to prevent an outbreak.

The third and final wave of hostility, in force and amplitude surpassing all previous racial outbursts, was touched off in December 1941 by Japan's assault on Pearl Harbor. This sudden, dramatic attack roused the racial fears and hostilities of white British Columbians to heights never before attained. In turn they loosed a torrent of racialism which surged across the province for the next eleven weeks. This outbreak of popular feeling demanded an immediate response from the King government. In attempting to placate white opinion it offered a succession of policies, each one aimed at further restricting the civil liberties of the west coast Japanese. As it proved, nothing short of total evacuation could quiet the public outcry.

The outbreak of war with Japan immediately raised the problem of public order for the King government because it greatly increased the likelihood of violent anti-Japanese demonstrations in British Columbia. It also created a new enemy alien problem, for the declaration of war altered the status of many Canadian residents of Japanese origin.[26] Faced with the prospect of racial incidents as well as that of an alien menace, the Dominion government quickly took preemptive action. A few hours after war was declared, thirty-eight Japanese nationals were interned on the grounds that they might endanger the community. At the same time the west coast Japanese fishing fleet was immobilized. On the advice of the RCMP, all Japanese-language newspapers and schools voluntarily closed their doors. Meanwhile Prime Minister King, senior police and military officers, and Vancouver's major newspapers all reassured the public and called for calm. As King told the nation in a radio address on December 8, "the competent authorities are satisfied that the security situation is well in hand. They are confident of the correct and loyal behaviour of Canadian residents of Japanese origin."[27]

But many west coast whites were not so easily mollified. Neither prompt federal action nor loyal protestations from leading Japanese did much to assuage their concern. War's outbreak once more opened the floodgates of fear and hostility. As a result the west coast quickly resumed its attack on the province's Japanese. Once again enmity was strongest in and around Vancouver and Victoria, long the province's two focal points of anti-Asian sentiment. In the week following Pearl Harbor some Japanese in Vancouver were victimized by scattered acts of vandalism. Several firms began discharging their Japanese employees. Fear of Japanese subversion again spread in the province.[28] In private, British Columbians began protesting to their members of Parliament. The weight of public concern also bore down on provincial newspapers. Columnist Bruce Hutchison informed the prime minister's office that at the *Vancouver Sun*, "we are under extraordinary pressure from our readers to advocate a pogrom of Japs. We told the people to be calm. Their reply was a bombardment of letters that the Japs all be interned."[29]

To encourage calm, police, government, and military officials issued further assurances that the Japanese problem was well in hand.[30] But their statements seemed to have little effect. Popular protest continued to grow, and in response alarm in government and military circles increased too. On December 20 F. J. Hume, chairman of the Standing Committee, told King:

In British Columbia particularly, the successes of the Japanese to date in the Pacific have to a great extent inflamed public opinion against the local Japanese. People here are in a very excited condition and it would require a very small local incident to bring about most unfortunate conditions between the whites and Japanese.[31]

Maj.-Gen. R. O. Alexander, commander-in-chief of the Pacific Command, was also concerned.

The situation with regard to the Japanese resident in British Columbia is assuming a serious aspect. Public feeling is becoming very insistent, especially in Vancouver, that local Japanese should be either interned or removed from the coast. Letters are being written continually to the press and I am being bombarded by individuals, both calm and hysterical, demanding that something should be done.[32]

Alexander feared that public demonstrations, which according to rumour were to be held in the near future, might lead to racial violence.

After a brief lull over Christmas the public outcry grew more strident than ever. Increasing numbers of west coast whites, regardless of all reassurance, were certain that the local Japanese community endangered west coast security. By early January 1942 patriotic societies, service clubs, town and city councils, and air raid precaution units, most of them on Vancouver Island or in the Vancouver area, had begun to protest.[33] Repeatedly they urged that all Japanese, regardless of citizenship, be interned as quickly as possible. Other spokesmen suggested somewhat less drastic action, but whatever the precise demands of the public, they all assumed the need for some form of Japanese evacuation. And with each passing day opinion seemed to grow more volatile. Even moderates like J. G. Turgeon, Liberal MP from Cariboo, were alarmed at the seeming danger. On January 6 he warned the prime minister:

> The condition in this province is dangerous, so far as the Japanese are concerned. If the Government do not take drastic action, the situation will get out-of-hand. The Government will suffer, and so will the Japanese, personally and through destruction of property.
>
> I am therefore forced to recommend that very strong measures to [*sic*] taken,—and quickly. Either delay, or lack of thorough action, may cause violence.[34]

Under heavy pressure, both popular and political, the federal government ordered yet another review of the Japanese problem. On January 8 and 9, 1942, a committee of federal and provincial government, police, and military officials met in Ottawa to discuss means of allaying west coast alarm. The central question explored was whether or not the Japanese should be removed from coastal areas; but the meeting could not agree on an answer. Several representatives who had just arrived from British Columbia, together with Ian Mackenzie, the meeting's chairman, argued that all able-bodied male Japanese nationals should immediately be removed. The majority of the delegates, however, few of whom had recently been in British Columbia, opposed such drastic action. Consequently the meeting submitted a moderate report which suggested both an extension of existing minor restrictions on the liberties of all Japanese and the creation of a quasi-military work corps for Canadian Japanese who wished to support the war effort.[35]

But the conference's report was only one opinion. From British Columbia there came ever more insistent demands for an evacuation program, and within the cabinet Ian Mackenzie, King's closest political friend from the province, pressed for such a solution.[36] Consequently, when the government announced its revised plans on January 14, the new policy bore the unmistakable imprint of west coast opinion. The King government accepted most of the

Ottawa conference's proposals, but in addition it proposed to remove all enemy aliens, regardless of age, sex, or nationality, from
protected areas soon to be defined in British Columbia. The program was aimed primarily at Japanese nationals although it embraced Germans and Italians as well. The statement also promised
that a Japanese Civilian Corps would soon be formed for work on
projects deemed in the national interest.[37] The covert hope was that
Japanese Canadian men would volunteer for it in large numbers,
thus permitting the government to remove them from the protected
areas without an unpleasant resort to compulsion.[38]

It was felt that, by yielding to some of the west coast's demands,
the partial evacuation policy would calm British Columbian fears.
Concerned for the safety of Canadian prisoners in Japan's hands,
anxious to avoid needless expense and disruption in time of war,
and touched with a lingering sense of justice and humanity, the
King government refused to make further concessions. But the plan
was also rather equivocal in that it neither defined the protected
areas nor promised when evacuation would begin. In effect, it still
gave the federal government considerable freedom of action. For a
few, brief moments the gesture seemed satisfactory. Premier John
Hart of British Columbia, whose government had already demanded similar measures, applauded the decision and the *Vancouver
Sun* praised the King government's common sense. The storm of
protest abated temporarily.[39]

Within ten days, however, agitation began to increase once
again. The public outcry mounted throughout February until, during the last week of the month, it reached unprecedented volume.
Pressed by the irrational fear of enemy subversion, thousands of
west coast whites petitioned Ottawa for the immediate evacuation
of all Japanese. Individuals, farm organizations, municipal councils, civil defence units, constituency associations, service clubs,
patriotic societies, trade unions, citizens' committees, chambers
of commerce—even the Vancouver and District Lawn Bowling Association—all demanded the total evacuation of Japanese from
coastal areas.[40] One group of prominent Vancouver residents telegraphed Ian Mackenzie that, "owing to wide spread public alarm
over enemy aliens on the Pacific coast and especially respecting
those astride vital defence points and with a view to stabilizing
public opinion and in the interest of public safety," they urged the
immediate evacuation of all Japanese.[41] Never before had west
coast race relations been so seriously strained.

Parliament reconvened on January 22 as the racial crisis
mounted. Members of Parliament from British Columbia, no

doubt as concerned as their protesting constituents, began to press for total evacuation. Howard Green, the Conservative member from Vancouver South, opened the attack in the Commons on January 29.[42] The threat of Japanese treachery confronted the Pacific coast, he said, and therefore all Japanese should be removed from the province. During the next three weeks other British Columbian members made similar claims in the House. In private they were even more insistent. On January 28 British Columbians in the Liberal caucus demanded that Japanese Canadians who failed to volunteer for the Civilian Corps be evacuated as quickly as possible. In succeeding weeks, as popular protest reached its greatest heights, King faced successive demands for relocation from provincial politicians, Conservative, Liberal, and independent alike.[43]

Meanwhile government officials in British Columbia sustained their pressure as well. At the height of the popular outcry the attorney-general of British Columbia told Ian Mackenzie:

Events have transpired recently which add to the danger we have always been subjected to by the presence of Japanese on this Coast.

I cannot urge too strongly the seriousness of this situation and the danger the people of British Columbia feel upon this matter.

Nothing short of immediate removal of the Japanese will meet the dangers which we feel in this Province.[44]

At the same time the minister of labour campaigned for total evacuation. The lieutenant-governor informed the prime minister that he had "rarely felt so keenly about any impending danger as I do about the Japanese on this coast being allowed to live in our midst." He suggested that at the very least Japanese males be quickly interned. Since mid-January senior officers of the Pacific Command had grown more concerned as well. By the time public protest reached its peak, they too subscribed to demands for total evacuation.[45]

It was Ian Mackenzie who ultimately bore the brunt of this storm of protest. First he received warnings and notes of alarm, then petitions urging evacuation, and finally demands that he resign. But on this matter Mackenzie had long shared the concern of his constituents. In the first weeks after the outbreak of war he grew convinced that all able-bodied Japanese men should be removed from strategic areas. In consequence he considered the partial evacuation policy inadequate. He also believed that the April 1 deadline was too remote. As pressure upon him grew, Mackenzie's alarm at the instability of public opinion increased in like proportion. On

Japanese men leaving for interior road camps, 1942.

A sign of the times, *Vancouver Sun*, February 26, 1942.

February 22, when news reached him of a series of mass protest
meetings planned for March 1, his anxiety reached a peak.[46] Two
days later he informed cabinet colleagues of the heated state of west
coast opinion and of a call for his own resignation. As he told the
minister of justice:

> The feeling in British Columbia in regard to the Japanese is so aflame that I
> consider we should take the necessary powers (if we have not got them now) to
> remove Canadian Nationals, as well as Japanese Nationals, from the protected
> areas.

> I have no report on how the Vancouver Corps has succeeded, but I greatly fear *disorder* from reports actually received, unless all able-bodied males of Japanese origin are immediately evacuated.[47]

Publicly Mackenzie appeared unperturbed, urging calm on his west coast correspondents, but privately he was extremely exercised.[48]

Within the cabinet others shared something of Mackenzie's alarm, particularly his concern for possible public disturbances. The prime minister agreed that there was "every possibility of riots" on the west coast, and feared that in such an event there would be "repercussions in the Far East against our own prisoners." The situation was awkward, he recognized, because "public prejudice is so strong in B.C. that it is going to be difficult to control."[49] Under such heavy external pressure, and alarmed by the evident danger of racial violence, the federal government finally took decisive action. On February 24, only hours after Mackenzie had written his warning to cabinet colleagues, the government approved an enabling measure which permitted total evacuation. Three days later the announcement was made that all persons of Japanese ancestry would have to leave the protected zones.[50] The King government had once more capitulated to public pressure.

In his *Theory of Collective Behavior*, Neil J. Smelser provides a model for the study of hostile public outbursts.[51] He suggests that five basic factors influence the development of mass hostility. First, the social setting must provide conditions which are conducive to the rise of such a movement. A second important component is that of social strain, the dynamic element which generates and sustains the hostile outburst. Its precipitating factors are a third influence for they crystallize hostility in the form of a social movement. Fourth, the structure and organization of the movement thus mobilized give the outburst its precise form. Finally, opposing influences usually attempt to contain the outbreak by employing various techniques of social control. In reference to this particular outburst of hostility, Smelser's model offers a useful tool of social analysis for, when viewed within this framework, the psychological forces which underlay the events of these eleven weeks assume a greater clarity.

That the structure of west coast society was conducive to this outburst there can be no doubt. British Columbia's traditional racial cleavage, in recent years marked by strong anti-Japanese feeling, had created enduring racial tensions which perpetually tended toward outbreaks of racial animosity within the white community. No obstacles prevented the general acceptance of racial prejudices.

On the contrary, the strength of the consensus encouraged widespread espousal of these negative beliefs. White society aired its biases openly and often, and its pronouncements met with virtually no contradiction. Racism was further legitimated by discriminatory law and custom, both of which enforced differential patterns of treatment among white and Oriental citizens. Thus the racial assumptions of west coast whites, the product of longstanding strains in race relations, created a climate of public opinion in the province which tended toward this eruption. The fact that similar minor incidents had occurred in recent years simply increased the likelihood that an outburst would occur.

In this instance, of course, the precipitating factor was North America's engagement in war on the Pacific, an event which suddenly imposed complex psychological strains upon white British Columbians. Owing to war in Europe, the level of generalized public anxiety in the province was already well above peacetime norms by December 7, 1941. Pearl Harbor raised this level appreciably, and in the following weeks a further increase took place.

In itself, the opening of a new theatre of war was an additional source of unease because it raised new uncertainties in an already war-troubled world. More specifically, the ambiguity which enveloped Japan's military activities in the weeks after December 7 also conditioned the growth of anxiety. The startling number of her targets, the suddenness of her assaults, the speed of her military expansion, and the seeming ease of her victories surprised and frightened many west coast whites. The enemy seemed everywhere in the Pacific. No one knew where he might next attack and some feared it would be British Columbia. In such conditions civil defence preparations themselves became a source of unease for they reflected the assumption that a Japanese attack was indeed imminent. During the first week of war air raid precaution units were called for duty, defence regulations were posted, and nightly blackouts were enforced. Far from offering reassurance, these activities further unsettled an already apprehensive public.

In the weeks that followed, a series of military reverses continued to play on west coast fears. By mid-January Japanese troops had overrun much of Malaya, the Philippines, Burma, and British North Borneo. They had occupied Thailand, captured Hong Kong (taking more than 1,600 Canadian troops prisoner), sunk Britain's most modern battleship, and crippled her Pacific fleet. Late in January they had laid siege to the island of Singapore. News of this swift succession of decisive victories dominated the front pages of the provincial press. These accounts repeatedly emphasized that

Japanese subversion and fifth column activity had played a central role in Japan's program of conquest. Already convinced of their own vulnerability, British Columbians grew more alarmed when worse news succeeded bad, and increasingly hostile toward the Japanese minority. The combined effect of Japanese militarism and the province's legacy of racial tension was to reveal the old image of the Yellow Peril in a new and lurid light. As many British Columbians peered through the fog of their anxieties, they saw little but the menacing outline of Japanese subversion. A growing sense of crisis narrowed their perceptions, which in turn intensified public unease. Thus social tensions and racial imagery were mutually reinforcing. Had British Columbians seen their Japanese neighbours clearly, they would have observed an isolated, defenceless minority, gravely alarmed by its plight and anxious to demonstrate its loyalty to Canada. But fear and prejudice obscured their vision. The local Japanese seemed nothing but a grave and growing threat.

A further sign of mounting social pressure was the increasing incidence of rumours of Japanese subversion. Some told of Japanese who owned high-powered vehicles and short wave equipment, who lived near sites of great strategic value, who swelled with insolent pride at Japan's successive victories. Others hinted at active Japanese disloyalty, and in the hothouse atmosphere of growing public tension stories grew to outlandish proportions. Military intelligence officers were informed in mid-January that Japanese in Vancouver had fixed infra-red and ultraviolet beacons on their roofs, devices which, when viewed through special binoculars, would guide enemy flights over the city.[52] Rumour is usually the product of serious social and psychological stress,[53] and these persistent rumours were one more indication of the growing racial crisis on Canada's west coast. The outbreak of war with Japan had spread a grave sense of looming threat among west coast whites. Yet for all its immediacy the threat remained somewhat vague and nebulous. The enemy was identified; his whereabouts were not. Rumours helped resolve this ambiguity. They suggested that some of the enemy were very close at hand. While this in itself was cause for concern, it also helped to clarify the confusions of war with a distant, elusive power. Because rumours singled out the nearest available enemy, they helped reduce the ambiguity which had spawned them in the first place. Once in circulation, they too stirred the ever-widening eddies of hostility and alarm.

It seems clear that a further, immediate reason for the renewed upsurge of protest in February was that many British Columbians, anxious for total evacuation, had misinterpreted the government's policy announcement of January 14. The *Sun* had taken it to mean that "all Japanese and other enemy aliens" were to be removed from protected areas, an assumption shared by several British Columbia members of Parliament. "My understanding," wrote Ian Mackenzie, "was that all able-bodied, adult enemy aliens would have to be removed from protected areas. My further understanding was also that all able-bodied *Canadian nationals* would have to be moved, but that *first* they should be given an opportunity to volunteer in the Civilian Corps."[54] Added complications arose from the failure of the federal government to implement its program immediately. Neither the evacuation plans nor the designated protected areas were announced until January 23, and the delay itself provoked some concern. When finally announced, the plans indicated that evacuation was not to be completed before April 1, a date which seemed far too remote to those who believed the Japanese threat was imminent. Once the plans were made public there was a further delay while the relocation machinery was set up. The task of arranging to move, house, and care for several thousand Japanese proved a time-consuming one and it was complicated further by the strong opposition of residents in the British Columbian interior, especially the Okanagan Valley, to proposals that all the Japanese be settled inland.[55] Several times the immediate departure of Japanese from Vancouver was announced and then postponed. Consequently few, if any, Japanese left their homes before mid-February. In the eyes of concerned west coast whites the government's partial evacuation policy increasingly seemed a mixture of confusion, delay, and prevarication. It appeared that Ottawa did not understand, let alone sympathize with, British Columbia's predicament.

Three elements thus combined to generate social strain in the province after the bombing of Pearl Harbor: reports of Japan's military campaigns in Asia, rumours of impending Japanese attack on British Columbia, and federal delays in implementing the wholesale evacuation policies advocated on the west coast. The first two projected a Japanese military threat to the province and assumed that the local Japanese community would play a subversive role in the anticipated conflict. The third expressed the frustrations of whites when the precautions they deemed necessary were not immediately taken. In each case the roots of this strain were fundamentally psychological.

The pattern of mobilization of this outburst is also revealing, for, by and large, British Columbians reached their conclusions about the Japanese menace with little prompting. More or less simultaneously, thousands recognized an obvious threat and identified the equally obvious solution. In the generation of this consensus, neither popular leaders nor popular journalism played a predominant role. Halford Wilson and MacGregor Macintosh, once the two chief critics of the west coast Japanese, were submerged beneath the rising tide of hostility. In fact, the protest movement had no preeminent leaders whatsoever. Nor did provincial papers become leaders of opinion, even though some took up the popular cry. During the crisis west coast journalism helped sustain the prevailing mood, but most papers merely reflected the popular mind. In other words the outburst was both widespread and largely spontaneous.

The very structure of the protest movement supports this contention for it clearly revealed how extensive was the anti-Japanese consensus. Although public anxiety had flared up immediately after Pearl Harbor, no effective anti-Japanese movement began to emerge until late January. In its earliest stage protest was random; it had no central leadership and no institutional focus. When the movement did begin to take form, protest was mobilized concurrently by a broad range of the traditional social, economic, administrative, and political organizations already entrenched in British Columbia. The Provincial Council of Women, the Vancouver Real Estate Exchange, the Canadian Legion in Gibson's Landing, the Kinsmen's Club of Victoria, the North Burnaby Liberal Association, the BC Poultry Industries Committee, the Corporation of the District of Saanich, the National Union of Machinists, Fitters, and Helpers (Victoria Local Number 2), and scores of other similar groups all pressed their demands for evacuation. Not only did these organizations represent major interest groups in the province, but their influence cut across most social, economic, and political bounds in west coast society. They represented the interests and opinions, the fears and hostilities of tens of thousands of British Columbians. If there were some provincial whites who did not share prevailing attitudes, they remained largely silent in the face of the consensus.

In addition, the forces opposing the outburst were relatively weak. In this case ultimate responsibility for control rested with the King government. Throughout the eleven-week crisis its chief concern remained constant: to reduce the level of racial tension in west coast society. For King and those of his ministers who were preoccupied with the problem, the first task was to prevent the torrent of racist rhetoric from spilling over into overt violence. Beyond that they wished to moderate racial hostility. But they had few tools at their disposal with which to achieve these ends. Physical protection of the minority by police or military forces was never seriously con-

Above, leaving for the interior, 1942. *Below*, camp life in the interior, 1942.

sidered. Nor, save in a limited way, was counter-publicity used to refute the claims of the nativists and encourage public calm. Instead the government employed appeasement to mollify British Columbia. Its first step, taken immediately, was a policy of selective internment and increased restrictions on Japanese civil liberties. The second was a plan to remove that segment of the Japanese population which seemed most immediately dangerous. The third and final step was wholesale evacuation. As a means of attaining the primary goal of lower social strain, the King government selected this as the path of least resistance. Whether any alternative policy could have succeeded is now a moot point.

That the King government chose this solution is not at all surprising, for west coast opinion weighed down upon a group of politicians quite susceptible to prejudice against Asians. Ever since Confederation, anti-Orientalism had pervaded the political culture of the province beyond the Rockies and on many occasions provincial representatives had thrust their opinions upon Ottawa. Usually their words had received a fairly sympathetic hearing, and past governments had repeatedly acquiesced in their major demands. Ian Mackenzie, on whom much of the burden of west coast opinion fell in 1942, had long been confirmed in his anti-Asian sentiments, though not outspokenly so, and on the eve of war in the Pacific most British Columbian politicians held the same convictions that he did. Consequently, when anti-Japanese feeling welled up after Pearl Harbor, they shared the public's growing concern and transmitted it with alacrity to Parliament and cabinet.

In Ottawa Mackenzie King also faced the rising tide of protest. His experience with west coast hostility toward Asians had been longer and more intimate than that of any other federal politician. In 1907 and 1908 he had held three royal commissions to investigate Oriental immigration and racial disturbances in Vancouver. In the 1920s and 1930s, as prime minister, he was repeatedly confronted by the issue. As was usual with King, his comments on the Oriental problem were always extremely circumspect. Prior to his premiership he had concluded that the roots of west coast tensions were economic, not racial, and he envisaged their satisfactory resolution through negotiation with Asian nations to seek mutually acceptable immigration levels.[56] In office, he proceeded to use both diplomacy and legislation to restrict immigration from China and Japan. During the later 1930s, however, when anti-Japanese feeling increased on the west coast, King felt constrained from any further restrictive action by international tensions. His view of the issue after the outbreak of war with Japan remains unclear. He did not share the anxieties of west coast residents, yet he ultimately accepted the possibility of a Japanese invasion of British Columbia.[57] Probably his primary concern was for the instability of west coast opinion and the threat to public order which it posed. If subsequent government policy is any measure of his thought, he was willing to adopt any expedient that would reduce public tension.

When the final announcement was made, the province did not immediately breathe a sigh of collective relief. Tension remained high for several days thereafter. In Ottawa Ian Mackenzie believed that public disorder was still possible. Slowly, however, the strain of racial crisis began to ease. The two mass meetings held on March 1 were quiet and orderly. Mackenzie received a note of praise from supporters in Vancouver. The flood of protests to Ottawa began to recede.[58]

When the cabinet approved the order which permitted evacuation, the editors of the *Sun* looked forward to the day the move would be complete. They hoped that the coast was "Saying Goodbye, Not Au Revoir" to the Japanese.[59] But while some had undoubtedly seen the crisis as a chance to solve the province's Japanese problem for all time, this scarcely explains the previous weeks' outburst of hostility. War with Japan had sharpened the animus, narrowed the vision, and intensified the fears of a community already profoundly divided along racial lines. In the minds of west coast whites, intimations of vulnerability and isolation had long nursed a sense of insecurity, and after Pearl Harbor many British Columbians had felt themselves exposed as never before to attack from Japan. In addition, they had grown convinced that the resident Japanese were a threat to the community's security. These beliefs had virtually no foundation in fact. In essence they were facets of the traditional Japanese image held by white British Columbians, stereotypes further distorted in the heat of war. Its fears fed by these perceptions, the west coast loosed a torrent of hostility. Sensitive to the public temper, and alarmed by the prospect of racial disturbance, the federal government attempted preventative action. But neither minor restrictions on civil liberties nor the promise of partial relocation satisfied west coast whites. They demanded total Japanese evacuation. In the end their wishes were met.[60]

By promising total relocation the new federal policy removed the apparent threat to provincial security which had prompted the outburst of mass hostility. But while white tempers were defused on Vancouver Island and in the lower mainland, in many interior com-

munities they were further aroused. As numbers of Japanese refu-
gees moved eastward on their own, and as the prospect increased
that thousands of evacuees would be sent to inland locations, whites
in many centres raised a new chorus of protest. From the Okanagan, for example, came claims that Japanese infiltration was
"assuming alarming proportions and if not forthwith stopped will
create serious defence and economic problems in the Valley."[61]
They were accompanied by a call for the removal of all Japanese
who had recently entered the valley and for the complete prohibition of any further Japanese arrivals. Whites in other inland cities
and towns made similar demands. For those in charge of the evacuation program the problem was serious. As the chairman of the
British Columbia Security Commission telegraphed Ian Mackenzie, "protests from interior points are such that without government intervention for necessity of cooperation from them it will be
practically impossible for us to evacuate Japanese to any of these
points."[62] Similarly, plans to move evacuees east of the Rockies
encountered vociferous local opposition, especially in southern Al-
berta where some Japanese were to be sent in order to work district
sugar beet crops.[63]

These subsequent flare-ups provided a basis in public opinion for
the many legal restrictions which hedged round the lives of the
evacuees. While inherent in the logic of the evacuation plan, two
new dimensions of federal policy, further curbs on Japanese civil
liberties and the alienation of Japanese property, were also exten-
sions of those deep-rooted racist sentiments brought to the fore by
recent events. Although the high pitch of popular protest was not
sustained throughout the war, nativism continued to lie close to the
surface of west coast society. It lurked behind federal initiatives to
repatriate Japanese at the end of World War II. It encouraged plans
to disperse the remaining minority throughout several provinces.
And it delayed the granting of the franchise to Japanese Canadians
once the war had concluded.

Yet, more openly than ever before, a small but growing number
of whites simultaneously declared support for the Japanese minority. Campaigns by whites in favour of Oriental civil rights were not
entirely new by the 1940s. During the interwar years, to a very
limited extent, west coast attitudes toward Asians had begun to
liberalize. British Columbia trade unionism gradually abandoned
its intense nativism. Undoubtedly racism persisted within the
labour movement, but union leaders and policies were no longer
outspokenly anti-Oriental and limited support for racial equality
could be found in union circles. Of greater importance was the fact

that Asian minorities had gained a political voice for the first time during the 1930s; the CCF took their cause to the public, calling for the franchise for second-generation Orientals, albeit with due regard for the party's political fortunes. Liberal protestantism also lost its obsession with the seeming need to assimilate Asiatics and commenced open advocacy of minority group interests. Together these various developments marked the dawn of a reassessment of traditional white assumptions about the Asian immigrant in British Columbia, and it was on these foundations that the first shift in attitudes during and after World War II was based.

The wartime advocates of the Japanese-Canadian cause demanded just treatment for all evacuees and urged positive government policies to extinguish anti-Orientalism forever. In the forefront of this movement were a handful of Protestant clergy and laymen and a few members of the CCF. Early in 1942 they formed the Vancouver Consultative Council, a group of between thirty and forty men and women from civil libertarian backgrounds.[64] Soon they were joined by the Fellowship for a Christian Social Order, a Christian socialist organization with branches in Toronto, Vancouver, and other Canadian cities. Both groups denounced racism and campaigned for government action to eliminate discrimination and encourage Japanese integration into Canadian society. They believed that the only way to solve the racial problem for all time was to disperse the Japanese community throughout Canadian society. In the words of Dr. Norman F. Black, a leading member of the VCC:

We feel very strongly that our Japanese problem can be solved only by prompt and systematic geographic and occupational dispersion ... *we foresee bloodshed on the streets of Vancouver* if, at the termination of the war, twenty thousand or ten thousand or even five thousand homeless and workless Japanese and Canadians of Japanese ancestry suddenly crowd back into this locality when war passions are still surging. The reasons for such anxiety are too manifest to require explanation. And we feel that, unless in the meantime these people have established real homes and become absorbed into the general currents of Canadian economic and social life, an intrinsically hopeless situation will inevitably develop.[65]

Similar sentiments were echoed by the provincial CCF.[66]

Late in the war this movement broadened as leaders of the second-generation Japanese joined church groups, civil libertarians, and CCF politicians in a protest against the federal disenfranchisement of those Japanese Canadians who lived outside the province of British Columbia.[67] An even more vigorous campaign opposed the King government's plan for mass Japanese deportation, a policy intended to send to Japan some 10,000 persons of Japanese ancestry who during 1944 and 1945 had declared their wish to go and had not retracted their decision before the Pacific war had ended; the majority of them had subsequently changed their minds and thus were to be deported against their will. In this instance protest was marshalled by Japanese-Canadian civil rights groups and the Co-operative Committee on Japanese Canadians, a Toronto-based coalition of local and national organizations, among them churches, youth clubs, trade unions, welfare councils, the YMCA, YWCA, and civil liberties associations. This was by far the most vigorous opposition yet mounted against anti-Oriental government policies. Ultimately it was successful for the King government relented and repatriated only those who still wished to be sent.[68]

These campaigns marked a fundamental shift in white attitudes toward Orientals, the first in the lengthy history of their presence in Canada. In British Columbia and across Canada liberal views on race relations were suddenly ascendant. In the later 1940s nativists still voiced their views in public but they were clearly on the defensive. One sign of this change in public opinion was the relative swiftness and ease with which discriminatory legislation was dismantled. The federal government repealed the Chinese Immigration Act in 1947, although sharp limitations on the number of entrants were to continue for years. Of greater symbolic significance was the removal of the franchise restrictions which had long been imposed upon all Asiatics. Chinese and East Indian Canadians gained the vote both provincially and federally in 1947. After a further two-year delay, symptomatic of greater white prejudice, Japanese Canadians were also given the franchise. Soon all of the legal disabilities affecting Orientals had been removed. By the early 1950s discrimination in law against residents of Oriental ancestry was a thing of the past. Undeniably nativism still lurked in white British Columbia, but its public spokesmen had vanished. Lacking public legitimacy, racial discrimination was henceforth forced to assume its many subtler forms.

The motives which lay beneath this major change in public opinion are too complex for analysis here. But among the many possibilities, four seem especially significant. First, and of most immediate importance, the end of the war and the Japanese dispersal had finally erased the image of a Japanese menace in Canada. Henceforth this minority group ceased to seem a military and economic threat. As a result, those attitudes which had once formed the core of anti-Japanese feeling could no longer be maintained. Second, the postwar revelations of German war atrocities cast racist doctrines into unprecedented disrepute in western societies. This revulsion underlay the growing trend toward public declarations of basic human rights, ideals which found open expression in the United Nations' charter and the liberal internationalist rhetoric of the postwar years. So articulate were the champions of this new idealism and so pervasive were their beliefs that by the early 1950s they had reduced Canadian nativists to virtual silence. In the third place, China had been a wartime partner of the Allies and this may have encouraged more positive public attitudes toward the Chinese in Canada, in any case a group which had already ceased to seem a major threat in the eyes of most British Columbians.

Finally, acculturation had greatly reduced the social distance between whites and Asians, particularly those of the second generation. In defiance of all that nativists had long predicted, the Chinese, Japanese, and East Indians had in varying degrees absorbed the social and cultural norms of western Canadian society. Thus they had taken great strides toward eliminating the fundamental source of British Columbian racism. The unassimilable Oriental was becoming assimilated.

9

THE DRIVE FOR A WHITE B.C.

From the late 1850s to the early 1940s anti-Orientalism was endemic in British Columbia. White society feared and disliked the Asian minority in the community and made its feelings abundantly clear in thought, word, and deed. While prejudice was by no means universal within the province, the racist consensus was nevertheless extremely broad. For the most part those who dissented from it kept their counsel to themselves. Once ingrained in the white mind, racist assumptions remained fixed there for almost a century. Their content was largely static. They expressed the same fundamental beliefs about Asiatics, the same unyielding animosity toward them, throughout this entire period. What fluctuated was the immediacy of the threat subsumed in these attitudes and the consequent intensity with which racist convictions were held. By themselves these beliefs did not generate anti-Oriental activity. They were a necessary, not a sufficient, condition of openly hostile action. What they did create was a reservoir of racial animosity which many kinds of incidents could tap readily and from which flowed numerous sorts of discriminatory acts. These ranged in scope from petty street violence and casual intolerance to restrictive legislation and massive population removal. Whatever their nature, however, all of these gestures were grounded in the continuing hostility of white British Columbians toward the immigrant from Asia.

During these years animosity was most intense in the heavily settled regions of the province: Vancouver, Victoria, the lower Fraser Valley, and the south half of Vancouver Island. These were the areas where most Orientals had congregated, where interracial contact occurred most frequently, where public opinion could circulate most freely, and where collective action by whites could be most easily mobilized. Yet racism was not confined to this corner of the province. It cropped up in most regions at one time or another. Furthermore, these sentiments were not the exclusive preserve of a few interest groups within the white population. At one time or another trade unionists, politicians, veterans, and journalists all played active roles in anti-Oriental campaigns. But they were far from alone in sharing racist opinions. Businessmen, housewives, missionaries, and many others were likely to agree, for nativism transcended most social, religious, economic, and political bounds in provincial society. In short, throughout British Columbia it became a cultural norm.

In the spreading of these beliefs, the press played a significant role. Most newspapers in British Columbia were heavily freighted with racist rhetoric and thus helped to circulate anti-Oriental opinion. Public leaders freely disseminated nativism from the platforms of the province. But these were secondary agents in the diffusion of racial attitudes. By and large, journalists and orators seem merely to have reflected beliefs already deeply entrenched in the popular mind. For the most part these attitudes circulated through the informal mechanisms of cultural transmission, passed by word and example from resident whites to newcomers and from one generation to another. Their ready acceptance was socially conditioned by the strength of this cultural norm. No sanctions in British Columbia curbed the free expression of racial prejudice. This pattern of informal, unrestricted circulation of attitudes facilitated the generation and maintenance of the racist consensus.

Popular anti-Orientalism alternated irregularly between quiescence and arousal. Sometimes these fluctuations were confined to a single interest group or community. On other occasions they were generalized and widespread throughout the province. Whenever racial outbursts occurred, they were provoked by one or more of a broad range of factors, including economic competition, high immigration rates, and distant war. But economic competition was often more apparent than real and even a handful of Asian newcomers could arouse hostility in a previously all-white community. War in Asia, of course, directly influenced the affairs of only a few west coast residents, most of them Oriental. Thus while migration, war, and economic rivalry sometimes touched the immediate interests of white British Columbia, they did not invariably do so. The periodic upsurge of racial hostility cannot be explained by conflicts of interest alone. Asiatic immigrants also left their mark upon the social psychology of white British Columbia and this must in large part account for the ebb and flow of prejudice in west coast society.

Leadership had only marginal impact upon fluctuations in popular racism in British Columbia. There were no nativists of truly demagogic proportions in the province, and only seldom did leaders leave a significant imprint upon public sentiments. This is not to suggest that anti-Orientalism was leaderless. A succession of

British Columbians, from Noah Shakespeare to Halford Wilson, became popular champions of the nativistic cause. Yet for the most part they were publicists and organizers, not magnetic leaders of men. In this way as well, upsurges in popular prejudice owed far more to broadly shared animosities, fears, and beliefs than to the agency of dynamic leadership.

Nor is there evidence to suggest that post-Darwinian racial theory directly influenced the course of British Columbian anti-Orientalism. The province's whites were guided by their own racial perceptions, not by the theoretical abstractions of a quasi-anthropology. In western thought a sharpened sense of racial awareness accompanied the rise of empire from the mid-nineteenth century onward, achieving full flower in social Darwinism. As a tool of social analysis the concept of race seemed to explain a broad range of racial, ethnic, and national differences. In the hands of intellectuals it gave rise to intricate theories of the relationship between race and culture. But in the grasp of those who lived in the west coast community, the tool was a comparatively blunt instrument. It gave the nativists little more than an accessible terminology, a useful set of categories with which to express their fears and hostilities.

Ultimately, several sources fed the anti-Oriental impulse in Canada's westernmost province. Among the more important were western images of Asia, continued migration from the Orient, recurrent economic rivalry, and intermittent conflicts of custom and of value. But what fused these disparate influences into a single racist imperative was one vital determinant much larger than all the rest: that psychological tension which inhered in the racially plural condition. White British Columbians yearned for a racially homogeneous society. They feared that heterogeneity would destroy their capacity to perpetuate their values and traditions, their laws and institutions—indeed, all those elements of their culture embraced by the White Canada symbol. These were vague and nebulous aspirations but, whatever their form, the Oriental immigrant seemed to endanger their fulfilment. Having encountered the Asian and his image, white British Columbians had condemned him as unalterably alien. He roused deep-seated fears for the cultural destiny of their society and seemed to prevent the achievement of that homogeneous "white" community for which they collectively longed. From these perceptions and aspirations grew the anxieties and prejudices which sustained the nativist drive within the west coast community. Fundamentally, then, racism was grounded in the irrational fears and assumptions of whites who lived in the farthest west.

TABLE 1

POPULATION OF BRITISH COLUMBIA BY RACIAL ORIGIN 1871-1921

Year	Total Population	Indians	Whites and Others	Chinese	Other Asians	% of Total Population which is Chinese	% of Chinese Population to White Population
1870	36,247	25,661	9,038	1,548	—	4.3	17.1
1881	49,459	25,661	19,448	4,350	—	8.8	22.4
1891	98,173	35,202a	54,061	8,910	—	9.1	16.5
1901	178,657	25,488	133,605	14,885b	4,681	8.3	11.1
1911	392,480	20,134	341,899	19,568	10,879	5.0	5.7
1921	524,582	22,377	459,456	23,533	16,206	4.5	5.1

Source: *Census of Canada*, 1871-1921.
aSource: Canada, Department of Indian Affairs, "Annual Report" (1891), *Canada Sessional Papers* (1892), no. 14, pt. I, 253.
bSource: Tien-fang Cheng, *Oriental Immigration in Canada* (Shanghai, 1931), p. 275.

TABLE 2

POPULATION OF BRITISH COLUMBIA BY RACIAL ORIGIN 1901-1941

Year	Total Population	Chinese	Japanese	East Indians and other Asians	Total Asians	% Chinese	% Japanese	% East Indian	% Asian
1901	178,657	14,885	4,597	84	19,482	8.3	2.6	.04	10.9a
1911	392,480	19,568	8,587	2,292	30,447	5.0	2.2	.58	7.8
1921	524,582	23,533	15,006	989	39,528	4.5	2.9	.18	7.5
1931	694,236	27,139	22,205	1,607	50,951	3.9	3.2	.23	7.3
1941	817,861	18,619	22,096	1,757	42,472	2.3	2.7	.21	5.2

Source: *Census of Canada*, 1901-1941.

aIn 1901 native Indians still composed a numerically significant proportion of the provincial population. The decennial census of that year reported 25,488 Indian residents in British Columbia. The ratio of Asians to white residents was 14.6 per cent. Thereafter the Indian population shrank while all other racial components of the community grew. As a result, the ratio of Asians to whites approached that of Asians to the total provincial population.

NOTES

ABBREVIATIONS

PABC Public Archives of British Columbia, Victoria
PAC   Public Archives of Canada, Ottawa
EAA   Department of External Affairs, Archives Branch, Ottawa

PREFACE

1. John Higham, *Strangers in the Land: Patterns of American Nativism 1860-1925* (New Brunswick, N.J.: Rutgers University Press, 1955), p. 4.

2. Michael Banton, "The Concept of Racism," *Race and Racialism*, ed. Sami Zubaida (London: Tavistock Publications, 1970), pp. 17-18.

3. Allan Smith, "Metaphor and Nationality in North America," *Canadian Historical Review* 51, no. 3 (September 1970): 247-75.

CHAPTER 1

1. Gordon W. Allport, *The Nature of Prejudice* (Reading, Mass.: Addison-Wesley, 1954), p. 191.

2. Ibid., pp. 20-23.

3. Raymond Dawson, *The Chinese Chameleon: An Analysis of European Conceptions of Chinese Civilization* (London: Oxford University Press, 1967), chap. 7.

4. Stuart Creighton Miller, *The Unwelcome Immigrant: The American Image of the Chinese, 1785-1882* (Berkeley: University of California Press, 1969), p. 201.

5. *Epitome of Geographical Knowledge, Ancient and Modern, Compiled for the Use of the Teachers and Advanced Classes of the National Schools of Ireland* (Dublin, 1854), p. 567. This text and other similar geographies were used in the colonial schools of British North America, those of Vancouver Island and British Columbia included.

6. For example see *The Colonist* (Victoria), May 3, 1884.

7. Government of Canada, *Report of the Royal Commission on Chinese Immigration* (1885), pp. 164-66.

8. Roger Daniels, *The Politics of Prejudice: The Anti-Japanese Movement in California and the Struggle for Japanese Exclusion* (Gloucester, Mass.: Peter Smith, 1966), pp. 65-78.

9. Government of Canada, Select Committee on Chinese Labor and Immigration, "Report," *Journals of the House of Commons* (1879), 14, testimony of J. S. Thompson, MP.

10. *Colonist*, Sept. 13, 1907.

11. For theoretical discussions of group norm prejudice see Muzafer Sherif, *Group Conflict and Co-operation: Their Social Psychology* (London: Routledge and Kegan Paul, 1966), pp. 25-26 and Allport, *The Nature of Prejudice*, pp. 39-41. Other comprehensive statements on the origins and nature of prejudice can be found in George E. Simpson and J. Milton Yinger, *Racial and Cultural Minorities: An Analysis of Prejudice and Discrimination* (New York: Harper, 1953) and James W. Vander Zanden, *American Minority Relations: The Sociology of Race and Ethnic Groups*, 2nd ed. (New York: Ronald Press, 1966).

12. *Colonist*, Nov. 1, 1884.

13. *Royal Commission* (1885), p. 49, testimony of John Flewin, Sergeant, Victoria Police Force.

14. Ibid., p. 87, testimony of James Young.

15. Margaret A. Ormsby, *British Columbia: A History* (Toronto: Macmillan, 1958), p. 281.

16. *Colonist*, July 13, 1884.

17. *The Industrial News* (Victoria), July 17, 1886.

18. During the early 1880s these reports were well-founded. In 1884 there were 154 Chinese women in British Columbia. Seventy were prostitutes and an unspecified number were concubines. Report of Commissioner Gray, *Royal Commission* (1885), p. lix.

19. Ibid., p. 89, testimony of James Young.

20. Ibid., p. 161, testimony of John A. Bradley.

21. *Colonist*, June 14, 1876.

22. Select Committee, 1879, p. 18, testimony of Dr. T. R. McInnes.

23. *Colonist*, Sept. 4, 1886.

24. *Royal Commission* (1885), p. 161, testimony of John A. Bradley.

25. *Victoria Times*, June 25, 1908.

26. Emily F. Murphy, *The Black Candle* (Toronto: Thomas Allen, 1922), p. 188.

27. Minutes of Evidence, Royal Commission to investigate losses sustained by the Chinese Population of Vancouver, B.C., 1908, 35-36, testimony of R. G. Chamberlain, Chief of Police, Vancouver, William Lyon Mackenzie King Papers, MG 26 J4, C31511-12, PAC. A. M. Stephen, *The Gleaming Archway* (London and Toronto: J. M. Dent, 1929). W. Peter Ward, "The Oriental Immigrant and Canada's Protestant Clergy, 1858-1925," *BC Studies*, no. 22 (Summer 1974), p. 47.

28. Report of Commissioner Gray, *Royal Commission* (1885), pp. lxi-lxii.

29. *Royal Commission* (1885), p. 156, submission of the Knights of Labor, Nanaimo.

30. *Cariboo Sentinel*, July 24, 1875.

31. *The Columbian* (New Westminster), Oct. 7, 1882.

32. Noah Shakespeare, Mayor, on behalf of the citizens of Victoria to the Marquis of Lorne, July 22, 1882, Government of Canada, *Sessional Papers* (1883), no. 93a, 13-14.

33. *Royal Commission* (1885), p. 71, testimony of Chief Justice M. B. Begbie. When Begbie referred to the law-abiding nature of the Chinese, he probably meant that they always met their business obligations. Many British Columbians, on the contrary, believed the Chinese a lawless element in west coast society.

34. Ibid., pp. 128-29, testimony of Robert Dunsmuir, colliery owner.

35. Andrew Onderdonk to Macdonald, June 14, 1882, Sir John A. Macdonald Papers, PAC.

36. Report of Commissioner Gray, *Royal Commission* (1885), p. xviii.

37. Government of Canada, *Report of the Royal Commission on Chinese and Japanese Immigration* (1902), p. 145, testimony of H. O. Bell-Irving, manager of a major fish packing company.

38. Ibid., p. 144, testimony of Bell-Irving.

39. W. A. Baillie-Grohman, *Fifteen Years' Sport and Life in the Hunting Grounds of Western America and British Columbia* (London: Horace Cox, 1900), p. 333. This work includes a chapter by Mrs. Baillie-Grohman on Chinese servants.

40. Ibid., pp. 333-61; on the paternalistic mode in race relations see Pierre L. van den Berghe, *Race and Racism: A Comparative Perspective* (New York: Wiley, 1967), pp. 27-29.

41. *Royal Commission* (1902), p. 278.

42. Judging by their attitudes toward the Chinese, North American whites were not much concerned about Asian sexuality, whereas attitudes toward blacks were highly charged with sexual imagery. For a valuable analysis of sexual attitudes in American race relations see Winthrop D. Jordan, *White Over Black: American Attitudes toward the Negro, 1550-1812* (Chapel Hill, N.C.: University of North Carolina Press, 1968).

43. For example see Marvin Harris, *The Rise of Anthropological Theory: A History of Theories of Culture* (New York: Thomas Y. Crowell, 1968); Thomas F. Gossett, *Race: The History of an Idea in America* (New York, Schocken Books, 1965); Richard Hofstadter, *Social Darwinism in American Thought, 1860-1915* (Philadelphia: University of Pennsylvania Press, 1945).

44. Ormsby, *British Columbia*, p. 303; Paul A. Phillips, *No Power Greater: A Century of Labour in British Columbia* (Vancouver: British Columbia Federation of Labour, 1967), 10; Donald H. Avery, "Canadian Immigration Policy and the Alien Question, 1896-1919" (Ph.D. thesis, University of Western Ontario, 1973), chap. II.

45. *Royal Commission* (1902), p. 240.

46. Ward, "Protestant Clergy."

47. E. O. S. Scholefield and R. E. Gosnell, *A History of British Columbia* (Vancouver: British Columbia Historical Association, 1913), pt. I, 185; *Colonist*, Mar. 28, 1861; Robert Edward Wynne, "Reaction to the Chinese in the Pacific Northwest and British Columbia, 1850-1910" (Ph.D. thesis, University of Washington, 1964), pp. 145-46.

48. W. E. Willmott, "Approaches to the Study of the Chinese in British Columbia," *BC Studies*, no. 4 (Spring 1970), p. 42. See also David Lai, "Home County and Clan Origins of Overseas Chinese in Canada in the Early 1880's," *BC Studies*, no. 27 (Autumn 1975), pp. 3-29.

49. *The Handbook of British Columbia and Emigrant's Guide to the Gold Fields* (London, 1862), p. 68; Florence Goodfellow, *Memories of Pioneer Life in British Columbia* (Wenatchee, Wash.: n.p., 1945), p. 14. For a description of the credit-

ticket system of immigration see Gunther Barth, *Bitter Strength: A History of the Chinese in the United States, 1850-1870* (Cambridge, Mass.: Harvard University Press, 1964), pp. 55-57.

50. *Royal Commission* (1902), pp. 134-67.

51. For wage rates in coal mines see Government of British Columbia, *Sessional Papers* (1899), 1169; for rates in lumber mills see *Royal Commission* (1902), p. 126.

52. Willmott, "Study of the Chinese," pp. 40-41; idem, "Chinese Clan Associations in Vancouver," *Man* 49 (March-April 1964): 33.

53. Leo Kuper, "Plural Societies: Perspectives and Problems," *Pluralism in Africa*, ed. Leo Kuper and M. G. Smith (Berkeley: University of California Press, 1969), pp. 7-26.

54. M. G. Smith, "Some Developments in the Analytic Framework of Pluralism," *Pluralism in Africa*, pp. 415-58.

55. H. Hoetink, *The Two Variants in Caribbean Race Relations: A Contribution to the Sociology of Segmented Societies*, trans. Eva M. Hooykaas (London: Oxford University Press, 1967), pp. 120-26; idem, "National Identity and Somatic Norm Image," *Ethnicity and Nation Building: Comparative, International, and Historical Perspectives*, ed. Wendell Bell and Walter E. Freeman (Beverly Hills and London: Sage Publications 1974), pp. 29-44.

56. Hoetink, *Two Variants*, pp. 106-10. For another historian's interpretation of Hoetink's theory see George M. Fredrickson, *The Black Image in the White Mind: The Debate on Afro-American Character and Destiny, 1817-1914* (New York: Harper and Row, 1971), pp. 131-32.

57. Government of Canada, *Senate Debates* (1886), 681.

58. In plural societies racial stereotypes usually serve several other important functions. In defining the social essence of racial distinctions they strengthen the communal identity of each racial segment by contrasting its own character with that of the others. Also, as Allport has suggested (p. 192), they rationalize, or justify, the conduct of one race toward the other. In particular they legitimize exploitation and other forms of differential treatment based upon race.

CHAPTER 2

1. The first Chinese on the north Pacific coast arrived with Capt. John Meares in 1788. Engaged in the transpacific fur trade, Meares brought fifty of them to act as carpenters and labourers, intending them to form the nucleus of a permanent settlement. In the following year, however, during the Nootka Sound dispute, they were sent back to China by the Spaniard Martinez who had seized Meares' boats. Charles James Woodsworth, *Canada and the Orient: A Study in International Relations* (Toronto: Macmillan, 1941), p. 5.

2. E. O. S. Scholefield and R. E. Gosnell, *A History of British Columbia* (Vancouver and Victoria: British Columbia Historical Association, 1913), pt. I, 185; *Colonist*, Mar. 28, 1861.

3. On anti-Chinese outbursts in the gold fields of California, see Leonard Pitt, "The Beginnings of Nativism in California," *Pacific Historical Review* 30 (February 1961): 23-38; Rodman W. Paul, "The Origin of the Chinese Issue in California," *The Mississippi Valley Historical Review* 25 (September 1938): 182-96; Mary Roberts Coolidge, *Chinese Immigration* (New York: Henry Holt, 1909); Elmer Clarence

Sandmeyer, *The Anti-Chinese Movement in California* (Urbana, Ill.: University of Illinois Press, 1939); Gunther Barth, *Bitter Strength: A History of the Chinese in the United States, 1850-1870* (Cambridge, Mass.: Harvard University Press, 1964).

4. Charles A. Price, *The Great White Walls are Built: Restrictive Immigration to North America and Australasia 1836-1888* (Canberra: Australian National University Press, 1974), chaps. 3 and 4.

5. W. Wymond Walkem, *Stories of Early British Columbia* (Vancouver: *News-Advertiser*, 1914), p. 123.

6. *The Handbook of British Columbia and Emigrant's Guide to the Gold Fields* (London, 1862), p. 62.

7. *Colonist*, Aug. 17, 1865.

8. Ibid., July 1, 1861.

9. *The Victoria Gazette*, Mar. 31, 1859.

10. Douglas to Newcastle, Apr. 23, 1860, Great Britain, *Imperial Blue Books on Affairs Relating to Canada*, vol. 39, Further Papers Relative to the Affairs of British Columbia, pt. IV (1862), 5.

11. *Colonist*, Mar. 6, 1860.

12. Duncan G. F. Macdonald, *British Columbia and Vancouver's Island, Comprising a Description of these Dependencies*... (London, 1862), pp. 299-302.

13. J. S. Helmcken, "Reminiscences," Helmcken Papers, 218-19, PABC.

14. Florence Goodfellow, *Memories of Pioneer Life in British Columbia* (Wenatchee, Wash.: n.p., 1945), p. 14.

15. Macdonald, *British Columbia and Vancouver's Island*, p. 299.

16. *Christian Guardian*, Feb. 15, 1860.

17. Douglas to Newcastle, Dec. 18, 1860, *Blue Book, 1860*, p. 25.

18. *Colonist*, May 10, 1860.

19. Ibid., July 1, 1861 and Mar. 8, 1862.

20. Matthew Macfie, *Vancouver Island and British Columbia: Their History, Resources and Prospects* (London, 1865), pp. 382-88.

21. *Cariboo Sentinel*, June 1, 1868.

22. A. Allan to [J. K.] Suter, Jan. 6, 1870, Alexander Allan Letterbook, PABC.

23. John Evans, Diary, Dec. 12, 1863, PABC.

24. *Colonist*, May 19, 1865.

25. Ibid., Jan. 27, 1871.

26. Ibid., Sept. 2 and 5, 1871; British Columbia, *Journals of the Legislative Assembly* (1872), 15-16.

27. *Colonist*, Feb. 27, 1872; British Columbia, *Statutes*, 35 Vict. c.37, s.13. In 1876, soon after several Chinese voted in Victoria's civic elections, the legislature extended the prohibition to all municipal electoral contests, British Columbia, *Statutes*, 39 Vict., c.1, s.9.

28. Ibid., 35 Vict., c.26, s.22.

29. *Colonist*, May 16, 1873.

30. British Columbia, *Journals* (1876), 37-38.

31. *Colonist*, July 22, 1875 and May 2, 1876.

32. Ibid., May 8, 9, and 10, and June 15 and 21, 1878. While racial tensions

were heightened, the Victoria City Council also stepped up its own campaign against the Chinese. In 1878 and 1879 it passed two by-laws clearly aimed at them, one to deal with sanitation in Chinese wash-houses, the other to prevent over-crowding in dwellings. Victoria, *By-Laws of the City of Victoria* (consolidated, 1877), nos. 42 and 56.

33. British Columbia, *Journals* (1878), 82; British Columbia, *Statutes*, 42 Vict., c.35; *Colonist*, Aug. 6 and 8, 1878.

34. Ibid., Aug. 9 and 11, and Sept. 18, 1878; Tai Sing v. Maguire, 1 *British Columbia Reports*, pt. 1, 101-13.

35. *Colonist*, Sept. 3, Nov. 1 and 5, and Dec. 11, 1878; Workingmen's Protective Association, *Constitution, By-Laws and Rules of Order of the Workingmen's Protective Association* (Victoria, 1878).

36. *Colonist*, Jan. 7, 1879.

37. Ibid., Oct. 10 and 13, 1879, and Mar. 9, 1880; Pierre Berton, *The Last Spike: The Great Railway, 1881-1885* (Toronto: McClelland and Stewart, 1971), p. 194.

38. British Columbia, *Journals* (1879), 2.

39. Canada, *Commons Debates* (1878), 1207-11; Select Committee, "Report," Canada, *Journals of the House of Commons* (1879), app. 4.

40. Onderdonk to Macdonald, June 14, 1882, Macdonald Papers, PAC.

CHAPTER 3

1. *British Columbian* (New Westminster), May 24, 1882.

2. *Colonist*, July 8 and 9, and Aug. 3, 1882.

3. *Inland Sentinel* (Kamloops), May 17, 1883; *Colonist*, May 15, 16, 19, and 27, 1883.

4. Morley Roberts, *The Western Avernus: or Toil and Travel in Further North America*, 2nd ed. (Westminster, 1896), p. 132.

5. *Free Press*, April 26, 1879. Statistics on mining accidents, however, do not bear out the miners' claim. See the annual reports of the minister of mines in the British Columbia *Sessional Papers* during the late nineteenth century. Since 1877 legislation had forbidden the employment of Chinese in responsible positions in mines.

6. Allan Donald Orr, "The Western Federation of Miners and the Royal Commission on Industrial Disputes in 1903 with Special Reference to the Vancouver Island Coal Miners' Strike" (M.A. thesis, University of British Columbia, 1968), pp. 44-51.

7. British Columbia, *Statutes*, 47 Vict., c.2, c.3, and c.4. Other anti-Chinese legislation passed during this session included an act to prevent graveyard desecration (introduced because of past objections to Chinese exhumations) and a measure which tightened existing franchise restrictions by declaring the Chinese ineligible to vote for school trustees. Ibid., 47 Vict., c.11 and c.27, s.10.

8. Macdonald to Smithe, Apr. 10, 1884, British Columbia, *Sessional Papers* (1885), 9.

9. Report of Commissioner Chapleau, *Royal Commission* (1885), pp. viii-ix.

10. Ibid., pp. cxxx, cxxxii-cxxxiii.

11. Report of Commissioner Gray, ibid., pp. lxxxii, cii.

12. Ibid., pp. lxxxvi-lxxxix; Report of Commissioner Chapleau, ibid., p. cxxxiii.

13. *Colonist*, Mar. 6, 1885; Canada, *Commons Debates* (1885), 3019.

14. British Columbia, *Statutes*, 48 Vict., c.13.

15. Onderdonk to Steven, n.d., Macdonald Papers, 122695-96a.

16. Canada, *Commons Journals* (1885), passim.

17. This provision was an amendment to the interpretation section of the bill. It declared that for the purposes of the act the term "person" was not intended to include Chinese or Mongolians. Canada, *Statutes*, 48-49 Vict., c.40, s.2.

18. Canada, *Commons Debates* (1885), 1585.

19. Ibid., 1582.

20. *Colonist*, May 22, 1885.

21. Ibid., Nov. 11, 1885.

22. Canada, *Statutes*, 48-49 Vict., c.71.

23. *Colonist*, Nov. 11, 1885.

24. Ibid., Jan. 20 and 30, 1886.

25. *Industrial News* (Victoria), Jan. 30, 1886.

26. *Colonist*, Mar. 14, 1886.

27. *Vancouver News*, Nov. 26, 1886.

28. Ibid., Dec. 7, 1886.

29. Ibid., Jan. 8, 1887.

30. Ibid., Jan. 9, 1887.

31. Ibid., Jan. 11 and 12, 1887.

32. *Colonist*, Feb. 11, 1887.

33. Ibid., Jan. 23, 1887.

34. *News*, Feb. 16, 1887.

35. Ibid., Feb. 25 and 26, 1887; *Colonist*, Feb. 26 and 27, 1887.

36. *Vancouver Daily World*, June 3, 1892.

37. Ibid., Apr. 22, 1889; *Colonist*, Dec. 19, 1889.

38. *Free Press*, Feb. 8, 1888.

39. *Industrial News*, May 29, 1886; *Free Press*, May 27, 1890 and Mar. 7, 1894.

40. Trades and Labor Congress of Canada, *Proceedings* (1891), pp. 10-13; ibid. (1893), p. 19.

41. Canada, *Commons Journals* (1885, 1887, 1891, 1892, 1893), passim.

42. *Colonist*, Feb. 28, 1904.

43. Executive Committee of the Chinese Consolidated Benevolent Association to Macdonald, Aug. 4, 1886, Macdonald Papers, 151852-56.

44. *Colonist*, Nov. 22, 1885; Jan. 31, 1897; Oct. 2, 1898.

45. "Report of the Commissioners appointed to inquire into the late epidemic outbreak of Smallpox in the Province of British Columbia," British Columbia, *Sessional Papers* (1893), 507-18.

46. *Colonist*, Oct. 26, 1892.

47. Ibid., Mar. 10, 1893; Victoria, *Annual Report* (1893), 35-36. As an incident in Calgary indicated, fear of the Chinese threat to public health was far from confined to the Pacific coast. Late in June 1892, while smallpox alarmed Victoria and Vancouver, the disease appeared in a Chinese laundry in Calgary. Soon the laundry's white neighbours were infected. Meanwhile civic authorities had quarantined the victims and burned the offending laundry to the ground. Anti-Chinese animus welled up when two whites died of the disease. Consequently tempers were high when the quarantined Chinese were released early on August 2. Late that evening a drunken mob of three hundred attacked the city's Chinese laundries and other Chinese dwellings. They demolished one building and forced the entire Chinese community to flee. Order was restored only when the local mounted police detachment intervened, and for the next several days the Chinese took refuge in the NWMP barracks while the Mounted Police patrolled the city. Inspector A. Ross Cuthbert to the Commissioner, July 22 and Aug. 19, 1892. RCMP Papers, vol. 68, file 521, PAC; Cuthbert to the Commissioner, Aug. 3 and 5, 1892, ibid., vol. 69, file 615.

48. Victoria, *Annual Report* (1892), 89.

49. *Daily News-Advertiser* (Vancouver), Aug. 18, 1896.

50. *Colonist*, Jan. 16 and 20, 1900.

51. Victoria, *Annual Report* (1893), 68.

52. *Colonist*, Nov. 26, 1892.

53. *Province* (Vancouver), Apr. 27, 1900.

54. Victoria, *By-Laws of the City of Victoria* (consolidated 1901), no. 354; Vancouver, *By-Laws of the City of Vancouver* (consolidated 1902), no. 373.

55. *Colonist*, Sept. 8 and 9, 1886.

56. Ibid., May 21, 1891; Ernest Hall and John Nelson, "The Lepers of D'Arcy Island," *Dominion Medical Monthly and Ontario Medical Journal* 11, no. 6 (1898): 3-10.

CHAPTER 4

1. Natural increase contributed little to the growth of the Chinese, Japanese, and East Indian communities in British Columbia before World War I. The great majority of Asian migrants during these years were male sojourners. As relatively few Oriental women resided in Canada, and as miscegenation was almost unknown, the number of children born of Asiatic ancestry was low.

2. The Japanese lost the franchise in 1895, the East Indians in 1907. British Columbia, *Statutes*, 58 Vict., c. 20, s.3; 58 Vict., c. 65, s. 3; 59 Vict., c. 38; 7 Ed. VII, c. 16; 8 Ed. VII, c. 14.

3. Ibid., 60 Vict., c. 1. For correspondence relating to the act's disallowance see Francis H. Gisborne and Arthur A. Fraser, comp., *Correspondence, Reports of the Minister of Justice and Orders in Council upon the Subject of Provincial Legislation, 1896-1920* (Ottawa: King's Printer, 1922), pp. 530-33.

4. British Columbia, *Statutes*, 61 Vict., c. 28. Laurier to Joseph Martin, Jan. 28, 1899, private and confidential, Laurier Papers, 29733, PAC. Chamberlain to the Governor-General of Canada, April 19, 1899, Canada, *Sessional Papers* (1899), no. 110, 25-26. Seizaburo Shimizu, Japanese Consul, Victoria to Aberdeen, May 10, 16, 20, and 28, 1898, British Columbia, *Sessional Papers* (1899), 716-18.

5. *Colonist*, May 2, 1900.

6. *Industrial World* (Rossland), Apr. 28, 1900.

7. *Colonist*, May 15, 1900.

8. British Columbia, *Statutes*, 64 Vict., c. 11 and c. 14. The Natal Act, recently approved in the colony of Natal, restricted immigration to those with knowledge of a European language. Chamberlain favoured it because it permitted exclusion while it avoided giving offence to friendly nations by declaring their peoples undesirable immigrants. Robert A. Huttenback, *Racism and Empire: White Settlers and Colored Immigrants in the British Self-Governing Colonies, 1830-1910* (Ithaca, N.Y. and London: Cornell University Press, 1976), pp. 139-42.

9. Dunsmuir to Laurier, Oct. 9, 1900, British Columbia, *Sessional Papers* (1901), 546-48.

10. British Columbia, *Statutes*, 2 Ed. VII, c. 34 and c. 38.

11. Ibid., 2 Ed. VII, c. 39.

12. Order in Council 245, May 26, 1902 and Order in Council 275, June 16, 1902. The orders were not rigorously enforced.

13. Memorandum of E. G. Prior, n.d., Canada, *Sessional Papers* (1903), no. 78, 36-38.

14. Laurier to Rev. A. Carmen, Apr. 29, 1899, Laurier Papers, 31995, PAC.

15. D. McNicoll to Laurier, July 8, 1899, ibid., 35129-30.

16. Laurier to J. Martin, Jan. 28, 1899, private and confidential, ibid., 29733.

17. Canada, *Commons Debates* (1900), 7056-57, 7408-09, 7412.

18. Ralph Smith, a prominent figure in the provincial labour movement and MPP from Nanaimo, was first appointed to the commission. But in November 1900 he was elected to the House of Commons and therefore resigned from the commission. Foley replaced him early in 1901.

19. *Royal Commission* (1902), p. 278.

20. Ibid., p. 279.

21. Ibid., p. 397.

22. Ibid., pp. 399-400.

23. Charlotte Reid to Laurier, Apr. 5 [1903], Laurier Papers, 72170-73.

24. *Colonist*, Feb. 14, 1901.

25. Ibid., Jan. 26, 1902.

26. Ibid., Apr. 20, 1902.

27. Alexander Robinson, Superintendent of Education, to F. H. Eaton, Secretary, Victoria School Board, Sept. 16, 1902, British Columbia, Superintendent of Education, Letterbooks, PABC.

28. *Colonist*, Oct. 30, 1902.

29. Ibid., Nov. 4, 12, and 13, 1902.

30. Ibid., Jan. 17, 1904 and June 15, 1905.

31. Ibid., Aug. 24, 27, 29, and 31, 1907. Later the board relented somewhat and permitted all Chinese born in Canada to attend public schools, whether their command of English was adequate or not.

32. *Times*, Nov. 14, 1907.

33. Ibid., Mar. 28, 1908.

34. *Colonist*, Apr. 9 and Oct. 15, 1908.

35. *The Province* (Vancouver), Feb. 11, 1908.

36. *The Paystreak* (Sandon), Nov. 5, 1898; *Atlin Claim*, Mar. 15, 22, and 29, 1902; *Province*, Apr. 10, 1905; *Daily News* (Nelson), Apr. 27, 1905; F. H. Hussey, Superintendent, Provincial Police to McBride, May 14, 1905, Richard McBride Papers, Letters Inward, Official, 1904/05, file 997, PABC; *Province*, Mar. 23 and 28, and Apr. 2, 1906; *Kelowna Courier*, Apr. 5, 1906. A similar incident occurred in the Yukon in July 1902. When five Chinese arrived in Whitehorse to establish a brickyard, they were quickly run out of town. Morris Zaslow, *The Opening of the Canadian North, 1870-1914* (Toronto: McClelland and Stewart, 1971), p. 118. Japanese workers were again expelled from Atlin in 1907. *Times*, Sept. 21, 1907.

37. *World*, Sept. 1 and Oct. 26, 1906.

38. *News-Advertiser*, Oct. 16 and 18, 1908; *World*, Oct. 17, 1908.

39. E. Blake Robertson to W. D. Scott, Dec. 27, 1906, Rodolphe Lemieux Papers, I, 74-76, PAC.

40. Canada, *Report of W. L. Mackenzie King, C.M.G., Commissioner Appointed to Enquire into the Methods by Which Oriental Labourers have been Induced to Come to Canada* (Ottawa: King's Printer, 1908), pp. 25-53.

41. The city editor of the *Province*, for example, declared that the Japanese "does not assimilate and never will. His sons and daughters will never be Canadians. They will always, in reality, owe allegiance to the Mikado." R. Brown, "White Canada," *Harper's Weekly*, October 5, 1907, pp. 1446-47. See below, chap. 6.

42. *News-Advertiser*, July 25, 1907.

43. Macpherson to Laurier, Aug. 20, 1907, Laurier Papers, 127979-80.

44. *Colonist*, Aug. 25, 1907.

45. Laurier to Macpherson, Aug. 27, 1907, Laurier Papers, 127981-82.

46. *News-Advertiser*, Aug. 13, 1907.

47. *Province*, Aug. 24 and 26, 1907.

48. *Colonist*, Sept. 10, 1907.

49. Contemporary accounts of the protest meeting and riot can be found in: *News-Advertiser*, Sept. 8, 1907; *World*, Sept. 9, 1907; *Province*, Sept. 9, 1907; *Colonist*, Sept. 8 and 10, 1907; McInnes to Oliver, Oct. 2, 1907, Governor General's Numbered Files, file 332, vol. 1, PAC; G. Payne, Secretary, Asiatic Exclusion League to Laurier, Sept. 9, 1907, Laurier Papers, 128836-40; testimony of Rufus D. Chamberlain, Chief of Police, and Charles Mulhern, Inspector, Vancouver Police, Royal Commission on Japanese Claims, Minutes of Evidence, 1907, William Lyon Mackenzie King Papers, MG 26, J4, c33816, c33833-34, c33838-39, and c33844-45, PAC.

50. Four of those who stood on the platform before the riot broke out were American. Two, Fowler and Young, were in town for the meeting while the other two, Von Rhein and Fraser, were American citizens resident in Vancouver, the latter, however, having been born in Canada. For a useful theoretical discussion of hostile outbursts see Neil J. Smelser, *Theory of Collective Behavior* (New York: Free Press, 1962), especially chap. VIII.

51. King to Laurier, Nov. 9, 1907, Laurier Papers, 131662-64.

52. McInnes to Oliver, Oct. 2, 1907, Governor General's Numbered Files, file 332, vol. 1. McInnes (who later changed the spelling of his name to MacInnes) was the son of Dr. T. R. McInnes, a former senator and lieutenant-governor of British Columbia and the brother of W. W. B. McInnes, once a flamboyant Liberal member of the House of Commons and later a leading figure in provincial politics. Four days after the riot he wrote to Laurier and volunteered reliable inside information

on the league and west coast public opinion regarding the Oriental question. His offer was accepted and throughout the life of the league he supplied frequent lengthy reports on its activities and influence.

53. *Province*, Sept. 21 and 24, 1907.

54. *Colonist*, Oct. 4, 1907; *British Columbian*, Nov. 1, 1907; McInnes to Laurier, Nov. 18, 1907, Laurier Papers, 131596-98.

55. McInnes to F. Oliver, Feb. 16, 1908, Governor General's Numbered Files, file 332A.

56. McInnes to Laurier, Jan. 9 and 26, 1908, Laurier Papers, 134909-12, 135595-98.

57. *Colonist*, Sept. 6, 1908.

58. Louis D. Taylor to Laurier, Oct. 12, 1907, telegram, Laurier Papers, 130446.

59. Elgin to Grey, Dec. 12, 1907, Governor General's Numbered Files, file 332, vol. 1, and Elgin to Grey, Jan. 4, 1908, ibid., vol. 2a.

60. Canada, *Report on Oriental Labourers Induced to Come to Canada*, pp. 53-54.

61. Ibid., pp. 76-80.

62. Charles J. Woodsworth, *Canada and the Orient: A Study in International Relations* (Toronto: Macmillan, 1941), app. E., pp. 294-95; for a detailed discussion of Lemieux' negotiations see Robert Joseph Gowen, "Canada's Relations with Japan, 1895-1922" (Ph.D. thesis, University of Chicago, 1966), pp. 142-91.

63. "Report by the Honourable Rodolphe Lemieux, K. C., Minister of Labour, of his Mission to Japan on the Subject of the Influx of Oriental Labourers into the Province of British Columbia, 1908," confidential, 9, Lemieux Papers, 1051.

64. R. L. Borden, *The Question of Oriental Immigration: Speeches (in part) Delivered by R. L. Borden, M. P. in 1907 and 1908* (n.p., n.d.), p. 9.

65. Canada, *Commons Debates* (1907-08), 699-753.

66. "Report of the Department of Labour for the Fiscal Year 1907-08," Canada, *Sessional Papers* (1909), no. 36, pp. 100-101. Subsequently this order was entrenched in statutory law. Canada, *Statutes*, 7-8 Ed. VII, c. 33.

67. In 1910 Parliament clarified the federal government's powers to prohibit immigration. The Immigration Act of that year permitted the Governor General-in-Council to bar the entry of immigrants of any race, class, occupation, or character which it deemed unsuited to the country. In this particular instance public opinion had little influence on the measure. It was merely a refinement of existing law and took its origins from within the civil service. Canada, *Statutes*, 9-10 Ed. VII, c. 38.

68. W. Templeman to Laurier, Nov. 5, 1908, Laurier Papers, 147227-30.

CHAPTER 5

1. *Canada Year Book*, 1915, 117; *Census of Canada*, 1911; W. Hopkinson to F. Oliver, Sept. 6, 1908, Laurier Papers, 144227-31. See table 2.

2. B. Lal, "East Indians in British Columbia: An Historical Study in Growth and Integration, 1904-1914" (M.A. thesis, University of British Columbia, 1976), pp. 13-49.

3. Canada, *Report of W. L. Mackenzie King, C.M.G., Commissioner Appointed to Enquire into the Methods by Which Oriental Labourers have been Induced to Come to Canada* (Ottawa: King's Printer, 1908), pp. 76, 80.

4. Lal, "East Indians," pp. 29-40.

5. Tom G. Kessinger, *Vilyatpur, 1848-1968: Social and Economic Change in a North Indian Village* (Berkeley: University of California Press, 1974), pp. 167-74.

6. Rajani Kanta Das, *Hindustani Workers on the Pacific Coast* (Berlin: W. de Gruyter, 1923), pp. 23-27.

7. Lal, "East Indians," pp. 50-97.

8. Ibid., pp. 98-129. For a description of modern American images of India and the Indians see Harold R. Isaacs, *Scratches on Our Minds: American Images of China and India* (New York: J. Day, 1958).

9. Scott, Memorandum re Immigration of Hindus to Canada, Nov. 2, 1906, Rodolphe Lemieux Papers, I, 82-83.

10. "Report by W. L. Mackenzie King, C.M.G., Deputy Minister of Labour, on his mission to England to confer with the British authorities on the subject of immigration to Canada from the Orient, and immigration from India in particular," Canada, *Sessional Papers* (1907-08), no. 36a, 7-8.

11. G. F. Gray, President, Victoria TLC, and others to [Scott], Oct. 15, 1906, Canada, Immigration Branch Records, Acc. 69/17, box 219, file 536999, PAC.

12. Ibid.

13. *Colonist*, Nov. 15, 1906.

14. C. Sivertz to Oliver, Dec. 17, 1906, Immigration Branch, Acc. 69/17, box 219, file 536999.

15. *World*, Oct. 19, 1906.

16. Ibid.; *Colonist*, Sept. 25 and Nov. 20, 1906; *Province*, Nov. 23, 1906.

17. Col. Falk Warren to Laurier, Jan. 2, 1907, Laurier Papers, 117771-74.

18. W. Munns, Secretary, Canadian Suffrage Association to Borden, Feb. 1, 1912, Borden Papers, 145287, PAC; Mrs. E. J. Kerr, Home Secretary, Woman's Missionary Society of the Methodist Church, Canada, to the Minister of Immigration [sic], Jan. 24, 1912, Immigration Branch, Acc. 69/17, box 219, file 536999.

19. Sunder Singh, "The Sikhs in Canada," *Empire Club Speeches, 1911-12* (Toronto, 1913), pp. 112-16; Eric W. Morse, "Immigration and Status of British East Indians in Canada: A Problem in Imperial Relations" (M.A. thesis, Queen's University, 1936), pp. 51-53; Canada India Committee, *The Hindu Case* (Toronto: n.p., 1915), p. 11.

20. In response to popular anti-Indian sentiment, the provincial legislature excluded all East Indians from the franchise during the session in 1907. W. J. Bowser, who introduced the bill, earned enthusiastic applause for his determination to keep British Columbia a white man's country. *Colonist*, Mar. 27, 1907; British Columbia, *Statutes*, 7 Ed. VII, c. 16.

21. *Memorandum Accompanying Report of W. L. Mackenzie King, C.M.G., Deputy Minister of Labour on his Mission to England to Confer with the British Authorities on the Subject of Immigration to Canada from the Orient, and Immigration from India in Particular* (Ottawa, 1908), p. 13; Elgin to Grey, Feb. 12, 1908, enclosing a telegram from the Government of India, Jan. 22, 1908, Governor General's Numbered Files, file 332, vol. 2a, PAC.

22. Laurier to Grey, Sept. 16, 1907, Grey of Howick Papers, 1581-82, PAC.

23. *Memorandum on Oriental Immigration*; "Report on Oriental Immigration," Canada, *Sessional Papers* (1907-08), no. 36a. In June 1908 a new order in council

required all Asians to possess $200 upon entry to Canada. *Canada Gazette,* June 20, 1908, 3276.

24. J. B. Harkin, *The East Indians in British Columbia: A Report regarding the proposal to provide work in British Honduras for the indigent unemployed among them* (Published under the authority of the Hon. Frank Oliver, Minister of the Interior, 1909), p. 3.

25. Ibid., pp. 3-4, 14; W. W. Cory to Laurier, Nov. 6, 1908, Laurier Papers, 147326-29.

26. Sivertz to Borden, Dec. 28, 1911, Borden Papers, 144735-36.

27. In re Narain Singh et al., 18 *British Columbia Reports,* 506. The orders were declared invalid because of inconsistencies and ambiguities in their construction.

28. Morse, "Status of British East Indians," pp. 71-80. While the order in council did not specifically exclude East Indians, in practice they were the only ones whose immigration was barred. The minister of the interior specifically exempted the Japanese, and Chinese immigration does not appear to have been curtailed.

29. Morse, "Some Aspects of the Komagata Maru Affair, 1914," Canadian Historical Association, *Report* (1936), p. 102; Lal, pp. 151-52.

30. Canada, *Commons Debates* (1914), 2639, 4214.

31. Re Munshi Singh, 20 *British Columbia Reports,* 243.

32. *News-Advertiser,* May 28, 1914; Canada, *Commons Debates* (1914), 4556-57.

33. June 2, 1914.

34. *World,* June 12, 1914.

35. *Western Methodist Recorder* 15, no. 1 (July 1914): 12.

36. R. McBride to Borden, June 23, 1914, Borden Papers, 17587.

37. *News-Advertiser,* June 24, 1914; Hopkinson to Cory, June 24, 1914, Governor General's Numbered Files, 332b, vol. 1b.

38. Minutes of a Public Meeting held in Dominion Hall, Vancouver, British Columbia, on Tuesday Evening, June 23, 1914, Borden Papers.

39. *British Columbian,* June 30, 1914.

40. "A Greater Britain on the Pacific," *Westward Ho! Magazine* 2, no. 1 (January 1908): 12.

CHAPTER 6

1. See above, chap. 1; Richard Austin Thompson, "The Yellow Peril, 1890-1924" (Ph.D. thesis, University of Wisconsin, 1957).

2. In emphasizing ritual suicide—hara-kiri—Puccini also stressed the cruel streak in the culture of Japan.

3. J. C. Calhoun Newton, *Japan: Country, Court, and People* (Toronto, 1899), pp. 280-401. Newton was an American missionary in Japan. His book was published in both the United States and Canada.

4. *Modern School Geography and Atlas,* 5th ed. (Toronto, 1876), p. 76. In an earlier edition, published in 1865, the text had depicted Japanese civilization as static. Seemingly the book's editors shared increasingly common assumptions about Japanese progressiveness.

5. Newton, *Japan,* p. 388.

6. For American perceptions of Japan after 1905 see Thompson, "Yellow Peril" and Roger Daniels, *The Politics of Prejudice: The Anti-Japanese Movement in California and the Struggle for Japanese Exclusion* (Gloucester, Mass.: Peter Smith, 1966), pp. 65-78.

7. "Asiatic Question," *Westward Ho! Magazine* 2, no. 3 (March 1908): 2.

8. Frank Buffington Vrooman, "Juijutsu and the Anglo-Japanese Alliance," *British Columbia Magazine* 8, no. 1 (January 1912): 64. For other examples see *Free Press*, Aug. 22, 1907; C. Phillips-Wolley, *The Canadian Naval Question* (Toronto: William Briggs, 1910), pp. 67-68.

9. Charles H. Stuart Wade, "The Pacific War of 1910," *Westward Ho! Magazine* 4, no. 6 (June 1909): 341-48. Episodes of the story appeared monthly in subsequent issues until May of 1910. In June the magazine's successor, *Man to Man*, took up the series and published the conclusion in its July-August issue. The quotation is from *Man to Man* 6, no. 7 (July-August 1910): 592.

10. Nigel Tourneur, "Naval Battle off Vancouver," *Westward Ho! Magazine* 4, no. 4 (April 1909): 215-18.

11. H. Glynn-Ward, *The Writing on the Wall* (Vancouver: *Sun*, 1921). H. Glynn-Ward was the pseudonym of Hilda Howard, local journalist and author.

12. Daniels, *Politics of Prejudice*, pp. 65-78.

13. For example see William Strange, *Canada, the Pacific, and War* (Toronto: Thomas Nelson and Sons, 1937); A. R. M. Lower, *Canada and the Far East—1940*, Institute of Pacific Relations Inquiry Series (New York: Institute of Pacific Relations, 1940); F. Leighton Thomas, *Japan: The Octopus of the East and its Menace to Canada* (Vancouver: n.p., 1932).

14. Aug. 7, 1921.

15. For example, see *Province*, Apr. 29, 1925, Sept. 30, 1933, and Nov. 2, 1935.

16. See above, p. 7.

17. *Royal Commission* (1902), pp. 337-39, testimony of J. Wilson, C. Phillips-Wolley, and W. H. Ellis.

18. Testimony of Hugh McRae, Nanaimo, Feb. 5, 1902, Evidence given at the Sittings of the B.C. Salmon Commission (typescript), Canada, Department of Fisheries, Acc. 67/24, box 137, file 2918, pt. 3, PAC. *Evidence Submitted to a Dominion Fishery Commission known as the British Columbia Fisheries Commission, 1905-1906* (Victoria, 1906), pp. 101-2, testimony of H. Wright. See also *Province*, Oct. 23, 1919 and *The Comox Argus*, May 27, 1920.

19. W. E. Payne to King, Jan. 25, 1923, Immigration Branch acc. 69/17; box 252, file 729921; *Province*, May 29, 1927.

20. "Chinese and Japanese," in *Canadian Problems*, ed. W. R. McIntosh (Toronto: R. Douglas Fraser, 1910), p. 53.

21. E. O. S. Scholefield and F. W. Howay, *British Columbia, from the Earliest Times to the Present* (Vancouver: S. J. Clark, 1914), II, 576. For a similar, later remark see Lukin Johnston, "British Columbia's Oriental Problem," *United Empire*, n.s. 13, no. 9 (September 1922): 570-76.

22. *Abbotsford, Matsqui, and Sumas News*, Nov. 10, 1924.

23. Letter to the editor, *Province*, Aug. 11, 1934 (magazine section).

24. Maj. Rowland Brittain to the Assistant Director of Intelligence, Sept. 5, 1908, Governor General's Numbered Files, file 332, vol. 2b.

25. *Province*, Apr. 29, 1933; *Sun*, Nov. 24, 1937. For examples of similar American attitudes see Dennis Ogawa, *From Japs to Japanese: An Evolution of Japanese-American Stereotypes* (Berkeley: McCutchan, 1971), pp. 16-22.

26. Canada, *Commons Debates*, Mar. 23, 1923, 1445-52; *Province*, Apr. 29, 1933; *Colonist*, Jan. 19, 1938.

27. George Godwin, *Columbia, or the Future of Canada* (London: Kegan Paul, Trench, Trubner and Co., 1928), pp. 35-36. For another example see *Canada's Oriental Province*, a pamphlet published in 1930 by Charles E. Hope, a leading Vancouver nativist.

28. *British Columbia Federationist*, Apr. 10, 1914.

29. *The Penticton Herald*, Jan. 1, 1920. For a fictional account of Japanese land purchases and the white response to it see George Godwin, *The Eternal Forest* (London: Philip Allan, 1929), pp. 106-13.

30. *Colonist*, May 13, 1905; *The Daily News* (Prince Rupert), Oct. 29, 1921; *Province*, Jan. 10, 1928.

31. *Royal Commission* (1902), p. 382, testimony of Steven Ramage, saw filer.

32. Laurier Papers, 117308-572.

33. Forrest E. LaViolette, *The Canadian Japanese and World War II: A Sociological and Psychological Account* (Toronto: University of Toronto Press, 1948), pp. 16-17.

34. See Table 2.

35. *Royal Commission* (1902), p. 327.

36. *Canada Year Book*, 1945, 175.

37. Charles H. Young and Helen R. Y. Reid, *The Japanese Canadians* (Toronto: University of Toronto Press, 1938), p. 30.

38. Ibid., pp. 15-17. Comparable sex ratios for the Chinese were 28 to 1 in 1911 and 15 to 1 in 1921.

39. Ibid., pp. 27-28.

40. Canada, Department of Labour, *Report of British Columbia Security Commission* (1942), p. 3.

41. Rigenda Sumida, "The Japanese in British Columbia" (M.A. thesis, University of British Columbia, 1935), pp. 53-55.

42. Ibid., p. 61; Young and Reid, *Japanese Canadians*, p. 28.

43. Sumida, "Japanese in British Columbia," pp. 46-51.

44. *Royal Commission* (1902), pp. 360-71.

45. By the mid-1920s the Japanese constituted approximately 8 per cent of the work force in the forest industries, including pulp and paper. Together with the Chinese and East Indians they comprised about 20 per cent of those employed in the industry. See British Columbia, "Annual Report of the Department of Labour," *Sessional Papers*, for the middle years of the decade.

46. W. A. Carrothers, "Oriental Standards of Living," in Young and Reid, *Japanese Canadians*, pp. 239-45.

47. *Royal Commission* (1902), pp. 360-70; British Columbia, "Annual Report of the Minister of Mines," *Sessional Papers* (1905), J225.

48. Young and Reid, *Japanese Canadians*, pp. 85-95.

49. The Methodist Church (and later the United Church) claimed the largest number of adherents among the Japanese, although the Catholic and Anglican

churches won significant numbers of converts as well. Tadashi Mitsui, "The Ministry of the United Church of Canada Amongst Japanese Canadians in British Columbia, 1892-1949" (M.S.Th. thesis, Union College of British Columbia, 1964).

50. Young and Reid, *Japanese Canadians*, p. 99.

51. Ibid., pp. 107-18.

52. Ibid., pp. 70-72; *Census of Canada*, 1901-1941.

53. Carrothers, "Standards of Living," pp. 291-92.

54. British Columbia, Attorney General's Files, file 2060-17-18, PABC; H. D. Wilson Papers, vol. I, files 19 and 20, PABC.

55. The other major exceptions could be found in hawking and peddling, laundering, and greengrocery sales, all heavily dominated by the Chinese.

56. For a fuller statement of this point and its theoretical underpinnings see above, pp. 19-22.

CHAPTER 7

1. Norbert MacDonald, "Population Growth and Change in Seattle and Vancouver, 1880-1960," *Pacifiic Historical Review* 39, no. 3 (August 1970): 305, 311.

2. See table 2.

3. Harry Keith Ralston, "The 1900 Strike of Fraser River Sockeye Salmon Fishermen" (M.A. thesis, University of British Columbia, 1965), p. 48; W. A. Carrothers, "Oriental Standards of Living," in Young and Reid, *Japanese Canadians*, table III, p. 251.

4. Ralston, "1900 Strike," pp. 47-51; *News Advertiser*, July 15 and 18, 1893; Petition to the Hon. C. H. Tupper, Minister of Marines and Fisheries, n.d., Trades and Labor Congress of Canada, *Proceedings* (1893), pp. 21-23.

5. Ralston, "1900 Strike," pp. 100-102.

6. Ibid., pp. 105-67.

7. E. P. Bremner to D. Mills, Aug. 11, 1900, Canada, Department of Fisheries, acc. 67/24, box 135, file 2864, PAC.

8. Percy Gladstone and Stuart Jamieson, "Unionism in the Fishing Industry of British Columbia," *Canadian Journal of Economics and Political Science* 16, no. 2 (May 1950): 146-59.

9. Testimony of H. Wright, *Evidence Submitted to a Dominion Fishery Commission known as the British Columbia Fisheries Commission, 1905-6* (Victoria, 1906), pp. 101-102.

10. *Federationist*, May 1, 1914.

11. Memorandum Re. Change in Policy Governing British Columbia Salmon Fishing and Canning Industries, December 17, 1919, Canada, Department of Fisheries, acc. 71E5, file 721-4-6, PAC, Record Centre, Ottawa.

12. C. C. Ballentyne to H. S. Clements, Nov. 22, 1919, telegram, ibid., vol. 20. For the fishermen's representations to the department see ibid., vols. 20 and 21, passim.

13. Order in Council PC 2552, ibid., vol. 21.

14. *Comox Argus*, May 27, 1920; *Colonist*, Nov. 12, 1921; J. G. Glenwright to the Minister, Jan. 13, 1922, Canada, Department of Fisheries, acc. 71E5, file 721-4-6, vol. 32; Neill to Lapointe, Feb. 12, 1922, ibid.

15. *Daily News* (Prince Rupert), Aug. 14 and 15, 1922.

16. The 40 per cent reduction applied primarily to gill-net licences. The department had already decided to reduce Japanese trolling licences by one-third, an amount the commission deemed satisfactory. Canada, British Columbia Fisheries Commission, 1922, *Report and Recommendations* (Ottawa 1923), pp. 11-13.

17. Memorandum Re. British Columbian Fisheries Reference as it Affects Citizens of Oriental Origin, W. A. Found, September 10, 1929, Canada, Department of External Affairs, vol. 1549, file 714, PAC.

18. *Province*, July 9, 1932; *Sun*, July 3, 1934; *Free Press*, Feb. 25, 1938; *Sun*, Mar. 13, 1939.

19. *World*, June 10, 1908; T. R. E. McInnes to E. J. Lemaire, Feb. 1, 1910, Laurier Papers, 166014-16; Resolution of the Associated Boards of Trade of the Okanagan Valley, Dec. 16 and 17, 1913, McBride Papers, Letters Inward, Official, 1913.

20. *News Advertiser*, Feb. 8, 1917; *World*, Nov. 6, 1917. Notwithstanding their aversion to Chinese immigration, the British Columbia Fruit Growers' Association urged the temporary removal of the head tax for agricultural labour (on the proviso that the entrants remain only a limited time) in order to meet the wartime labour shortage on provincial fruit farms. *Province*, Feb. 14, 1917.

21. G. O. Buchanan to President of the Council, Jan. 16, 1919, British Columbia, Premiers' Correspondence, 1920, Correspondence Inward, file 60, PABC; M. A. Middleton to Oliver, Dec. 24, 1919, ibid.; W. E. Chapple to Oliver, Sept. 2, 1920, ibid.; J. Greig to Oliver, July 20, 1921, Premiers' Correspondence, 1921, Correspondence Inward, file 60; *Province*, Feb. 6, 1920; *Penticton Herald*, June 10, 1920; *Vernon News*, Apr. 21, 1921.

22. *Herald*, Dec. 4, 11, and 23, 1919 and Jan. 8 and 15, 1920; *Sun*, Jan. 16, 1920; *Kelowna Courier*, Jan. 22, 1920.

23. Ibid.

24. *Province*, Feb. 20, 1919.

25. *Times*, May 16, 1919.

26. *Province*, Jan. 14, 1920.

27. Ibid., Sept. 14, 1921; *Colonist*, Nov. 29, 1921.

28. Ibid., Mar. 1, 1922; *Times*, Mar. 23, 1922.

29. *Province*, Apr. 23, 1923.

30. D. Stuart to T. A. Crerar, May 8, 1922, Crerar Papers, box 117, ser. III, Queen's University Archives.

31. W. E. Payne to King, Jan. 25, 1923, Immigration Branch, acc. 69/17, box 252, file 729921.

32. British Columbia, "Annual Report of the Department of Agriculture," *Sessional Papers* (1922), U147. In 1921 there were 850 square miles of improved farmland in the province. M. C. Urquhart and K. A. H. Buckley, *Historical Statistics of Canada* (Toronto: Macmillan, 1965), p. 352.

33. Patricia E. Roy, "The Oriental 'Menace' in British Columbia," *Historical Essays on British Columbia*, ed. J. Friesen and H. K. Ralston (Toronto: McClelland and Stewart, 1976), p. 245.

34. Vancouver, Trades Licenses, 1921, Vancouver City Archives.

35. *Province*, Feb. 18, 1922. Fewer than 300 of the 1,000 Asian students in city schools were segregated at this time.

36. *Times*, Aug. 29 and Sept. 6, 1922; *Colonist*, Sept. 6 and 14, 1922.

37. *Times*, Sept. 4, 1923. Segregation was also enforced in other communities, notably in Steveston in 1925 when the trustees barred the school doors to Japanese entirely. Tadashi Mitsui, "The Ministry of the United Church of Canada Amongst Japanese Canadians in British Columbia, 1892-1949" (M.S. Th. thesis, Union College of British Columbia, 1964), pp. 132-34.

38. *Province*, Oct. 17, 1919 and May 4, 1921. The following poem, published early in 1919, suggests the veterans' mood.

A WHITE B.C.
By the Bellman—Apologies to Kipling.

"What is it black agin' the sky?" the war worn veteran cried.
"Its the C. P. R. Mounteagle, a-comin' up the tide."
"What is it crowdin' up her decks?" the war worn veteran said.
"It's the Chinks they're shipping in, old top, 500 bucks a head."
"They're shipping out our own boys to fight the Bolshevik,
And they're letting in the yellow men by hundreds every week."

"I need a job, and need it bad," the war worn veteran said.
"You'll never find it here, old top," the longshore loafer said.
"But I fought for King and country, and they told me when I went,
My job would be awaiting, and every effort spent."
"You're out of luck; your dope's all wrong," the longshore loafer said.
"Your pals aren't so unlucky that lie in Flanders, dead."

"Oh, they're bringing in the yellow men, so don't downhearted be;
They're filling this old Province from the boundary to the sea.
That ain't the worst for soldiers, for the lid's tight on right here;
Religious cranks and pro-hi's have cut out all your beer."
"I thought I fought for liberty," the war worn veteran said.
"You're right, old longshore loafer, I surely should be dead."

Clipping from the *Vancouver Critic*, Immigration Branch, vol. 121, file 23635, vol. 4.

39. *Times*, Mar. 21, 1919; *Province*, May 6, 1921.

40. (Vancouver: *Sun*, 1921).

41. *Argus*, May 5, 1921; *Daily News* (Prince Rupert), Sept. 20, 1921; *Herald*, July 30, 1921.

42. *Province*, May 6 and 13, and July 20, 1921.

43. *Free Press*, Sept. 26, 1921; *Argus*, Oct. 27, 1921; *Daily News*, Dec. 14, 1921.

44. "Asiatic Exclusion League of Canada, formed to keep this Dominion for the white man, by stopping any further Oriental immigration" (Vancouver, 1921).

45. C. F. Macaulay to David Lloyd George, Oct. 31, 1921, External Affairs Records, vol. 1285, file 43, PAC.

46. D. A. Smith to W. D. Noyes, Feb. 10, 1922, Presbyterian Church in Canada, Papers of Mission to the Chinese in Canada, 1888-1925, box 5, United Church Archives, Victoria University, Toronto.

47. British Columbia, *Journals* (1921), Nov. 1, 1921, 32; ibid. (1922), Nov. 20, 1922, 60; ibid., Dec. 5, 1922, 137-38.

48. 13 Geo. V, c.25 and c.65; *Province*, Nov. 22, 1922 and Dec. 24, 1922.

49. J. P. to Messrs. Richard Hall and Sons, Nov. 21, 1922. Premiers' Correspondence, 1922, Correspondence Inward, file 60; *Province*, Aug. 5, 1922.

50. Oliver to King, Oct. 11, 1922, King Papers, MG 26, J1, vol. 70, 67076-77.

51. *Colonist*, May 18, 1922.

52. British Columbia, "Annual Report of the Minister of Labor, 1922," *Sessional Papers* (1923), S8.

53. *Province*, Feb. 2, Apr. 27 and Oct. 31, 1921, and Feb. 24, Oct. 10, Nov. 15, and Dec. 8, 1922; *Times*, Oct. 10, 1921; *Fraser Valley Record* (Mission), Oct. 12, 1922.

54. F. C. Blair Memorandum, Apr. 12, 1921, Immigration Branch, acc. 70/47, box 70, file 827821, vol. 6; 11-12 Geo. V, c.21.

55. Canada, *Commons Debates*, May 8, 1922, 1509.

56. E. B. Robertson to J. G. Mitchell, June 29, 1914, Immigration Branch, vol. 121, file 23635, vol. 3.

57. Robertson to W. W. Cory, Feb. 5, 1919, ibid., vol. 4.

58. W. D. Scott to J. A. Calder, Feb. 25, 1919, ibid.

59. Jolliffe to Scott, Feb. 7, 1922, ibid., vol. 5.

60. Memorandum of Conversation with Dr. Chilien Tsur, July 28, 1922, King Papers, MG 26, J4, c61104-10; Draft Memorandum for Chinese Consul, L. C. Christie, Oct. 3, 1922, ibid., c61335-39.

61. King Diary, King Papers, MG 26, J13, Feb. 24, 1923.

62. 13-14 Geo. V, c.38, s.5. Order in Council PC1272, July 10, 1923, passed under this act, required the registration of all Chinese living in Canada.

63. King to Rowell, May 14, 1923, King Papers, MG 26, J1, vol. 93, 77876-77.

64. A. F. Barss to Oliver, Feb. 4, 1924, Premiers' Correspondence, 1924, Correspondence Inward, file 60; R. C. Neish to Meighen, Mar. 6, 1925, Meighen Papers, vol. 96, 54785-86, PAC; Barss to A. M. Manson, Apr. 25, 1927, British Columbia, Attorney General's Papers, file 2060-17-18, PABC; W. J. Bonavia to S. F. Tolmie, Jan. 15, 1930, Premiers' Correspondence, 1930-33, file 0-4-G.

65. *Province*, July 27 and Nov. 6, 1927, Nov. 30, 1928, and Apr. 13, 1929.

66. Ibid., July 17, 1927, June 29, 1929, and May 15, 1934.

67. Petition to MacLean, received Feb. 11, 1928, Attorney General's Papers, file 2060-17-18, 870-88.

68. MacInnes to MacLean, Apr. 21, 1928, Pattullo Papers, vol 28, file 6, 1-2, PABC. The merchants' support for the B.C. group, however, was half-hearted at best. P. E. Roy, "Protecting their Pocketbooks and Preserving Their Race: White Merchants and Oriental Competition," in A.R. McCormack and I. Macpherson, eds., *Cities in the West: Papers of the Western Canada Urban History Conference—University of Winnipeg, October 1974* (Ottawa: National Museums of Man, 1975), p. 122.

69. P. H. Smith to J. A. Clark, May 28, 1924, Immigration Branch, vol. 85, file 9309, vol. 12; *Province*, Jan. 12 and 19, 1927. The veterans explained this latter demand as a response to the confiscation of British property and the deportation of British residents in China.

70. L. Healey to Members of the House of Commons, Feb. 8, 1927, Premiers' Correspondence, 1927, Correspondence Inward, file 60. The Klan persisted for at least two years but played no significant role in promoting popular anti-Orientalism. Its existence, however, was symptomatic of the public temper.

71. H. Thornley to Premier, Apr. 6, 1925, Premiers' correspondence, 1925, Correspondence Inward, file 60; Thornley to Meighen, May 5, 1925, Meighen Papers, vol. 96, 54832-33; *Province*, Feb. 3, 1925.

72. *Colonist*, Mar. 24 and 31, 1925; *Times*, Apr. 28 and May 12, 1925; C. Davies to Oliver, Sept. 25, 1925, Premiers' Correspondence, 1925, Correspondence Inward, file 60.

73. The suggestion was that the head tax be refunded to Chinese who wished to return to China. *Colonist*, Dec. 3, 1925; Memorandum to C. Stewart, Jan. 26, 1926, Immigration Branch, vol. 121, file 23635, vol. 6.

74. It claimed a membership of 1,700 in 1929. Minutes of the founding meeting of the White Canada Association, Nov. 27, 1929, Premiers' Correspondence, 1929, Correspondence Inward, file 60.

75. Ibid.

76. *Colonist*, Dec. 11, 1929.

77. Hope to Tolmie, Dec. 19, 1929 and Mar. 30, 1931, Premiers' Correspondence, 1930-33, file 0-4-G; Hope to R. B. Bennett, Mar. 30, 1931, Immigration Branch, acc. 69/17, box 208, file 462229; Hope to King, Nov. 23, 1935, External Affairs Records, vol. 1756, file 815; idem, "Canada's Oriental Province" (Vancouver: n.p., 1930); C. E. Hope, "British Columbia's Racial Problem," *MacLean's*, Feb. 1, 1930, pp.3-4, 62-63 and Feb. 15, 1930, pp. 8, 45-48.

78. *Province*, Apr. 15, 1931.

79. British Columbia, *Journals* (1923), Nov. 27, 1923, 106; ibid. (1924), Dec. 17, 1924, 158-59; ibid. (1928), Mar. 14, 1928, 176-77.

80. The underlying assumption was, of course, that whites were more productive than Orientals and therefore at the same wage rate had a competitive advantage over Asians. The law apparently did reduce the number of Orientals employed in the industry. 16 Geo. V, c.32; British Columbia, Report of the Department of Labor, 1926, *Sessional Papers* (1927), F42; Report of the Department of Labor, 1927, ibid. (1928), L41-42.

81. Geo. V, c.49; petition to J. D. MacLean, received Feb. 11, 1928, Attorney-General's Papers, file 2060-17-18, 870-88.

82. Canada, *Commons' Debates*, 1924-1926, passim; Neill to J. H. King, June 13, 1924, King Papers, MG 26, J1, vol. 106, 89985-88.

83. Interview between King and the Japanese Consul, Apr. 2, 1925, King Papers, MG 26, J4, vol. 80, file 634, c61268-70; Governor General to the Secretary of State for Colonies, May 26, 1925, coded telegram, Canada, Governor General's Numbered Files, vol. 209, file 332, vol. 17b.

84. Oliver to King, Jan. 21, 1927, King Papers, MG 26, J1, vol. 147, 124777.

85. S. Tomii to R. Forke, May 29, 1928, External Affairs Records, vol. 1430, file 799, pt. I. For details of the agreement see O. D. Skelton to Tomii, Nov. 26, 1928, ibid.

86. As far as immigration from India was concerned there had been only minor changes in exclusion regulations. In 1919 existing restrictions were sufficiently relaxed to permit the entry of wives and children of East Indians then living in Canada. The move was prompted by a resolution of the Imperial War Conference in 1918. Prime Minister Borden considered the gesture desirable from the point of view of relations with India. Borden to Calder, Mar. 16, 1919, telegram, Borden Papers, vol. 41, 18110-11; Order in Council PC641, March 26, 1919, ibid., 18157-59.

87. F. Leighton Thomas, *Japan: The Octopus of the East and Its Menace to Canada* (Vancouver: n.p., 1932); *Province*, Apr. 29, 1933; I. Mackenzie to King, Feb. 14, 1936, External Affairs Records, vol. 1430, file 799, pt. II.

88. Their criticism of the Chinese Immigration Act in 1923 offers one example. Noyes to C. Stewart, Mar. 7, 1923, Immigration Branch, acc. 70/47, box 71, file 827821, vol. 9; S. Gould to the Minister, Apr. 19, 1923, ibid., vol. 8.

89. S. S. Osterhout and others to King, Apr. 3, 1923, ibid., vol. 9.

90. W. Peter Ward, "The Oriental Immigrant and Canada's Protestant Clergy, 1858-1925," *BC Studies*, no. 22 (Summer 1974), pp. 40-55.

91. Theordore H. Boggs, "The Oriental on the Pacific Coast," *Queen's Quarterly* 33, no. 3 (February 1926): 320.

92. Ibid., p. 323.

93. *Colonist*, May 12, 1925.

94. *Province*, Mar. 16 and Apr. 14, 1920; *Times*, Mar. 18, 1920; *Colonist*, Apr. 4, 1920.

95. *Times*, Mar. 14, 1921; *Province*, June 18, 1924 and May 2, 1928.

96. Ibid., Mar. 23 and Apr. 1, 1931; 21 Geo. V, c.21.

97. H. F. Angus, "Canadians of Oriental Race," *The Anvil* 1, no. 1 (January 1931): 2-4; idem, "Underprivileged Canadians," *Queen's Quarterly* 38, no. 3 (Summer 1931): 445-60.

98. *Province*, March 27, Sept. 1, and Nov. 13, 1934; *Colonist*, Mar. 31, 1936; *Times*, May 5, 1938.

99. *Province*, Sept. 24 and 25, 1931.

100. Woodsworth's defence of Asian civil liberties during the 1930s contrasted sharply with his nativistic response to all immigrants, especially Orientals, a quarter-century earlier. J. S. Woodsworth, *Strangers Within Our Gates; or Coming Canadians* (Toronto: F. C. Stevenson, 1909).

101. *Province*, Nov. 9, 1934; *Colonist*, Sept. 26, 1935; Canada *Commons' Debates*, Feb. 20 and 27, 1936, 373-91 and 573-77.

102. *Free Press*, May 4, 1938; *Sun*, July 4, 1938.

103. Native Sons of British Columbia, "Argument Advanced by Native Sons of British Columbia in Opposition to Granting of Oriental Franchise" (New Westminster: n.p., n.d.); *News Herald* (Vancouver), June 15, 1936.

104. J. Edward Sears, "Orientals and the C.C.F.," radio address, MacInnis Papers, box 41, folder 8, Special Collections, University of British Columbia Library; *Colonist*, Sept. 25, 1935; H. F. Angus, "Liberalism Stoops to Conquer," *Canadian Forum* 15, no. 179 (Dec. 1935): 389-90.

CHAPTER 8

1. A. R. M. Lower, *Canada and the Far East—1940* (New York: Institute of Pacific Relations, 1940), pp. 23-28.

2. *Sun*, Nov. 17, 1937.

3. *Sun*, Nov. 24, 1937; *Colonist*, Jan. 19, 1938.

4. Canada, *Commons Debates*, Feb. 17, 1938, 550-75.

5. *Province*, Feb. 22, 1938.

6. *Province*, Feb. 2, 17, 18, and 24, 1938; *Sun*, Feb. 10, 12, 14, and 28, 1938.

7. Two representative letters to King are: Dr. R. S. Hanna to King, Feb. 14, 1938, King Papers, MG 26, J2, vol. 147, file I-209; Forgotten Native of Japanada

to King, n.d., ibid. Letters to Wilson in 1938 can be found in the Wilson Papers, vol. I, file 1.

8. Pattullo to King, Jan. 26, 1938, King Papers, MG 26, J1, vol. 256, 218388-89; Mackenzie to King, Feb. 26, 1938, ibid., vol. 253, 216060; King to Mackenzie, Mar. 1, 1938, ibid., 216062-63A.

9. *Sun*, Mar. 23, 1938.

10. The Board of Review estimated that about 120 Japanese were then living illegally in the province. Board of Review [Immigration], *Final Report*, Sept. 29, 1938, p. 38.

11. British Columbia, *Journals*, Dec. 9, 1938, 120; *Sun*, Oct. 12 and 18, 1938.

12. H. L. K[eenleyside], Memorandum, June 11, 1940, Department of External Affairs Records, vol. 2007, file 212, pt. I; *Province*, Aug. 7 and 15, 1940.

13. See also Wilson Papers, vol. I, file 4; *Sun*, June 29 and Aug. 10, 1940; *Province*, Aug. 21 and 24, 1940.

14. K[eenleyside], Memorandum, June 11, 1940, External Affairs Records, vol. 2007, file 212, pt. I; J. G. Turgeon to King, Aug. 7, 1940, King Papers, MG 26, J1, vol. 297, 252824-25; King to E. Lapointe, Aug. 8, 1940, ibid., 252828.

15. Canada, Privy Council, Minutes and Documents of the Cabinet War Committee, vol. II, Minutes, Oct. 8, 1940, 2, PAC.

16. L. R. LaFleche to F. C. Blair, June 2, 1938, Canada, Department of National Defence Records, file H.Q. 6-0-7, Department of National Defence Archives, Ottawa.

17. Brig. C. V. Stockwell to the Secretary, Department of National Defence, Sept. 4, 1940, Defence Records, file H.Q.S., v.s. 38-1-1-1, vol. 5.

18. Supt. C. H. Hill to the Commissioner, Aug. 25, 1938, Canada, Immigration Branch Records, vol. 86, file 9309, vol. 16; Asst. Comm. R. R. Tait to Keenleyside, Oct. 28, 1940, External Affairs Records, vol. 2007, file 212, pt. I. The entire contents of this file substantiate the observations made in this paragraph.

19. The RCMP did, however, identify a small number of Japanese who might endanger the state in time of war and these individuals were arrested and detained immediately after war on Japan was declared.

20. Pattullo to King, Sept. 23, 1940, King Papers, MG 26, J1, vol. 293, 248363; King to Pattullo, Sept. 27, 1940, T. D. Pattullo Papers, vol. 70, file 4, 21, PABC; Wilson to the Finance Committee, City of Vancouver, Sept. 24, 1940, Wilson Papers, vol. I, file 4; A. D. P. Heeney, Memorandum for the Prime Minister, Sept. 27, 1940, King Papers, MG 26, J4, vol. 361, file 3849.

21. Report and Recommendations of the Special Committee on Orientals in British Columbia, December 1940, typescript, King Papers, MG 26, J4, vol. 361, file 3849. The committee also recommended that, because testimony before it almost unanimously favoured a complete end to Japanese immigration, the government should forbid it when the international situation permitted the move. This recommendation was not published because King feared it might strain existing relations with Japan and inflame anti-Oriental opinion in British Columbia. Canada, Privy Council, vol. IV, Minutes, Jan. 2, 1941, 8-9; Keenleyside to G. Sansom, [Jan. 3, 1941] External Affairs Records, vol. 1868, file 263, pt. IV; Additional Statement by the Members of the Special Committee on Orientals In British Columbia for consideration by the Prime Minister and members of the Cabinet War Committee, n.d., King Papers, MG 26, J1, vol. 307, 259432-33.

22. Keenleyside to King, Dec. 2, 1940, King Papers, MG 26, J1, vol. 289, 244808-10.

23. *Province*, Jan. 9 and Feb. 11, 1941; *Times*, Feb. 26, 1941; *Sun*, Apr. 8 and July 26, 1941. One sign of growing suspicion was the increasing sensitivity of west coast whites to Japanese using cameras. For example see *Free Press*, Feb. 8, 1941.

24. Keenleyside to Comm. S. T. Wood, Feb. 20, 1941, External Affairs Records, vol. 2007, file 212, pt. II; Asst. Comm. F. J. Mead to the Commissioner, Feb. 28, 1941, ibid.; H. F. Angus to Mayor F. J. Hume, July 25, 1941, ibid.

25. F/O W. A. Nield, Report on the State of Intelligence on the Pacific Coast with Particular Reference to the Problem of the Japanese Minority, July 27, 1941, Defence Records, file H.Q., S67-3, vol. 1.

26. All Japanese nationals immediately became enemy aliens and restrictions imposed upon them were also imposed upon all Japanese Canadians naturalized after 1922.

27. Forrest E. La Violette, *The Canadian Japanese and World War II: A Social and Psychological Account* (Toronto: University of Toronto Press, 1948), p. 44; Declaration of the Existence of a State of War Between Canada and Japan, Dec. 8, 1941, King Papers, MG 26, J5, D58190-94; *Sun*, Dec. 8, 1941; *Free Press*, Dec. 8, 1941; *Province*, Dec. 8, 1941.

28. After Pearl Harbor the major daily newspapers in Vancouver and Victoria published a steady stream of letters on the Japanese problem, most of which voiced suspicion of the west coast Japanese and demanded federal action to remove the threat which they posed. For reports of vandalism see *Province*, Dec. 8, 9, and 11, 1941. For rumours of Japanese subversion see Weekly Internal Security Intelligence Report, Dec. 13, 1941, Western Air Command, Defence Records, file H.Q. S67-3, vol. 1. With the exception of fishermen, most Japanese who lost their jobs were soon reabsorbed by the labour market. Hill, Intelligence Report, Dec. 16, 1941 and Jan. 13, 1942, External Affairs Records, file 3464-G-40, Department of External Affairs, Archives Branch (EAA).

29. Hutchison to Pickersgill, [Dec. 16, 1941], King Papers, MG 26, J4, vol. 347, 239219-20.

30. *Province*, Dec. 19, 1941; Hill to the Commissioner, RCMP, Dec. 20, 1941, External Affairs Records, file 3464-H-40C, EAA.

31. Hume to King, Dec. 20, 1941, External Affairs Records, vol. 1868, file 263, pt. IV, PAC.

32. Alexander to Chief of the General Staff, Dec. 30, 1941, Defence Records, file H.Q. 6-0-7. Alexander's concern was shared by those officers commanding Canada's Pacific coast naval and air forces. Commodore W. J. R. Beech to the General Officer Commanding-in-Chief, Pacific Command, Dec. 27, 1941, ibid.; Air Commodore L. F. Stevenson to the Secretary, Department of National Defence for Air, Jan. 2, 1941, Defence Records, file H.Q., S67-3, vol. 1. In Ottawa the Chief of the General Staff did not subscribe to these fears. Lt. Gen. K. Stuart to Keenleyside, Dec. 26, 1941, External Affairs Records, file 3464-H-40C, EAA.

33. Petitions to the federal government can be found in King Papers, MG 26, J2, vol. 294, file P-309, vol. 14; Ian Mackenzie Papers, vol. 24, file 70-25, vol. 1; ibid., vol. 25, file 70-25, vols. 2 and 3; ibid., vol. 25, file 70-25E, PAC; External Affairs Records, file 773-B-1-40, pts. I and II, EAA.

34. Turgeon to King, Jan. 6, 1942, ibid., pt. I.

35. Conference on the Japanese Problem in British Columbia, Minutes, Jan. 8 and 9, 1942, External Affairs Records, vol. 1868, file 263, pt. IV, PAC; Mackenzie to King, Jan. 10, 1942, Mackenzie Papers, vol. 32, file x-81; Keenleyside to Mackenzie, Jan. 10, 1942, ibid. The minority recommendation for partial evacuation was appended to the report.

36. Mackenzie to King, Jan. 10, 1942, ibid.; Pacific Command to National Defence Headquarters, Jan. 12, 1942, telegram, Defence Papers, file H.Q. 6-0-7.

37. Statement of the Prime Minister, Jan. 14, 1942, Mackenzie Papers, vol. 24, file 70-25, vol. 1. Two protected zones were ultimately defined. The larger embraced the area west of the Cascade Mountains, a range which ran parallel to the coast about 100 miles inland. The smaller encompassed the city of Trail and vicinity.

38. Mackenzie to B. M. Stewart, Jan. 23, 1942, Mackenzie Papers, vol. 32, file x-81, vol. 2; Keenleyside to Mackenzie, Jan. 26, 1942, ibid.; Keenleyside, "The Japanese Problem in British Columbia," Memorandum to N.A. Robertson, Jan. 27, 1942, ibid.

39. *Sun*, Jan. 14, 1942; the lull was obvious to military intelligence officers in British Columbia. Maj. H. C. Bray to the Director, Military Operations and Intelligence, National Defence Headquarters, Jan. 29, 1942, Canada, Department of Labour Papers, Lacelle Files, vol. 174, file 614.02:11-1, vol. 1, PAC.

40. See above, n. 33.

41. M. C. Robinson and others to Mackenzie, Feb. 23, 1942, Mackenzie Papers, vol. 25, file 70-25, vol. 2.

42. *Commons Debates*, Jan. 29, 1942, 156-158.

43. ,Mackenzie to Robertson, Jan. 28, 1942, Mackenzie Papers, vol. 32, file x-81, vol. 2; R. W. Mayhew to King, Feb. 12, 1942, King Papers, MG 26, J1, vol. 330; G. G. McGeer to King, Feb. 13, 1942, Gerald Grattan McGeer Papers, box 2, file 9, PABC; O. Hanson and others to King, Feb. 21, 1942, King Papers, MG 26, J1, vol. 336.

44. R. L. Maitland to Mackenzie, Feb. 17, 1942, Mackenzie Papers, vol. 32, file x-81, vol. 2.

45. G. S. Pearson to A. Macnamara, Feb. 17, 1942, Labour Records, Lacelle Files, vol. 174, file 614.02:11-1, vol. 2; *Sun*, Feb. 16, 1942; Lt. Gov. W. C. Woodward to King, Feb. 11, 1942, King Papers, MG 26, J1, vol. 336; Alexander to the Secretary, Chiefs of Staff Committee, Feb. 13, 1942, Defence Records, Chiefs of Staff Committee, Miscellaneous Memoranda, vol. 3, February 1942; Joint Services Committee, Pacific Coast, Minutes, Feb. 19 and 20, 1942, ibid.

46. Mackenzie to L. St. Laurent, Feb. 14, 1942, Mackenzie Papers, vol. 24, file 70-25, vol. 1; Mackenzie to King, Feb. 22, 1942, King Papers, MG 26, J1, vol. 328.

47. Mackenzie to St. Laurent, Feb. 24, 1942, Mackenzie Papers, vol. 25, file 70-25, vol. 2. At the same time Mackenzie sent similar letters to colleagues King C. G. Power, J. L. Ralston, A. Macdonald, and H. Mitchell.

48. Mackenzie to J. R. Bowler, Feb. 26, 1942, ibid.

49. King Diary, Feb. 19, 1942, King Papers, MG 26, J13.

50. Order in Council P.C. 1486, Feb. 24, 1942; *Commons Debates*, Feb. 27, 1942, 917-20.

51. (New York: Free Press, 1962), chap. VIII.

52. Weekly Internal Security Intelligence Report, Jan. 17, 1942, Western Air Command, Defence Records, file H.Q. S67-3, vol. 1. For another example of rumour see Gwen Cash, *A Million Miles from Ottawa* (Toronto: Macmillan, 1942), pp. 25-26.

53. On the nature and significance of rumour see Gordon W. Allport and Leo Postman, *The Psychology of Rumor* (New York: Russell and Russell, 1965), especially chap. II.

54. *Sun*, Jan. 14, 1942; Mackenzie to Stewart, Jan. 23, 1942, Mackenzie Papers, vol. 32, file x-81, vol. 2. The emphasis was Mackenzie's.

55. Although some fruit and vegetable growers in the Okanagan Valley requested Japanese workers for the duration of the war in order to ease the wartime labour shortage, the proposal roused a strong outburst of bitter opposition in the valley. Protest was channelled through municipal councils, newspapers, boards of trade, and dissenting farm organizations. Proposals that the Japanese be moved east of the Rockies met opposition from several provincial governments. *Penticton Herald*, Jan. 15, 22, and 29, 1942; *Kelowna Courier*, Jan. 22 and Feb. 12, 1942; Keenleyside, Memorandum for Robertson, Feb. 4, 1942, External Affairs Records, file 3464-G-40, EAA.

56. W. L. Mackenzie King, *Industry and Humanity: A Study in the Principles Underlying Industrial Reconstruction* (Toronto: Thomas Allen, 1918), pp. 75-76.

57. King Diary, Feb. 20, 23, and 24, 1942, King Papers, MG 26, J13.

58. Cash, *A Million Miles*, p. 33; *Province*, Mar. 2, 1942; *Colonist*, Mar. 3, 1942; A. Thompson to C. N. Senior, Feb. 27, 1942, Mackenzie Papers, vol. 25, file 70-25, vol. 2.

59. *Sun*, Feb. 26, 1942.

60. While racial tensions swelled in British Columbia after Pearl Harbor, a similar crisis occurred on the American Pacific Coast. There, as in Canada, residents in coastal areas who were of Japanese origin, were forced to move inland to camps constructed for their reception. The American decision for evacuation, however, was based solely on military considerations and was taken by military officers who had been given a free hand by President Roosevelt. There seems to have been no collaboration between the Canadian and American governments in the decision-making process, and, while the events of the two evacuations ran in close parallel, neither country's policy appears to have had much influence upon that of the other. For accounts of the American evacuation see Morton Grodzins, *Americans Betrayed: Politics and the Japanese Evacuation* (Chicago: University of Chicago Press, 1949); Stetson Conn, "The Decision to Evacuate the Japanese from the Pacific Coast (1942)," *Command Decisions*, ed. Kent Roberts Greenfield, prepared by the Office of the Chief of Military History, Department of the Army (New York: Harcourt, Brace, 1959), pp. 88-109; Roger Daniels, *Concentration Camps USA: Japanese Americans and World War II* (New York: Holt, Rinehart and Winston, 1972).

61. E. W. Barton to Stirling, Mar. 6, 1942, Mackenzie Papers, vol. 24, file 67-25, vol. 1.

62. A. Taylor to Mackenzie, Mar. 4, 1942, telegram, ibid.

63. *Lethbridge Herald*, Mar. 17 and 19, 1942.

64. Interview with Rev. Howard Norman, July 26, 1973.

65. Black to G. Dorey, Jan. 4, 1943, United Church of Canada, Board of Home Missions, United Church Archives, Toronto.

66. Grace MacInnis and Angus MacInnis, *Oriental Canadians — Outcasts or Citizens?* (n.p., n.d.) , pp. 17-20.

67. Carol F. Lee, "The Road to Enfranchisement: Chinese and Japanese in British Columbia," *BC Studies*, no. 30 (Summer 1976), p. 52.

68. Ibid., 60; LaViolette, *The Canadian Japanese and World War II*, chaps. X and XI.

A NOTE ON THE SOURCES

Any study of popular attitudes must necessarily draw upon a broad range of sources. Moreover, until after World War II, British Columbians were always extremely open about their racial prejudices and, as a result, left behind abundant evidence of their antipathies. Consequently this book has selectively employed a wide variety of sources. Provincial newspapers offered a rich record of event and opinion, in particular the major dailies published in Victoria and Vancouver, where anti-Orientalism was most persistent and intense. The regional weekly press, while not as fruitful a source, also helped to reveal the breadth of the anti-Oriental consensus, as did special interest publications and other periodicals. As samples of public opinion, the successive federal enquiries and royal commissions on Oriental immigration held during the late nineteenth and early twentieth centuries were useful as well.

The major manuscript collections examined also reflected the nature of public sentiment, and in addition, revealed much about the formation of government policy with regard to Orientals. In the Public Archives of Canada the various prime ministerial collections proved of great value, especially those of Laurier, Borden, and King, all of which contain an abundance of representations from ordinary people and special interest groups, as well as policy memoranda. The Ian Mackenzie papers were indispensable for the post-Pearl Harbor period. Among the departmental record groups, those of the Immigration Branch and the Department of External Affairs were particularly helpful. External Affairs and the Department of National Defence also maintain their own archives, each of which yielded valuable information on the problem during the 1930s and 1940s.

Several manuscript collections in the Public Archives of British Columbia also rewarded investigation. The files of successive twentieth-century provincial premiers, especially those of McBride and Pattullo, offered illumination. The Attorney-General's papers, a major source for the study of the social history of the province, were informative as well.

In recent years the encounter between whites and Asian immigrants in other countries has attracted scholarly attention. For comparative purposes one might begin by examining the following studies: Stuart Creighton Miller, *The Unwelcome Immigrant: The American Image of the Chinese, 1785-1882* (Berkeley: University of California Press, 1969); Roger Daniels, *The Politics of Prejudice: The Anti-Japanese Movement in California and the Struggle for Japanese Exclusion* (Gloucester, Mass.: Peter Smith, 1966) and his *Concentration Camps USA: Japanese Americans and World War II* (New York: Holt, Rinehart, and Winston, 1972); Charles A. Price, *The Great White Walls are Built: Restrictive Immigration to North America and Australasia, 1836-1888* (Canberra: Australian National University Press, 1974); and Robert A. Huttenback, *Racism and Empire: White Settlers and Colored Immigrants in the British Self-Governing Colonies, 1830-1910* (Ithaca, N.Y., and London: Cornell University Press, 1976).

RECENT WORKS

Since this book was first published, several studies which touch on the subject have appeared. Useful short introductions to the histories of the three Asian minorities are: W. Peter Ward, *The Japanese in Canada* (Ottawa: Canadian Historical Association, 1982); Hugh Johnston, *The East Indians in Canada* (Ottawa: Canadian Historical Association, 1984); and Jin Tan and Patricia E. Roy, *The Chinese in Canada* (Ottawa: Canadian Historical Association, 1985). Harry Con et al., *From China to Canada: A History of the Chinese Communities in Canada* (Toronto: McClelland and Stewart and the Multiculturalism Directorate, Department of the Secretary of State, 1982) is a thorough survey, particularly strong on the organizational life of the Chinese Canadian community. Peter S. Li's *The Chinese in Canada* (Don Mills: Oxford University Press, 1988) emphasizes the theme of institutional racism. Ken Adachi's *The Enemy That Never Was: A History of the Japanese Canadians* (Toronto: McClelland and Stewart, 1976) is the work of a sensitive journalist commissioned by the National Japanese Canadian Citizens Association. A comprehensive survey emphasizing the wartime evacuation and its aftermath, the book unfortunately does not draw upon Japanese-language sources. The only general overview of the East Indian community is Norman Buchigani's *Continuous Journey: A Social History of South Asians in Canada* (Toronto: McClelland and Stewart and the Multiculturalism Directorate, Department of the Secretary of State, 1985). Hugh Johnston's *The Voyage of the Komagata Maru: The Sikh Challenge to Canada's Colour Bar* (Delhi: Oxford University Press, 1979) is a lively account of the dramatic confrontation between would-be East Indian immigrants and Canadian government officials in 1914.

Two major, recent studies of Canadian immigration policy are Freda Hawkin's *Canada and Immigration: Public Policy and Public Concern*, 2d edition (Montreal and Kingston: McGill-Queens University Press, 1988) and her *Critical Years in Immigration: Canada and Australia Compared* (Montreal and Kingston: McGill-Queen's University Press, 1989). Both are concerned principally with policy formation and implementation at the ministerial and senior bureaucratic levels.

The issue of racism has also attracted considerable scholarly interest. Some years ago I published a short essay which excited rather more controversy than any brief piece would seem to warrant: "Class and Race in the Social Structure of British Columbia," *BC Studies* 45 (Spring 1980): 17-35. For an exchange of views on the subject see Rennie Warburton, "Race and Class in British Columbia: A Comment," *BC Studies* 49 (Spring 1981): 79-85 and W. Peter Ward, "Race and Class: A Reply," *BC Studies* 50 (Summer 1981): 52. Rennie Warburton and David Coburn, eds., *Workers, Capital, and the State in British Columbia: Selected Papers* (Vancouver: University of British Columbia Press, 1988) includes several neo-Marxist essays which also take issue with my views on the origins of anti-Asian feeling in western Canada. Patricia E. Roy's *A White Man's Province: British Columbia Politicians and Chinese and Japanese Immigrants, 1858-1914* (Vancouver: University of British Columbia Press, 1989) is an exhaustive survey of west coast opposition to Asians in the years before World War I. Two studies examine the treatment of the Japanese in Canada during World War II: Ann Gomer Sunahara, *The Politics of Racism: The Uprooting of Japanese Canadians during the Second World War* (Toronto: James Lorimer, 1981) and Patricia E. Roy et al., *Mutual Hostages: Canadians and Japanese during the Second World War* (Toronto: University of Toronto Press, 1990). Both books draw on archival materials not open for research when my book was written but, while they add new details to our knowledge of those events, neither alters our basic understanding of the processes and motives which led to the decision to expel the Japanese from coastal British Columbia.

INDEX